Lioness

Publisher: Lioness Books

Editor: Dr. Melissa Caudle

Cover Designer: Rebeca @Rebecacovers
Internal Design: Meital @meitals_design

IN LIBRARY IN-DATA-PUBLICATION

Conversations with my Body/Dr. Elana Maryles Sztokman

ISBN Second Edition ebook: 978-1-957712-02-4
ISBN Second Edition paperback: 978-1-957712-03-1

1. Memoir   2. Autobiography   3. Woman's Literature

Conversations with my Body

Essays on My Life as a Jewish Woman

Second edition

Elana Sztokman

This book is dedicated with love and
appreciation
to my beautiful soul sister

Chana Erin Griver

With an ocean of gratitude between us.
Thanks for sharing the journey.

Contents

"To lose confidence in one's body is
to lose confidence in oneself."
— Simone de Beauvoir

"Every woman knows that, regardless of
all her other achievements, she is a failure
if she is not beautiful."
— Germaine Greer

Preface to Second Edition

A lot has happened in the world since I first published this book in the summer of 2020, especially in the American and Israeli circles where my identity mostly resides. A rough version of the ride: The end of Trump's first term, several election cycles in Israel, the end of Covid, a respite from Bibi Netanyahu as Prime Minister of Israel, some thoughts of relief, January 6, a war in Gaza, Netanyahu's return to power, a year of anti-Bibi pro-democracy protests, Putin's invasion into Ukraine, scary climate catastrophes around the world, the rise of gazillionaire wealth-hoarders, October 7, hostages, another war in Gaza, cries of genocide and ethnic cleansing, more rockets, more death and destruction, a year of anti-war protests, still hostages in Gaza, a second Trump victory, more climate catastrophes, Trump and Bibi in cahoots, Elon Musk running the world, and the end of feelings of relief. That's on the global, political scale. Hard days. Very hard days.

I've had changes in my life, too, mostly good ones. Kids getting married, grandchildren born, I earned a second Master's Degree, I published another book called *When Rabbis Abuse: Power, Gender, Status in the Dynamics of Sexual Abuse in Jewish Culture*, I started a blog called "Toxic Tactics" and then paused it because it was too much, I started a Substack called "The Roar" which is still going strong, I moved to Jaffa for a while, I became involved in several women's peace initiatives, I engaged several clients doing peace and gender work, and I

i

started a podcast called "Women Ending War" with a Palestinian co-host, Eva Dalak. I'm working, all the time, as are so many amazing people, to respond to these events and strive towards repair.

My attentions have shifted but not entirely. I left Orthodoxy behind, and with that, the intensity of my focus on Orthodox feminism. My feminist interests expanded beyond the world that I came from. I joined interfaith dialogue groups. I studied group facilitation. I began deeper explorations of patriarchal language. I spent time focusing on sexual abuse and emotional abuse, not just in Jewish culture but also in political discourse more broadly. I studied sustainable building. In October 2023, a minute before the major explosion in Israel/Palestine, I completed my master's degree in environmental science from Tel Aviv University, thinking that I would swing away from my laser focus on gender and begin attending to the environment, an issue that has been a quiet priority of mine for many years. For months before the catastrophe, I had actually been in conversations with some wonderful people in the Gaza rim about a plastic waste and sustainability education initiative – discussions that have since disappeared into the ether, along with so much else, as a result of the war. I never quite left gender behind – how could I? – nor have I launched a career in sustainability. But now this mishmash of interests competes for my mental and emotional attention while I try not to panic over the state of the world.

The events of October 7 and what followed comprise their own story of disruption – logistical, emotional, political, and ideological chaos. I spent months looking after two of my displaced daughters and their babies while their husbands were called up to reserve duty. My son was also in reserve duty for months, and my youngest daughter was in the midst of her compulsory service when the war broke out. That is a lot of war on my doorstep. Actually, "disruption" is too mild description of the year that followed. But it is nothing compared to what has since been happening to the people of Gaza. The situation is only escalating, with no end in sight. Maybe my situation *is* mild, relatively speaking.

I have been writing my way through much of this. On my Substack, I have been documenting political events and my feelings about them, as well as my own ideological evolutions. I have turned all of that into a book that is scheduled to come out in early 2025 called *In A Jewish State: How I was trained in pro-Israel advocacy, and how I learned to talk back to my culture, find my own humanity, and fight for peace.* It is my first major literary foray into Israeli/Palestinian politics. It is also the first book that could potentially be called a memoir, or at least some of it. And the topic represents the issues that occupy much of my attention these days.

All of this takes me back to this book, *Conversations with my Body,* and why I'm rereleasing it now, of all things – a minute before I leave it behind to focus more intensively on peace work. When this essay collection first came out in 2020, some of the feedback I received was that my narrative was "unclear". I have no "arc" to my life story. At book events, I was sometimes asked, "What's your *point*, exactly?" Well, I didn't have a *point*. In what I structured as a bunch of essays around different themes, I had no real beginning or ending. I had no moment of "triumph", no vindication, and no redemption. This wasn't even necessarily a conscious choice. I think it reflected a certain truth about myself, which is that I did not really know what my life story is about. Literarily speaking, the book was never intended as a memoir, so it hadn't bothered me that much that there was no real story.

Well, maybe it bothered me *a little*.

Those discussions with my readers forced me to ask myself what my own personal lessons were from all this. Even as my attention was turning away from issues of Orthodoxy and body, I felt like I needed to clarify for myself what I was trying to say about life, first to myself and then perhaps to others – my readers, my kids, and my companions on this journey.

I have studied a lot about writing, and at a certain point I began to more zealously explore the world of memoir. A tough lesson I learned from one particular teacher was this: To write a good memoir, first you have to look at your own *shame*. She gives her memoir-writing students an assignment to write down the things that we are most ashamed of in our lives.

Face your shame.

Oy vey.

I got this assignment, and took out a pen and paper and started writing. It wasn't one thing but rather a whole list. The process distracted me for hours, and I could not sit down at my computer for the rest of the day. I surprised myself about how many aspects of my life fit into that category of *shaming*. It was as if clots of coal and dust had been scattered throughout my body and soul that I was just carrying around hoping nobody would notice. I needed to hold this realization for a moment – not just for the sake of writing memoir, which I wasn't even sure that I wanted to do, but also for the sake of my own honesty with myself. I needed to face certain truths about where I've been and what I've done. I need to reconcile with an actual life story.

One of my discoveries in that process – perhaps it should not have been so surprising – was about how many items on that shame list revolve around my aspects of my *body*. My body size, my stomach, my chin, my hair, my sexuality, my loud voice, my voice, my accent, my laugh, my size, my appetite. I began to recall experiences and incidents in my life that left me wallowing shame. Comments, exchanges, meals, arguments, awkwardness, sadness, regrets, remorse....

And then I had an "aha" moment. I realized that much of what I put together in this essay collection is precisely about that. (Apparently some of my readers saw it more clearly than I did.) I understood that this entire compilation can be described as a chronicle of body shame – of the ways in which the societies that I belong(ed) to have been training women to internalize body shame. It's all in here. Well, perhaps not all of it. I left a few things out.

It took some time – countless walks on the beach, several solo-travel adventures, many massages, spontaneous dancing in the kitchen, endless journaling, invaluable friend-sisters, and lots of therapy – but I think I know now what my story is. It still isn't a story of triumph, but it does have a certain clarity.

And the story climax is this: *I've made a conscious decision to let go of the body shame and move on.*

I have learned to accept myself, exactly as I am. My skin, my sounds, my hunger, my ideas, my brain, my quirks, my passions, my loves, my art, my music, my flaws, my idiosyncrasies, my mistakes, my rage, my addictions, my sadness, my fat, my scars, my normalness, my abnormalness, my beauty, my magic.

I wouldn't call my conclusion "self-love", which I sometimes feel is an overused new-agey slogan that doesn't always help me. To cite Lizzo[1] among others, it's not so much "body positivity" as much as it is "body neutrality". It's just being at home with whatever I am, and not making such a thing of it. No judgment at all. Just *being*.

I also wouldn't necessarily call this a *conclusion*. It's more like an *intermission*. Body issues are often a life-long struggle, a constant revisiting of the same issues from a different location. If you've spent most of your early life being shamed for who you are, that isn't something that you're likely to fully get over. But you *can* kind of learn to accept that voice inside your head, acknowledge it, say hello to it, laugh at it, and then move on.

That's mostly where I am. Letting go. Moving on. Act II will commence when the lights come back on.

As part of this journey of letting go, I've decided to revisit this book and re-release it. Because the first time I released it, I was hesitant. I didn't do much to share or market it or even tell people about it. I had a small handful of events that I didn't want to advertise. I did not put it on Amazon or anywhere also really. I was too ambivalent within myself about whether I wanted

---

[1] Ruth La Ferla, Lizzo Embraces 'Body Neutrality': The singer Lizzo, who has a new swim line, has moved on from "body positivity." *New York Times,* March 27, 2024 https://www.nytimes.com/2024/03/27/style/lizzo-yitty-swim-swimwear-line.html ; Jessi Kneeland, *Body Neutral: A Revolutionary Guide to Overcoming Body Image* (Penguin Life 2023)

anyone to read it. That is how I know for sure that the book contained sources of shame.

So I decided that now, right before my new memoir will be coming out – and before I embark on a chapter focusing on other more pressing issues – I am going to let go of all that shame I felt in even publishing the book. Put all that behind me, too.

My body is *not* my life story. It's just a thing.

In peace, love, and acceptance,

Elana
Modi'in, Israel
November 2024

Prologue:
A personal reckoning
with my body

I turned fifty years old this year. I did not mark the event by giving away cars, nor by flying my friends and family to Morocco for the weekend. Instead, on the day itself, I spent the morning taking my daughter wedding dress shopping, and then spent the afternoon meeting with a group of women to establish a new women's political party in Israel. It was a nearly perfect day for me, a kind of a neat summary of Elana@50 – the personal and the political; the private and the public; my family but also the world; drawing on love while stoking my fire; my intense drive for political change for women alongside a stirring desire to focus on the blessings around me. Perhaps it was an eclectic reflection of my life as a Jewish woman – weaving my public work toward women's empowerment along with my real, everyday experiences of putting that all aside in order to build loving and healthy relationships.

Sounds nice, right?

PROLOGUE

Except that a moment later, the world crumbled into little pieces.

Before Corona hit, 2020 was set to be a year of intense activity for the world and for me. "The year 2020," I said in January, "is going to be a year of two weddings and two elections." The weddings would be for two of my children, each of whom got engaged to their loves in 2019. And the elections were the American presidential election and the Israeli election for the Knesset. All of these were big and significant points of importance for me. That all *did* happen in 2020, but those events seemed like background noise to the string of upheavals that transpired.

To be sure, I always have my head in multiple places. As an American-Israeli from New York living in Israel for nearly 30 years, I am involved in political systems in both Israel and America, both of which had elections in 2020. I serve as Vice-Chair for Media and Policy for Democrats Abroad-Israel, a position that holds a political and moral urgency especially in the Trump era. And as a feminist activist in Israel, I am the founding Chair of the *Kol Hanashim* Voice of Women party that we formed on my fiftieth birthday and that ran in the March 2020 general elections intending to achieve deep-rooted systemic change for women all around Israel. It was going to be a complicated but exciting year, I thought.

By the time the Israeli elections rolled around on March 2, attention turned to Covid-19, and it became clear that everything was shifting and entering completely uncharted territory in all realms – politically, economically, socially, medically, scientifically, and culturally. Within days after the election, my husband and I bought a new freezer and a food cabinet that we dubbed our "end of the world pantry" and madly filled it up, like we were on an episode of *Laverne and Shirley*. While I was panicking, our four kids all moved back home along with a few significant others, a stranded niece, and a lone soldier. We miraculously found beds for everyone, and together we hunkered down. We made a small, impromptu garden wedding for my daughter and her now-husband two weeks earlier than planned in order to avoid lockdown (at least she had the dress), and an even smaller garden wedding for my son and his now-wife. By another miracle everyone stayed healthy, and here we are. Although 2020 turned into what Israelis might call a *balagan* – chaos – we're still standing. Thank God.

Well, it's not quite the end of the world (*yet*). However, something is different. This is the year that everything stopped – while in some ways everything changed. Roads and airways cleared, but the house became a flurry of activity. We were stockpiling food, and at the same time cooking and eating tons. School buildings closed while the students in the family transformed the house into a big study hall with devices lighting up in every corner. Some of us lost jobs and direction while others pivoted to entirely new realms. And most jarring, relatives and friends have gotten sick, and some have died of Covid. But the lack of connection makes it all feel a bit far off and surreal, even as the stories flood our living room. The numbers of dead are staggering, and yet we do not even know all the names and faces of the victims. The world is in some ways screaming – between Black Lives Matter in the States and Bibi Go Home protests in Israel, the communal outcries are in many ways unprecedented. But at the same time, the distancing between people has never cast a greater silence. And the multi-faceted fears that swirl around our spaces often feel unmanageable. I have regular protests right on my corner, which I sometimes participate in and sometimes don't. Sometimes I feel too emotionally drained from all of it. A year of contradictions, confounding, and a lot of crying.

This is not how I planned the year, but as we know, people plan, and God laughs. (The original expression is that "man plans," but I've obviously fixed that). The truth is, I had started the year thinking that 2020 would be the year I was going to finally impact transformative change on behalf of women in Israel via political action. Starting the party was quite a grandiose act that was many years in the making, and I had big dreams. Yet, not only did our party not even come close to achieving our goals; instead, all hell broke loose in Israeli politics. Covid became an excuse to trample individual rights, as the first-ever sitting Prime Minister on trial threatens democracy while receiving fat paybacks from the taxpayers still struggling with economic collapse. Ministers come and go, as do managers of the pandemic crisis, and the government has had so many about-faces in how to contain the pandemic that governance seems like a farce. The once great "hope" to replace Bibi – Benny Gantz – has been reduced to a shred of nothing, and now the new potential competitor has emerged from the right flank, effectively obliterating what remained of Israel's left. The long-envisioned normalization with Arab nations has left discussions of a diplomatic accord with the Palestinians in the gutter, and "peace" has lost all real meaning, replaced instead with grotesque arms-deals. And perhaps most significantly in my mind, Covid has particularly threatened the well-being of women, who are fading out of the workplace, regressing to home-managers, and increasingly at risk from violence. Yet, the issue of women's equality is nowhere on the public agenda. *Nowhere*. Like so many other topics and issues, it has faded behind the big story of the pandemic and all that came with it.

The erasure of women's needs from the public agenda is taking place around the world. In fact, over the past year, whenever I felt like it was too hard to watch Israeli politics, I would take a peek over the Atlantic to see what Trump has been doing to America, and some days I would thank God that I'm not living there right now. Sometimes, when I would see Trumpist America screaming for their rights to shop without a mask, calling science a "hoax," allowing police to tear-gas anti-racism protesters, or idealizing White Supremacist ideologies, I would wonder if I'm living in an episode of the *Twilight Zone.*

Has America always been this way? I often ask myself. *Has Israel?*

What an insane year – unlike anything anyone could have imagined. And even though Joe Biden and Kamala Harris thankfully won the election, it still does feel, at times, like we are nearing the end of the world.

Something is happening in me, too. I've also turned in many ways from activist to observer, from noisemaker to quiet homemaker. I am in a pause of sorts, so overwhelmed by what I see in the world that I cannot bring myself to take a step. *To do what? To go where? To try what?* This experience has been a moment for me to turn inward. Like many people, the hunkering down at home has sent me on a path of personal reckoning and cleaning house – literally and figuratively. For example, to make room for the new family additions, we rearranged a few rooms, threw out old pieces of furniture, and finally removed useless storage (how quickly CDs, video cameras, and dictionaries became obsolete). It feels like the end of something. Maybe a lot of things. It may be the beginning of things, too, although it's hard to see what's next when there is so much fog around you.

In some ways, this has been cathartic for me. Like many others, I have been cleaning through mountains of old files, transferring boxes of archives to flash drives, clearing spaces, and often asking myself what I *actually* need.

One of my happier discoveries was just how much I have crafted over the years. The pile I made that started with the label "Portfolio" became larger than I could have imagined. I collected essays, articles, and blogs that have been published in different places. I regularly wrote for *The Forward* for nearly ten years and discovered that I had over 200 essays published there. I never counted them quite this way, but once I did, it gave me pause. I also have an entire box of old journals, even though I am an inconsistent-at-best journal-writer. I am inspired to journal from Virginia Woolf, who considered journal-writing an essential practice for writing women, but I am not so good at maintaining routines. I have gone through what I thought were long periods of not journaling. Nevertheless, I have apparently pulled out many words over the years from my ever-rattling brain.

For me, the writing is about leaving breadcrumbs in this world. It's about feeling like I've actually existed. It's also about chronicling my own evolution. As I read some of my earlier works, I realized that I have changed through the writing process. Some of what I wrote earlier I would not write today – some of it was too judgmental, while some of it was too soft. Many of my ideas have crystallized over time, while in other instances, I am even more ambivalent than ever.

I have certainly changed in some noticeable ways. When I started my writing career, I was still mostly Orthodox, trying to justify *halakha*, or Jewish law, and find my place within that. Today, I do not engage with the halakhic process or see myself in that world at all. But my changes are about more than just my religious practice. They have something to do with what I want out of life. About how I define freedom. About what permissions I give myself to think for myself. I am a much freer person today than I was all those years ago, even if my Jewish identity does not yet have a proper home. Maybe it never will. Maybe I am not even looking for that anymore. I'm not sure.

I can track many of these processes in my writing, in subtle shifts. I wonder if my readers detect that, too.

I find myself trying to make sense of all this, finding some kind of story or clear arc in my life. Perhaps it's another outcome of the whole end-of-the-world atmosphere: *What exactly have I done with my life?*

I stared at this mountain of writing and thought to myself: *The answer is in this pile.*

As I started poring through all these pages, I discovered a milestone that had not occurred to me until then. This year marks the 25th anniversary of what I have come to think of as my feminist awakening. Although these kinds of complex shifts are generally hard to mark with a precise date and time, there were two events in 1995, when I was 25 years old, that I consider significant watersheds in my life – one public, and one personal.

PROLOGUE

The public activity that I think of as the beginning of my feminist journey was forming an organization called Mavoi Satum, literally "The Dead End" to help *agunot*, literally "chained women," a term for women stuck in unwanted marriages. At the time, I was a young religious mother of a two-year-old toddler living in Jerusalem – and pregnant with my second child. I spent most of this pregnancy alone with my child as my husband was away for four months doing his army service. We lived up on a second-floor walk-up – 45 stairs, to be exact, which I know because I counted them every day – and I was struggling. I was new in the country. I had no money, no real job, very few friends, no car, no particular career aspirations, and not enough knowledge of working Hebrew or Israeli culture to make my daily life easy or comprehensible. I had sort of harbored an idyllic dream of moving to Israel and living on a farm somewhere, but that wasn't happening. Instead, I was drowning.

To create some kind of structure or community, I joined a women's organization in the neighborhood called ESRA, literally "Help" (an ironic name now that I think about it. Was I helping others or helping myself? Hmmm.). We met every few weeks to discuss what is called "*chesed*," or charity work. We would sit around the table, eat, share life updates, and then review cases of women in the community who needed support – new mothers who needed diapers, women in the hospital who needed visitors, or mourners who needed meals. It was a classic Jewish women's activity, and quite a lovely gathering, even if I was the only one around the table under the age of 65.

Little did I know that one of these meetings was destined to alter the trajectory of my life. One day, we heard a different kind of story. It was about a woman named

Gratzia, who was an *agunah* – literally a "chained woman" who could not get divorced. Israeli divorce law follows Orthodox interpretations of *halakha*, or Jewish law, which holds that divorce is subject to the will and volition of the husband. As a result, women who want to get divorced are often victims of extortion by their not-yet-ex-husbands. Some women wait for years while their husbands make demands. Women in this situation, *agunot*, cannot remarry or have children or get on with their lives. Men, on the other hand, who hold their wives hostage, have no such constraints. They have ways of remarrying and even having children while their first wives are still in chains, so to speak, tied to a non-existent yet still abusive marriage while their husbands are free. There are estimated to be thousands or even tens of thousands of women in this situation in Israel and around the Jewish world.

I knew about the *agunah* situation from growing up in Flatbush, a modern-Orthodox neighborhood in Brooklyn, New York where every once in a while, my community rallied around a woman who was denied a divorce. We would show up at the workplace of some recalcitrant husband and hold posters and chant – sometimes for weeks or months – until he gave the *get*, the bill of divorce.

However, with Gratzia, this was the first time that I encountered an actual *agunah* in person who had a name and a face, and who was asking me *personally* for help, so to speak.

The story of Gratzia shook me, and I got involved. I went to meet the late Leah Ain Globe, a then-80-something Jerusalem activist, on behalf of agunot, who introduced me to Judith Djemal, another young mother like me who was also keen to *do something*. At Leah Globe's instructions, Judith and I raised money to help Gratzia pay for legal representation, which ultimately led her to obtain her divorce. As a result of this experience, we realized that this seemingly simple tactic of making sure that women had legal representation could radically change women's lives. In December 1995, Judith and I went to the Not-for-Profit Authority, each of us with newborn babies in tow, and opened up an organization to help agunot called Mavoi Satum, literally, "The Dead End," a name coined by Leah Globe that accurately reflected the situation many of these women were in. I co-chaired the organization for seven years along with the amazing Gloria Menzin, a retired Jerusalem businesswoman and widow who built a fabulously successful granola company from her kitchen while raising five children solo. Although I am no longer involved in the organization, it is still around – its dedicated leaders still fighting the fight, helping *agunot*, and advocating for systemic change in the way Jewish women get divorced in Israel so that this situation might be eliminated once and for all.

The work with *agunot* was an important part of my life during the years when I was first crafting a vision of my own adulthood. But at the time I saw it mostly as a public activity to advance social change for women. I was not an *agunah*, so it wasn't personal. I was helping others, not myself. Right? *Right?*

The other major milestone from 1995, which may or may not have been impacted by my work with *agunot*, was personal. I stopped covering my hair. It sounds like a little thing, but I feel like the act of taking off my hat has become, in retrospect, a formative event, and I think it is a reasonably accurate description of the moment in which I started to make a shift. And interestingly, as I turned fifty, it also marked the halfway point of my life until now.

When I was pregnant with my son – who was born around the time we started Mavoi Satum – I was BIG. Huge, actually, or so I thought at the time. On top of all that, I was diagnosed with gestational diabetes, which meant I had to eat a special diet, prick my finger for blood seven times a day, and make my way to the Hadassah Ein Karem hospital on the outskirts of the city twice a week, preferably without my toddler, despite not having a car or a job or any real support network. I have no idea how I did all that. I read in one of my journals from the time that I felt like God was carrying me up the stairs. Maybe she was.

One day, eight months pregnant in the Middle Eastern heat, I was crouching down at the bottom of the slide in the park, waiting for my daughter to land in my arms, and I suddenly noticed how uncomfortable I was. I was wearing a long skirt, and my hair was tied up in a hat. I just felt heavy, hot, and ridiculous – and alone.

What the hell am I doing?

That was the sentence that erupted in my head. Like, who was I trying to please? Who was I trying to impress? Who was I listening to, dictating how I should dress? It was as if I finally *noticed* how I was feeling, like I woke up and started hearing my own voice, which I hadn't heard in quite a long time.

The next day, I went out and bought myself a pair of maternity pants, and a few months later, after my son was born, I took off my hat.

That was the moment I started talking back to my culture. It was the moment I started paying attention to myself. That moment, I believe, was the beginning of my feminist journey.

For the most part, this feminist journey has seemed like a public one. I have since been involved in many organizations; I completed a doctorate on gender, education, and society; I have written four books about gender; I have taught gender in places around the world and spoken at dozens of conferences; I have been involved in synagogues and community-building everywhere I have lived; and most recently, I tried my hand at politics. It's a story of advancing social change for women in a very public way.

Yet, what I realized as I contemplated the path of these past 25 years is that there is also a very personal story as well, one that I do not often write about, but which is no less significant.

I was sitting with a dozen other women in Gloria's living room in Jerusalem, the board members of Mavoi Satum, listening to an extraordinary speaker. The year was 1998, and the speaker had my attention. Her name is Dr. Karen Abrams Gerber, a brilliant and clairvoyant coach and facilitator specializing in gender issues and organizational life who has since become a cherished friend. She had come to teach us about the dynamics of leadership among women, and what she said completely threw me off guard.

"What brings you here?" she asked innocuously at first.

I thought to myself; *I know exactly why I'm here.* We were there to help *agunot.* Isn't it evident?

"But why are *you* here?" Karen asked us again, looking, it seemed, at each one of us. It felt like such an easy question to answer. *There is a terrible injustice in our midst, and we are here to fix it. Simple.* We wanted to help women, to ease women's suffering, and to bring justice and equality to the divorce system in Israel. We were engaged in the process of advancing social justice in the Jewish world. We went around the room, explaining what felt like the obvious.

"Those are all lovely answers, but that's not what I'm asking," Karen replied. "I mean *you*. Why are *you* here, working on this issue?"

I didn't understand. Karen turned to me. "Elana, you're not an *agunah*. None of you are *agunot*. Not one of you! So why are *you* here doing this work? Why do you identify so strongly with these women? Why do these women, of all the people suffering in the world, grab hold of your emotions this way?"

The questions stumped me because I had never thought about it that way. But Karen was right. For one thing, she introduced us to the question of whether we were objectifying others. That was a big *aha!* moment for me. But it was more than that. There are a lot of people suffering in the world, and yet this was where I felt the urgency of putting my attentions. I did not know why. My husband did not beat me, and I was not filing for divorce. I didn't have a close friend or a neighbor or a sibling who was an *agunah* at the time. There was no palpable reason why I should identify specifically with *agunot* instead of, say, starving children, tortured animals, or victims of the Rwandan civil war. I couldn't readily explain why I was dedicating tens of hours of volunteer time each week to this organization dealing with this almost obscure problem of chained women. At the time, I had no real tools to investigate the answer, either.

"You need to ask yourselves why you identify with *agunot*," Karen said. "And, by the way," she added, "it's a good idea for you to invite actual *agunot* to join your board."

She was right, of course, on both counts. I was both perplexed and ashamed in my new and unseasoned self-awareness. I knew then – though I know better now – that the answer to this question was vital for me in order to understand myself and my life, but it would take me many years to find a real answer. Still, this event set that process in motion.

It set other crucial processes in motion, too. The conversation taught me how patronizing it was for us to be helping people who had no seat at the table, who were still voiceless "others." It taught me about the challenges that women sometimes have in really listening to one another instead of just assuming that we know what the other person is going through. Mostly, Karen's session taught me one of my first real lessons in the idea that the personal is political: Everyone in the room had a personal story, a reason for getting involved in this issue. We may not have been *agunot* in the classic sense, but something about being chained to *halakha*, anchored to men's will, resonated with all of us – and scared or outraged us enough to make it our life's work. And while it was possible to try and do the work of social justice without delving into our own stories, that path of working on society without addressing our own spirits and traumas would end up being significantly flawed.

It took me a long time to figure out the answer to Karen's questions – I would say, probably 15 years. It took a lot of unpacking and journaling, and more than a few painfully confronting events in my life, for me to have the courage to say the truth about how I felt about my life.

The process that began during those years – when I met Gratzia, started Mavoi Satum, took off my hat, worked on my dissertation, and contemplated Karen Abrams's questions about why I identified with "chained women" – propelled me onto a path of unpacking Orthodox Judaism from its patriarchal structure. It sent me to Orthodox feminism, where I became involved in many public campaigns and activities, not only around divorce but also around religious leadership, ritual, politics, economic equality, and more. Eventually, it sent me outside of Orthodoxy, and possibly outside of Jewish thought altogether, looking for a path of light somewhere else.

When I think about this journey that I am on, I realize that the personal and political have always been intricately connected, even if it is sometimes hard to admit. My involvement with Orthodox feminism was about fighting for social change for women while battling with my voices inside my head about my own body, my relationships with Judaism, and my life in general. It is all somehow connected. And even years later when I left Orthodoxy behind, that feminist journey of weaving the personal and political is still with me. I'm still in that, very intensely.

Throughout this journey, I have been writing. In the hundreds of essays that I've written – both published and unpublished – as well as my books, blogs, and even some social media exchanges, I'm narrating my life. I'm narrating a story even though I'm not sure what my arc is or how the story ends, but I'm narrating.

PROLOGUE

As a result of this process, and perhaps urged on by months of hunkering down and cleaning the house, I have decided to mark 25 years since my feminist awakening by telling my story. I have collected some of these essays to try to weave together some kind of chronicle of my life and my work. My story may not be coherent; it certainly isn't linear and does not have a neat ending, but I want to take stock and observe where I've been – perhaps to help me decide where I'm headed next.

One of my key discoveries along the way – and I'm still discovering – is how much patriarchy lives in the female body. My body holds my pains and traumas, as well as the traumas of my grandmothers and their grandmothers. I have spent the past 25 years unpacking how I was socialized into my relationship with my body and myself. It has been quite a journey and has taken me far and wide – to Australia, Hawaii, India, Hungary, Rwanda, and back home. It has taken me through cultures and religions and spiritual heights and emotional turbulences. It has not always been easy, but I'm traveling with my eyes fully open.

I decided, therefore, that my first collection of essays would be dedicated to body issues. The volume is not comprehensive, but rather a start. It focuses on issues of so-called "modesty," as well as issues of voice, hair, sexuality, food, fat, and body-commentary. This first volume is a starting point. Perhaps in a certain way, it is where all our lives begin.

This collection is personal and political, and it is a reminder for me to be whole and to stand up tall and not to feel shame or guilt for my travels or my ideas or my choices. This is who I am—all of it.

This volume is very different from my previous books, which all used my researcher's hat, and anthropologically explored the lives of women other than myself. This time, the primary subject here is me. Every essay, even those that tackle public events and do not initially seem like they are about me, are personal, even subtly. Inspired by Brené Brown's invocation to allow vulnerability, I am exposing myself here and praying that it will be okay, and worth the risk.

My hope is that the writing touches you. And that perhaps together, we can make changes not only for ourselves as individuals, but for the collective, those of us who have struggled with the way we have been constructed. If we understand that we are not alone, that the burden is on us but not on us alone, perhaps together we can make real change.

Dr. Elana Hope Maryles Sztokman

December 2020

Modi'in, Israel

"Modesty" they call it... as if

"You are not a mistake.
You are not a problem to be solved.
But you won't discover this until you
are willing to stop banging your head
against the wall of shaming and
caging and fearing yourself."

— Geneen Roth

When I think about my life as a Jewish woman, the most dominant feature emerging from my memories is the demand to be "modest." This mandate filters through so many of my experiences even at a young age: getting dressed, eating, walking, my voice, my hair, and, most emphatically, my sexuality. It has taken me years, if not decades, to face my own feelings about it all. I'm still doing it, even at fifty years old. It has taken me this long to have an honest conversation with myself. Digging deeper, I have discovered that even simply asking myself what I feel or what I want has been a rebellious act. Giving myself permission to want, to desire, to think for myself – these have been daring activities for me.

Today, I don't even know what "modesty" means. It's such an idiotic word. Ideally, the word "modesty" should convey a certain gentleness of demeanor vis a vis the other, as in taking care not to impose one's gaze on another human being. It should invoke an idea that I am no better than another person, that all people are equal creatures of God, equal in worth before the Divine Spirit. It should reflect an internal equanimity, a spiritual appreciation of one's minor place in the universe, and an understanding that one does not see himself or herself as inherently better than the other. Only God can judge people. All that we humans can do is accept one another and continuously strive to make ourselves better.

But "modesty," as it is used in the world I come from, is not that. It's never that. It's not a spiritual demeanor, an internal stance, a personal quest for growth, or a framework for building kind and compassionate relationships among people in which no one person claims a high and mighty stance among her or his peers. The word has evolved into something else entirely. Today, when rabbis or principals or Republicans talk about "modesty," there is only one issue they have in mind: covering and controlling women's bodies.

"Modesty" has become a code word for women's and girls' body cover, which is used as a marker for the virtuousness for the men around them. The length of the skirt, sleeve, or neckline is used as a measuring stick of religious identity and societal control. The more female skin is covered, the more virtuous the girls – or rather, their surrounding communities consider themselves to be. In fact, it is taken quite literally in some cases. One Jewish community recently came out with an actual "modesty ruler," to be used by girls measuring their skirts around their knees. I wrote about this trend at length in my book, Educating in the Divine Issues: Gender issues in Orthodox Jewish Day Schools, *co-authored with my dear friend, Dr. Chaya Gorsetman.*

This distorted, misogynistic view of modesty is a blight. And it affects us – it affects ME.

Tellingly, the topic that never comes up in these conversations about the so-called "modesty" is what girls and women experience. *It is always about how girls* look *– according to controlling, sexually-obsessed, heterosexual men – never how girls and women* feel. *As a result, there is very little communal discussion about what girls and women go through when living out these rules.*

In this section, I have compiled a few essays that I have written on this subject from the perspective of someone who tried for years – decades – to adhere to these rules but eventually left them behind. Everything I write here comes from life experience, even when I use my researcher's hat. It's all personal. Very, very personal.

Between Baalat Teshuva and Britney Spears[2]

This was one of my first published essays in which I shared my journey from yeshivah girl to Orthodox feminist. It is at times crude, but it remains an accurate depiction of my life at the time.

When I was an 18-year-old yeshiva high school graduate from Brooklyn, one of the biggest questions on the minds of my female friends and me — right after, who will get engaged next? — was, who is going to "frum out" in Israel? You know, it's what happens during that post-high school yeshiva experience in Israel: the skirts get longer, the bowing gets deeper during prayers, which also increase in frequency. The phrases *"Baruch hashem"* (thank God) and *"bli neder"* (no vow) go from a mere drizzle in one's vocabulary to a full-blown hurricane, and obedience to one's teachers

---

[2] November 23, 2009, originally published at *The Forward*. Reprinted with permission.
https://forward.com/sisterhood/119459/between-baalat-teshuva-and-britney-spears/

completely overtakes all ability to think independently, express flexibility, and demonstrate a sense of humor. Yes, frumming out. I went through a somewhat modified version myself. I spent around 5-6 years wearing floor-sweeping skirts, spent my first four years of marriage wearing a head covering (*baruch hashem,* that's over), and for a while, actually believed that reward and punishment were readily apparent in everyday life. (A few major terror attacks relieved me of that notion.)

I'm about to turn 40, and I'm (*baruch hashem*) over most of that now, as are many of my contemporaries. I often talk with my friends over Shabbat lunch about our journeys back and forth between religion, God, and self. Although the journey is enlightening, I wonder how much of the pain is necessary. Put differently, some days, I'm angry at my teachers.

I thought about all this recently at a somewhat surprising place. I gave a talk about Orthodox feminism to a group of Americans on an Israel Women's Network mission to Israel, headed by a Minnesota State Senator, a Reform Jewish woman whose three adult daughters all became ultra-Orthodox — or what is mislabeled "*baalei teshuva,*" or "returnees," (as if people who are not Orthodox by definition need to repent, as if becoming Orthodox is some kind of return from something, as if Orthodoxy is the only lifestyle that is authentically Jewish). It turns out, the Senator was coming to Israel to visit her daughter, who had recently gotten married in Safed, and she converted the visit into a feminist mission. *Now that,* I thought, *was novel.*

During my session, we discussed many of the troubling trends in Israel around religion and gender: increased pressure for gender segregation in public spaces, the frightening tolerance for violence against women who are deemed non-conforming, and of course, the weary struggle of *agunot*. Following the session, the Senator approached me and said, "So tell me, please. What is the great attraction of Orthodoxy?"

Her question was weighted with frustration. "I brought my daughters up with all the right ideas," she said. "We always had gender equality in our community and our synagogue. We raised them to be activists, committed to equal rights. I don't understand why girls would turn their backs on this in favor of Orthodoxy." Her pain was palpable.

Why, indeed? Returnee activists will undoubtedly use this as "proof" of the superiority of their lifestyle, but I don't buy that. In fact, the polarized juxtaposition of Western culture versus ultra-Orthodoxy is at the root of women's entrapment. As if it's either one or the other: If you don't want to be a superficial, mindless, materialistic sex-object, cover-up and come to us. The returnee movement feeds on people's dissatisfaction with what Dr. Beverly Gribetz calls "great, big, shopping-mall America," with Paris Hilton and Britney Spears as models of femininity.

But of course, there are worlds in between. It's just not so easy for an impressionable 18–25-year-old sincere spiritual seeker to unravel the subtleties and summon the courage to say, "None of the above."

Moreover, the ultra-Orthodox "answer" to modern life is wrapped up in an impregnable God-rhetoric. A friend of mine, a stay-at-home mother of six, once said, "I just have to remember that even when I'm picking up dirty socks, I'm doing God's work."

Yeah, right, I thought. "That's the biggest crock I've ever heard," I responded.

She didn't like that. She was too exhausted and too reliant on the rhetoric to keep herself happy amid her servitude.

I don't have a good answer for the Senator or for my Orthodox acquaintances who want to know why (or whether) I'm still Orthodox. But I do, nevertheless, have prayer, and I pray that the Senator will find her daughters again.

Post-script

Although this essay began with discussions of Orthodox women's clothing, it ended up being about expectations of behavior. I don't think that's an accident. These issues are all connected. We are told to dress "modestly" in order to keep us in our place.

Over the years, I have gotten a lot of angry push-back from religious women over essays like this. Religious women sometimes feel like I don't sufficiently respect their choices. That I'm not "live and let live" enough about women who choose to be religious, to cover their bodies, to or drench dirty socks with sexist positivity. When I point out that I come from that world, that I'm basing my ideas on my own life experiences as well as on scholarship, it doesn't even necessarily help. Since this essay was published in 2009, I have learned to temper some of my language with more compassion and understanding, to try to do a better job of respecting everyone's life choices, and to more gently frame my belief systems in my own journey and experiences rather than in absolute, all-encompassing opinions. Today I am probably less likely to say out loud that the notion of picking up dirty socks as a spiritual act is a crock of shit. Although I certainly still think it – maybe now even more emphatically than I did then.

Indeed, although I have been learning how to better navigate hard conversations with women, my underlying sentiments have not changed that much, and perhaps have even gotten stronger. I feel even more strongly today than I did then that religious and cultural Jewish leaders often infuse their messages with layers of sexism and use spiritual language to keep women servile. They seem to think that if they tell women enough times that dedication to mindless servitude is God's way, women may believe it enough to keep the gendered order of things.

I think this phenomenon may even be getting worse in some corners of Jewish life. And even as I respect women's choices, I wholeheartedly believe that female subservience, while perhaps the will of some men, is absolutely not the will of God. But it is not always safe for me to say that out loud.

Perhaps more than anything, this essay reminds me of how hard it is to have these conversations with people who are invested in their culture – even women struggling to believe that dirty socks are holy. However, these conversations are hard. We are up against God rhetoric. It's not easy.

But it also raises another question that has haunted me in my life: Which is more important, hanging on to my truth, or hanging on to relationships? Put differently, if a relationship is one in which your most important truth, that truth which gives you your basic freedom, is not valued or understood, should you put that aside in order to keep a relationship? Or are connections with people who do not understand my desperate need for freedom not worth the pain that they invariably cause?

I have made some painful choices on this subject. But I still question at times whether I have done the right thing. I don't think I could have done it any other way and come out whole. But in some ways, I'm still not whole.

On Skirts and Daughters[3]

In general, I am reluctant to write about my kids because their stories are their own to tell. I also rarely give out parenting advice because, well, I don't have the parenting thing figured out. This essay breaks both of those rules – although my daughter gave me permission to write about her at the time. But I take no responsibility for the accuracy of my parenting ideas.

I remember well the time I decided to stop wearing trousers in favor of skirts. At the age of 19, I was becoming more "religious" following my yeshiva education, and I packed up my slacks and put on those hard, straight denim skirts that were popular in my Brooklyn day school. But it wasn't long before I opted for the long, flowy, floral, and paisley one-size-fits-all down to the ankle types, otherwise known as "floor sweepers". In those skirts, I was comfortable. I could sit cross-legged on the floor, I could feel my body move in the fabric, and

[3] 2005 (originally written in 2001). Published in Mandy Ross and Ronne Randall, eds. *For Generations: Jewish Motherhood.* (UK: Five Leaves). Reprinted with permission. Adjusted for US spelling.

I was less cloistered. In a certain sense, it was more "beautiful" to me, maybe even more feminine.

It wasn't until years later when I was a young married woman and changed my appearance again by taking off my beret and pulling on my jeans, that it occurred to me that those shapeless skirts that my Dad used to so easily disparage as "unflattering" were actually a form of rebellion. I was making an unconscious statement. Wearing those skirts was my way of saying that how I *feel* is more important than how I *look*, that I had enough of the tight, molded and squeezed sensations that came with the classic Orthodox girls' uniform of the straight skirt. How odd to think that in the world of modern Orthodox Judaism, a young woman can rebel by becoming more religious.

The oppression of women via the clothing that they are expected to wear is an old story. Although we have come a long way from corsets and bustles, and the acceptance of women's trousers in the workplace seems to indicate growing respect for women as professional equals, still, societal expectations of women continue to be reflected in styles of dress. An ultra-Orthodox colleague of mine ironically echoed the feminist sentiment when he described how he feels that mini-mini-skirts, cropped tops, and sheer-tight dresses turn women into sex objects. A religious hairdresser neighbor recalled her own transition from being secular to religious as one in which she was searching for a world in which women were viewed as more than their external appearance. *Hmmm*, I thought, as she finished doing my color. Would my grey hair encourage people to appreciate my mind?

And moreover, must I forego all beauty products to consider myself a feminist truly? Something tells me that we are beyond that – or maybe not. Maybe we were never quite there.

The issue is complicated. For observant Jews, the answers are so often provided before we have finished asking the question. Jewish law tells women to cover themselves up for the purposes of sexual propriety. "*Shok isha erva, kol isha erva*" says the *Shulchan Aruch*, a central authority on Jewish law. "A woman's thighs are forbidden, a woman's voice is forbidden." As predictable as these ancient assertions are, so too are their modern-day aggadic interpretations – from the apologists who try to convince us that women are actually on a "higher" (read "different") level, to the fundamentalists who chide us that this is God's will and that feminism is not a Jewish value. On the other side of the fence, post-modernists tell us that everything is subjective, that all Jewish law is context-dependent and socially constructed, anyway. It's a classic example of women's subjugation – these laws succeed in turning us into silent and invisible beings for the sake of community and familial wellness. Women subject to men's gaze, women as objects of man's desire.

Meanwhile, we women with physiques and psyches, body issues, food issues, voice issues, and control issues, spend our money on therapy and yoga, diets and wardrobes, in a feeble attempt to help us sort out the pieces of the puzzle. Caught between our respect for tradition and our respect for ourselves, between adherence to codes and adherence to our own inner voices, we are returned to the ongoing tension between autonomy and submission, in search once again for our own reflections and practice of what it means to be a Jewish woman.

MODESTY

I see young girls in the park across the street from my house, the oldest one under the age of ten, wearing a wool tartan dress with long sleeves, thick tights, and shoes, looking after two younger siblings. *She's growing up too fast,* I think to myself. Already she's a little mother, already she's covering her body – and she hasn't even hit puberty yet. She won't be climbing trees, riding a bike or jumping hurdles any time soon. Already she is taught that her body is about how others see her rather than how she feels. In summer she'll be hot from the sleeves and in winter she'll be cold from the stockings. And when she wants to hide her body, when she feels flawed and imperfect, she has many tools at her disposal for covering up and hiding the perceived blemishes.

I'm grateful that my eight-year-old daughter, Avigayil, is permitted to wear trousers this year in her religious school. So far, she is empowered in terms of her own appearance, freely choosing clothes that are comfortable, warm, and physically enabling – and that look nice to her when she looks in the mirror. She seems comfortable with her body in that healthy, youthful way. But of course, the skirt rule begins next year at our school. And I worry about that. I've started to speak informally to other parents and the principal about extending permission for trousers at least until the age of 11 or even 12 (though in reality, I would prefer to do away with the rule altogether – but first things first). Why are we telling them so young that their bodies are sexual objects, that they should be paying so much attention to the way men see them? So far, I haven't met with much support for these thoughts. After all, I've been told, there are so many more important and pressing issues on the agenda. Is this where we should be focusing our energies when we have to deal with more important questions like the curriculum, bus schedules, and homework?

Maybe it's the influence of Mary Pipher's *Reviving Ophelia* that stays with me, the notion that these early years are crucial for girls' sense of self-worth, that in a few short years they'll experience the infamous "drop" – the drop in self-esteem and self-image that puts them at high risk of eating disorders, depression, drug and alcohol exposure, and conflicts about their sexuality, among other things. The religious community is no longer able to maintain the delusion that it is somehow immune to these ills. Anorexia alone is so widespread among religious adolescent girls that all pretense of sweeping it under the carpet is gone. And maybe the growing numbers of abused women in the Orthodox community will ultimately propel us to re-examine the messages that we send our young women about self within relationships. Maybe.

Consciousness. I would like to see the Orthodox community become more attentive to girls' subjective experience. What are the girls feeling? How do they experience their own bodies? How does the girl in the park see herself? I want to be able to have a conversation about the impact of dress codes on girls within the religious, educational system. So far, I haven't found too many partners for the conversation. But I'm still looking.

My three-year-old daughter, Yonina, is going through the famous "dress stage." I understand from other parents that all girls go through it. My mother reports that when I was in kindergarten, I had one dress only that I insisted on wearing every day. Thank God Yonina has two or three – that helps with the laundry. And not any dress will do, only the ones that flow high when she spins around fast, like a pinafore. Despite an early effort to gently persuade her of the merits of trousers in the rainy, snowy winter, I swiftly abandoned my cause. Like

12

any good struggling parent, I addressed the conflict between my own vision and my child's desires by casting aside my own needs and going with hers all the way. Now I help her find matching tights and headbands. Every morning in preschool, she runs to her friend Ruthie, and they compare dresses, colors, shoes, hair, and twirling around. It's their own sweet ritual. And despite myself, it always makes me smile. For some reason that feminist researchers may never come to understand, this stage seems important, and apparently inevitable. Besides, so far, she hasn't let the dress stop her from riding her tricycle, going down the slide, rolling on the floor, or jumping from the third stair. And I guess that's what ultimately counts.

Our messages are complicated. The laws of "modesty" may encourage a form of self-respect. But they can also be inhibiting, objectifying, and oppressive. Sure, secular society often shows women as sex-objects. But in the religious world, women often aren't seen at all. And so, I remain torn between my desire to be seen and my desire not to be seen too much, between wanting my daughters to use their legs and not wanting them to be seen only for their legs. Finding the balance between my sometimes-conflicting values is my challenge as an educator, a mother, and essentially as a grown-up girl.

Post-script

My daughters have grown quite a bit since this writing. Avigayil is 27, and Yonina is 23. And I'm thrilled to say that they both wear exactly what they want. Thank God. But the problem of insufficient attention to the body needs of girls in many communities has not gone away. And the feeling of having multiple sets of eyes on our bodies and expectations coming at from all directions, has also, unfortunately, stayed with me for all these years. I think my daughters are fine, but I'm not so sure about myself.

My Body Is Not Just an Object in Your Landscape[4]

The day that I heard that even feminist-leaning girls schools were overly policing girls' dress, I felt dejected and deflated. Outraged, actually. But I know that this issue is not the exclusive domain of religious schools. I have been in state schools and non-Orthodox schools that are also obsessed with dress code. It's all about control. And it is still infuriating.

A religious girls' high school in Jerusalem came out with a new rule: discussions about girls' clothing choices could no longer occupy more than twenty minutes out of every hour of staff meeting time. It makes you wonder how much time some Jewish educators spend talking about students' dress. And it's a question not just for Orthodox schools but for Jewish schools across the spectrum.

Certainly, the Orthodox community has its own particular obsession with girls' dress. In the Orthodox world, girls' so-called "modesty" – a code-word that has

[4] April 2, 2014. Originally published in *The NCJW Journal.* Reprinted with permission. https://ncjwa.org.au/wp-content/uploads/2014/04/NCJWA-Council-Bulletin-Vol-90-No-2-Pesach-2014.pdf

nothing to do with actual humility but simply refers to the length of skirts, sleeves, and necklines – has become the ubiquitous missive for almost all things deemed religious. Girls receive the unequivocal message that to be religious means to cover the body.

It's a message that comes across loud and clear to the students. Indeed, many girls have a hard time answering the question, "How religious are you?" or "What do you feel about Torah observance?" without going directly into discussions about their skirts and sleeves. Even among boys, questions about their religious identity are often answered with responses such as, "I would like my wife to cover her hair when I get married" as if to say the head-covering choices of the future imagined spouse are an adequate description of a boy's connection to God and Torah.

It's not just Orthodox educators, however, who expend disproportionate time and energy on students' appearance. I've been to many staff meetings that featured prolonged discussions about the perceived horror of students' lax attention to uniform rules. Teachers complain about how much time is wasted in class, getting their students to tidy up their appearance. Educators complain that it's impossible to teach students who are so unkempt and irreverent as if that untucked shirt says everything about a person's character.

I believe what these stories have in common is a misguided notion that education is first and foremost about control – an attempt to control the school environment by controlling students' bodies. I understand why control is valued. When you are given the task of managing a thousand or so children, or when you are given 56 minutes to teach 27 children five pages of text five or seven times in a row each day, control can be key to maintaining one's own sanity and getting through your task list for the day.

But this is not really education, is it? Do we really want students who are more committed to obedience than to free-thinking and independent creativity? In our post-Holocaust world, this question should give us all pause.

Furthermore, there is something deeply troubling about the language of body-control that characterizes these discussions. In the religious world, control over the female body is about maintaining a certain perception of sexual purity: as if to say, if girls cover their bodies in a certain way, then they will not engage in sexual behavior with the opposite sex, and this makes girls "religious."

There are many flaws in that line of thinking, the first of which is that there is no immutable connection between clothing choices and sex. We need to recognize that girls' and women's clothing choices often have little to do with their sexual choices and have much more to do with fashion tastes, body shape, and if they're lucky, physical comfort. (Although perhaps in our society at large, women's comfort often takes a back seat to fashion expectations, which is a whole other set of problems).

Furthermore, where a woman's choice of clothing reflects her sense of her own sexuality and sensuality, that may have absolutely nothing to do with her sexual behavior with other people, and may just be how she chooses to carry herself. We are all sexual beings, and how we feel in our own bodies is not about who we are sleeping with but rather how alive we are within our own skin. If only women's physical sensations in our skin and our clothes were something recognized as valuable for us as human beings – and by the way, nobody else's business. The entire rationale that says that women and girls have to cover our bodies to the max in order to prevent us from being sexually attractive to the men in charge or having unapproved sex sends the immutable message that our bodies are not our own but belong to the men and boys around us, who get to make all the rules.

Plus, the connection between girls' body cover and so-called religiousness reinforces the deeply distorted idea that religious identity is a function of women's and girls' external appearance – rather than, say, a function of a person's approach to Godliness, compassion, and relationships with other human beings.

At the risk of stating the obvious, I would just like to point out that my body is not merely an object in someone else's landscape. It is just my body, the one that enables me to move and breathe and think and eat and run and function in my life. From my perspective, I would rather see girls wearing shorts and t-shirts volunteering in an aged-care facility than see girls wearing long skirts and sleeves hanging around the mall. Our bodies are here to facilitate our lives as we try to do good things in the world.

Significantly, the language of female body control often has more to do with men's presumed needs than with women's and girls' needs. This, unfortunately, spreading thought – that is, that a (heterosexual) man who wants to live in a world in which there are no sexual "distractions" should demand all females to adhere to extreme body cover – is, as we all know, causing tremendous grief to women everywhere who are asked to hide behind partitions, walk on the other side of the road, switch seats on airplanes, and more. Women and girls are increasingly being asked to adjust our own bodies to create a landscape for men that is free of apparitions of the female body.

Perhaps Jewish educators should be rethinking the emphasis on body-control. If we want to educate for care and compassion, for an awareness of the world around us and the needs of the other, then the obsession with students' appearance is not only distracting but detrimental. We need a different model. When we believe in our children and our students, when we trust them as human beings with open hearts and minds, when we allow ourselves to let go of the need to control their bodies and instead make space for them to grow as people, that's when the real process of Jewish education can take place.

Post-script

In essays like this one, I wear a lot of hats: Parent, teacher, researcher, observer. Perhaps less obvious is that I am also always wearing one more hat: that of the religious girl. I may be an adult, but I'm writing to give the girl inside of me a voice.

There is a saying among doctoral students that all dissertations are personal. Writing about religious girls in school was my way of writing about myself without having to wear my heart on my sleeve. But today, I would like to say this out loud – that when I write about what girls might be feeling when their bodies are being obsessively controlled, I am often writing from my own heart and life experiences – even memories buried deep.

Dignified in Pants[5]

This essay was written in response to an essay in the Forward by a young religious woman who described her commitment to wearing skirts and hair-covering as "dignified." It reminded me of the rabbis who tell girls to cover up to "respect ourselves." I bought into that line for way too long. Today I know that it's rubbish. They are just words that are told to girls to admit that men are leering at girls' bodies. So much for "dignified".

Just because I wear pants, it doesn't mean I lack dignity. Or self-respect. Or even modesty. This is why I find pieces like this one, suggesting that dignity for a woman means excessive body-cover, so offensive.

When rabbis or anyone else claim that women need to cover their skin, their elbows, ankles, and necks for the sake of "dignity" or "self-respect" or "protecting sexuality," what that means is that people who dress like me are not dignified. We are overly sexualized. We

---

[5] February 6, 2012. Originally published at *The Forward*. Reprinted with permission.
https://forward.com/sisterhood/150237/dignified-in-pants/

might as well be walking naked on the subway platform. But it is just not true.

My body is mine alone, and I project that in my clothes - not floor-sweeping skirts, not scarves to my forehead or necklines that choke. No, I wear pants, sometimes jeans, sometimes shorts and, yes, sometimes even sleeveless tops. I wear clothes that are comfortable, that feel good, that let me move and sit on the floor or in a chair, that enable me to ride a bike or climb a tree if I so choose, that let me wear my hair in a ponytail or a scrunchie or even just down. Ultimately my hair is mine alone, as are my elbows, my neck, my ankles, and skin. Before I look in a mirror, I look inward and ask myself how I feel about my body at this moment, and I let my inner voice of self-respect guide me.

In addition, Gavriella Lerner's assertion of choice, followed by an admission that she does what she believes is expected of her according to *halakha,* is a classic Orthodox non-sequitur. As in, I *choose* to do what I'm told.

I would like to challenge this dubious claim of choice this way: If your rabbi came out tomorrow and said that you do *not* have to dress this way, how would you dress, really? And be honest. And don't answer fast. Because religious girls and women are *never* asked that question, so they barely even know how to address it. What would you *desire* on your body? Comfort and desire are not concepts that any religious woman is raised to consider for herself. And by the way, desire to obey *halakha,* to be a good girl, is not the kind of desire I'm talking about. I am talking about actual body desire.

It is naïve to think that *halakha* says unequivocally that this is how women should dress. The idea that pants are "*kli gever*" (men's clothing) was disproved generations ago. And there has been so much cultural variation in expectations of women's dress — in fact, in Maimonides' times, it was the men who wore dresses — that notions of some kind of monolithic *halachic* way are beyond absurd. It's just social convention.

I'm also troubled by the author's attempt to disassociate from others who are more excessive than her in body-cover rules. Orthodox Jews are masterful in their ability to look at other Orthodox Jews and say, "We're not like *that*." It's the Jewish version of Goldilocks: I cover just the right amount of skin — not too little and not too much. I have just the right amount of enthusiasm for *halakha*, not too little, not too much.

It's living a life based on the Orthodox obsession with the female body in some form or another. It is the same rationale that allows a man to think of little Naama Margolese as "immodest" or to call a female soldier a "slut." It is all the same rhetoric that turns non-conforming women, women who dress "different" — women like me — into the strange other. This is not Judaism; it is social dysfunction.

Orthodoxy needs a new vision about what it means to live a Torah life. The big lie that sleeves and skirts make us religious just isn't working anymore.

Post-script
Here, too, the anger that is so palpable was coming from my personal identification with girls who are being body-policed. Although at this writing, my feelings on the matter were unequivocal, it took me years to get to that place where I could hear these thoughts in my head, and have the courage to say them out loud.

I cannot help but wonder how girls in Orthodoxy are faring today. Do they have more body autonomy, self-awareness, and confidence to listen to themselves than I did? Are they exposed to body positivity through the Internet and through feminist movements? Or are the struggles that I documented in my doctoral research, and that I experienced in my own life, still dominant?

I wait for the next generation of writers, researchers, and thinkers to answer those questions.

Olympics 2016: Two Cultures, One Sexual Gaze[6]

The iconic Reuters photo of Olympic volleyball players Doaa Elghobashy of Egypt wearing a hijab opposite Kira Walkenhorst of Germany wearing a bikini is one of the most important photos in the conversation about women's bodies – because it illustrates how women get it from all sides. We are placed in a dichotomy of men's makings. And all sides are wrong.

Some people look at this photo and see the beauty of diversity at the Olympics. Maybe. But I also see something else. I see women in two different cultures trapped in their cultures' demands about women's bodies and appearance: opposite cultures, the same problem of sexual objectification.

On the right, we have women athletes who, no matter what their physical and mental accomplishments, are

---

[6] August 10, 2016. Originally published on my blog, *A Jewish Feminist.*
http://jewfem.com/index.php?option=com_easyblog&view=entry&id=541&Itemid=513

forced to abide by rules intended to maximize their sexual appeal to gazing heterosexual males. The beach volleyball athletes have been among the most objectified, photographed from behind, valued for their cleavage and skin, and commented on for sexual appeal of their skin rather than for their athletic prowess. You are more likely to come across a photo of a volleyball player's behind than one of her slamming the ball.

On the left, we have a different form of sexual objectification from a radically different culture, one similarly controlled and dominated by men who view women primarily as sex objects. In the culture on the left, the response to this outlook is to maintain extreme, maximum coverage for women. It is the opposite response to the same position of men believing women are primarily objects to look at, the same men controlling their culture by maintaining norms of women's body cover/uncover.

Both women have overcome their positions as sexual artifacts to achieve a place in the Olympics. That is incredible. Doubly incredible - like Ginger Rogers doing everything Fred Astaire did but backward and in high heels. Women often have to work within the rules of their cultures to achieve their dreams for this life. Sometimes that is doable, and sometimes it just isn't. So this is a picture of women choosing to abide by the rules of their cultures, no matter how sexist and misogynistic, and succeeding in overcoming these excessive obstacles in order to great things and to be outstanding.

But it doesn't address the deeper problem. In neither of these cultures are women allowed to prioritize their own comfort or desire. Women in both cultures – secular and religious cultures – are molded from the age of zero to be conscious of being watched and gazed upon. In neither

24

secular nor religious culture are women and girls allowed to just *be* with their bodies, to dress for *comfort*, to choose based on their own feelings and a sense of their own contours rather than on proscriptions of the men dominating their cultures. This is a problem worldwide, the absence of legitimacy for women's comfort and women's desires and women's body autonomy. And so with all the different types of inspiration that this picture generates, it also generates a very strong outrage that women still have to put up with this.

Portrait of women in the world, 2016.

Post-script

Which is more empowering for a woman, a hijab or a bikini? It's the kind of question that religious leaders love to put to women in order to gain our compliance with their rules. But the question is a trap. The answer is neither and both. The male gaze comes at us from all sides. The bikini is not necessarily "liberated", especially in the context of sports that mandate objectifying uniforms and are often covered by ogling photographers more interested in women's behinds than their powerful ball-throwing arms. But neither is the hijab.

Still, maybe my answer is also skewed. I am someone who no longer covers my hair and shoulders but also does not wear bikinis. And why not? Why not really? I say it is because I don't want to be objectified by modern, secular standards of patriarchy. But maybe it is because I have also internalized a deep shame about my body.

After all, my mother used to tell us that the reason why we could not wear short sleeves was not just because it was immodest but also because our arms were ugly, and that flabby thighs should not be seen. It's not just the patriarchy that comes at us from all sides; it is also the shame. All sides teach us shame. Today, I am wondering if my rejection of "extreme" body revealing is also holding my own body shame.

When Modest Is Hottest[7]

The "modesty" obsession is not the exclusive domain of Orthodox Judaism. It is a plague, and it is everywhere – state schools, non-Jewish schools, even liberal schools. It is about control. But perhaps people like me – graduates of the "modesty" system who have taken back the conversation with our bodies – have an important contribution to make to the entire issue.

The obsession with covering girls' knees is no longer the territory of religious schools alone. Earlier this month, according to a report in *Ha'aretz*, a group of 12th-grade girls at the Israeli state Ben Zvi High School in Kiryat Ono were asked to cover their knees for yearbook photos, or stand behind a bench to hide their legs. Their exposed knees, they were told, were not "respectful" of the school." No boys were asked to cover their knees.

The truth is that the spread of the "modesty" obsession from religious school settings to public school settings has been going on for some time, in both Israel and the United States. In Israel, already in 2012, parents at the

---

7 December 14, 2015, originally published in *The Forward*.
https://forward.com/life/327103/when-modest-is-hottest/
Reprinted with permission.

secular junior high school Gevanim in Kadima complained that the principal was sending girls home for wearing pants that were deemed too short, and for holding "pants checks" for girls at the entrance to the school. In Ben Zvi, girls were also reportedly not allowed to wear sleeveless t-shirts for school photos, and those who did found their arms covered via Photoshop.

But it's not just Israel. In the United States, "modesty" (a tragic misnomer for an idea that has nothing to do with humility) has become a catchphrase for body-policing as well. Schools around the country have been imposing dress codes on girls against pants that are "too tight," strapless dresses for an eighth grade dance, tops that are considered too low-cut, and even a kindergarten girl whose skirt was considered too short.

In many cases, public shaming is considered acceptable practice in the name of imposing so-called "modesty." Principals and teachers have no compunction against humiliating students, with such practices as rounding up the girls for a spot-check of their knees; making girls wear a "shame suit"; refusing entry to girls at their high school dance after being made to flap their arms up and down and turn in circles in front of male administrators whose stated goal was to make sure that girls had "no curvature of their breasts showing"; or simply yelling at female students, as the Ben Zvi teachers did, in front of the whole school.

Much of this public shaming for the sake of "modesty" is of course familiar to me, as it probably is to any other female graduate of an Orthodox day school, where teachers and rabbis would routinely stand by the front door checking our knees. "Skirting" in Orthodox schools, accompanied by this kind of public shaming, has become so routine that even when it is protested – as it was by an outraged student of the Yeshivah of Flatbush last year — educators are mostly unwilling to show remorse or reflection on these common practices.

Still, despite their familiarity, it is worthwhile to look at the kinds of ideas that are used to justify the shaming-for-modesty educational practices. The rationales are different but similar in religious and secular settings. Religious educators often cite a kind of esoteric piety, like the need for girls to be "pure," or the unsubstantiated idea that covering one's body is the most important commandment in the Torah for women and girls, or even the frightening rationale that women's body cover saves people's lives. Last week, I attended a talk by a religious woman who described how, when she was diagnosed with breast cancer, she took it upon herself to speak less gossip and practice more "modesty" in order to heal the cancer. She ironically noted that it didn't really have the desired effect.

There is an intriguing overlap between Jewish and Christian religious rhetoric around policing girls' bodies. Christian fundamentalists also use the "modesty" language, and in fact have coined the chilling term "modest is hottest" – to reinforce the idea that girls should dress to be modest and "hot" at the same time. This term underscores how the sexualizing of women's and girl's bodies is coming at us from all directions. There seems to be no culture in which girls are safe from the male sexual gaze.

In secular settings, girls' bodies are described as "distracting" to boys, or "disrespectful" of the surrounding community. But these ideas seem to be overlapping between worlds. In my doctoral research, I also came across a similar rationale of girls as "tempting" or "distracting" boys, like putting unkosher food in front of them – with little consciousness about the implications of comparing girls' bodies to food. One rabbi talked about how it is "not nice" for girls to make themselves so tempting to boys, reinforcing the idea that girls' existential purpose is to sweetly serve the (sexual? culinary?) needs of men and boys. And by contrast, the girls in the secular Ben Zvi high school were reportedly yelled at and humiliated with comments such as, "School is not a place for licentiousness."

Ultimately, these approaches have as little to do with religiousness or Torah as they do with respectfulness or education. They are about one thing: controlling girls' sexuality. The predominant idea around so-called modesty is to ensure that girls do not engage in sexual activity, do not emote any sexual energy, do not feel any sexual feelings, and do not relate to themselves as sexual beings. To wit, one Wisconsin school sent out elaborate dress code instructions for prom night under the banner of "A night to protect her character." As if to say, if a boy and a girl engage in any kind of sexual activity, it "ruins" the girl's character while having no impact on the boy. As Nina Bahadur writes in *Huffington Post*, the implication is that "God forbid a young woman make choices about what she'd like to do with herself and a consenting partner. The implication is that a girl who doesn't 'protect her character' isn't brave, courageous, or worthy of respect. And of course, there's no mention of what boys should be doing to 'protect' their reputations."

Girls receive this message across all kinds of settings, at all ages, across religions, across countries, and across schools and educational systems. It doesn't seem to matter what religious outlook they hold by, whether they are prepubescent or lesbian or asexual, what they look like or what kind of clothes they actually like. The

29

message in all these cases is that female human beings, from the time we are born, are objects in a man's world, and are meant to internalize that objectivity. We are meant to hang on tight to the knowledge that we are watched and owned by men who make the rules about our body, to think about that gaze whenever we choose our clothing, whenever we walk in public, whenever we speak, whenever we move.

We are also meant to believe that our skin is owned by our surroundings and our community. We show "respect" for our communities by not being seen – hiding under cloth or behind a bench. The exposure of boys' skin has no such consequence of disrespect; only girls' skin is perceived as insolence. Only girls are expected to know their place in society.

In some encouraging but sort of complicated news, women and girls have been protesting all this slut-shaming. Girls everywhere have started to revolt, with walkouts, social media campaigns like #iam-morethanadistraction, petitions, and girls coming to school en masse on particularly hot days in crop tops and tank tops.

In the Christian world, within a growing community of formerly-evangelicals, bloggers and activists have been exposing the dangers of the "modest is hottest" movement. One blogger at the religion site Patheos writes, "As young as 6, 8, and 10 years old, my friends and I were viewed by our parents and leaders as potential objects of lust and temptation. The fact that a teen or grown adult man could become sexually aroused by our uncovered knees and shoulders was viewed as normal." But it gets worse. She continues, "Modesty became eroticized, virginity fetishized, our bodies both infantilized and hyper-sexualized. Worse, our bodies became disposable. Our bodies were simply vessels for the gift of purity, and our value was determined by how many fingerprints were on the box. If someone 'unwrapped' you before your wedding day, you became a cup of spit, a licked candy bar, a white sheet rolled in the mud. Consumed. Polluted. Spent." Another Christian blogger writes, "Modesty, rather than offering believers an alternative to the sexual objectification of women, often continues the objectification, just in a different form." Another blogger also writes about the connection between modesty and eating disorders, in a fascinating piece titled "How modesty made me fat."

In Jewish settings, the movement is less pronounced. Certainly Melissa Duchan tried to lead a revolution in Flatbush. And the girls at Ben Zvi and other secular high schools in Israel are taking to social media. But this revolution hasn't taken off yet. Signs seem to indicate that modesty obsession is getting worse and not better in the Jewish world.

In addition, some of the protests seem to be leading in odd directions. The reason why I claimed that the protests are at times complicated is because it can be hard for us to figure out what the opposite of "modest" is. In some feminist circles, the desire to protest excessive male gaze and ownership of our bodies has been to bare it all. Slut walks, FEMEN, Free the Nipple, and even Dove have promoted public female nudity as an antidote to sexism and male ownership of our bodies. This movement towards nudity as empowerment has even taken hold in some Orthodox settings.

I get this. I can see how empowering this can be. After all, Nobel Prize Laureate Leyma Gbowee brought peace to Liberia by standing naked in front of the generals negotiating the end of the war. The men were so horrified by the women's nudity that they stayed in the board room until a settlement had been reached. That is real power. Still, I worry about the idea that the antidote to male ownership of the female body is unrestrained nudity. It is supposed to be about taking ownership of our sexuality. And for some women I'm sure it is. But it also ironically reinforces the idea that the world really prefers women naked, and provides lots of unintended material for the male gaze on women.

Moreover, what worries me more is what it means for schoolgirls trying to liberate themselves from male gaze. I have a hard time getting behind protests that seem to have been dictated by ideas of femininity emerging from the fashion industry — a culture notoriously misogynistic. I find it hard to see girls protesting for the right to wear whatever short shorts the fashion industry has determined are right for us. It feels like we are running from one brick wall to the other, from one set of bodily expectations to another extreme. Put differently, skimpy clothes are marketed to girls and not to boys because the world wants to see exposed girls' bodies.

As blogger Juliet C Bond wrote earlier this year, "In a society where children are exposed to thousands of ads each day depicting women and girls in tight-fitting clothing, licking things, gyrating against random objects, and laying suggestively across anything from cars to cartons of yogurt, young girls get the message very early on, that their worth is inextricably tied to their sexuality. What a confusing edict we hand to girls: in order to be considered attractive, you have to look like these women in the ads. Yet when girls wear these clothes, they are punished or humiliated when they attempt to look like those same women. "

Rather than focus on the idea that bodily freedom means maximum skin exposure and maximum public displays of sexuality, I would rather see our girls focus on fighting for the right to wear the same things that boys get to wear – comfortable clothes! I don't want to hold up fashion as a paragon of feminism, or to take a Madonna-like view of my sexuality which is that it is for public consumption on my own terms. There is a certain feminist empowerment in that, for sure, in ownership of our sexuality and the choice to go topless if we want. And I will forever defend women's rights to go topless if they so choose. But I think that this misses a deeper message. I think more important than the freedom to go topless is the freedom from gaze. I want girls and women to be able to do what men are able to do, and that is to be to feel our own skin and not worry too much about who is watching us or trying to consume us.

Post-script

It is obvious in this essay that even as I rejected the so-called "modesty" of my upbringing, I still struggled with complete body freedom for women. I remember that when I wrote this essay, I believed that I had found the great balance, or a kind of middle-ground, between Orthodoxy and, say, Madonna. Like I was a fountain of wisdom, lighting a path of moderation between extreme cover and extreme uncover. While I still bristle at the fashion industry's sexualization of girls, there is more going on here. The truth is, I found Madonna's complete body freedom too confronting. I was still clutching my pearls. It wasn't just finding a golden path; it was also about holding on to the idea that women should not be showing so much skin. And of course, the reluctance to show my skin also reflected my own deeply embedded body shame. So there's that.

Today, I'm not entirely in the same place I was then. I mean, yes to equality, yes to girls' freedom and better choices, yes to longer shorts options. I'm not quite ready to participate in Free the Nipple protests. But I am definitely experimenting with my own self-imposed limitations, my own chains in a way, and I am drilling down deeper about my discomfort with women's body exposure. I've still got an internalized patriarchal gaze that I have not fully dislodged.

Also, I have come to understand that for some women, body exposure is its own form of healing from body trauma. For many survivors of sexual abuse, being comfortable in one's own skin, in private and in public, is a vital step towards body wholeness and self-ownership. I am still in a place of grappling with all that myself. The process was not done when I wrote this essay, and it is not done now.

What Banning Facebook is Really About[8]

When we talk about modesty, we are not just talking about how girls dress. We are also talking about how girls are expected to behave. This includes sexual activity as well as more mundane body movements – climbing trees, riding bicycles, and doing somersaults. But ultimately, it's about instilling an entire demeanor of self-restraint, of not living fully. Just for girls.

Facebook is forbidden among Chabad teenage girls, as The Sisterhood reported. This reflects a blatant double standard, the report points out, because the movement has widely embraced technology to spread its message while refusing to allow its own youth to use these tools.

But Chabad's double standard in its relationship to secular society is only one part of the problem. It seems to me that the story of girls being forbidden from using Facebook and other internet tools is less about Chabad's missionary stance and more about their view of women and girls. After all, it is only a girls' school that is handing

---

[8] April 10, 2012. Originally published at the *Forward*. Reprinted with permission. https://forward.com/sisterhood/154558/what-banning-facebook-is-really-about/

out $100 fines and having mothers monitor students' computer use.

Moreover, the practice of banning girls from the computer largely revolves around one concept: modesty. The Facebook ban is just the latest in a long string of insidious practices in the Orthodox community — not just Chabad, to be sure — aimed at restricting women's and girls' freedom. These practices are promoted under the term *tzniut*, or "modesty," but really are nothing more than classic misogyny.

In different Orthodox communities, public pronouncements about modesty by rabbinic leaders over the past decade have included: forbidding women from wearing high heels that make noise, forbidding women from talking on cellphones in public, forcing women to wear overcoats on top of their clothes when they go to weddings, even in summer, forbidding women from wearing the color red and forbidding women from blogging. The list goes on. One Orthodox community established a "kashrut department" for supervising clothing stores to check the length of the skirts and sleeves of the merchandise. This practice was justified by a group called "The Committee for the Sanctity of the Camp," to combat what they called "damaging our camp's modesty" due to women and girls "breaching" conventions.

"Modesty" now supersedes kashrut as the identifying mark of Orthodoxy. A group of rabbis recently announced that kashruth certificates for summer hotels should include the extent of a resort's "modesty" — that is, how women are dressed around the hotel. "The Gedolei Yisrael feel that regarding *mehadrin kashrus* certification for hotels, the issues of kashrus and *tznius* mustn't be addressed separately....*Mehadrin kashrus* for hotels and resorts ....must include *tznius* standards to prevent stumbling blocks for *frum* [observant] visitors."

Yet none of this has anything to do with "modesty," or even about Jewish law. Forbidding women's use of cellphones or girls' use of Facebook is not about religiousness or Torah. These are rules made by men who believe that women's silence and invisibility will make their lives somehow easier or better.

It is worth remembering what "modesty" actually is. The Talmudic interpretation of Bilaam's unwitting blessing of the Israelites in the desert with the famous passage, "How fair are your tents O Jacob, your dwellings, O Israel," argues that this verse is a tribute to the "modesty" of the Israelites, who positioned their tents with the doors facing away from each other, allowing each family their privacy. "R. Johanan said: This verse....indicates that [Bilaam] saw that the doors of their tents did not exactly face one another, whereupon he exclaimed: Worthy are these that the Divine presence should rest upon them!" It's an injunction to control your own behavior, not to watch how the other is dressed.

True "modesty," considered an expression of the Divine presence, is about relationship with the other — as in taking care not to impose one's gaze on another Jew through his or her private window or door. It is about humility, such as that credited to Moses, a type of submissiveness in which one rejects an artificial sense of self-importance and fully accepts the notion that all people are equal creatures of God.

Yet, the concept of "modesty" as it is often promulgated has lost its essential meaning and been crudely manipulated and misused. What once referred to a spiritual demeanor, an internal, personal quest for growth, a framework for building kind and compassionate relationships among people has evolved into something else entirely. Today, when rabbis talk about *tzniut*, there is only one issue they have in mind: women's bodies. And that is just not Torah.

Post-script

After reading these essays, in which I constantly struggle to understand the modesty obsession, it occurred to me what "modesty" really means. When men tell women to be modest, they are really saying, Be small. Keep yourself hidden. Do not take up space in the world. The world does not belong to you. Keep your body unobtrusive. Not just body – also your spirit. Don't let your persona occupy a place in the world. When men tell women to be "modest" what they are saying is that the world belongs to them and that our presence threatens that ownership.

The concept of "modesty", which can be a worthwhile spiritual practice in certain contexts, is co-opted – despite its potential authenticity – and exploited as a persuasive tool to get us to disappear for them. To get us to stop taking up space, speaking, thinking, and wanting to be full participants in the world. It is intended to get us to participate in the process of moving over and becoming invisible so that men can continue to own the world unfettered and unencumbered. Let's at least call it what it is. And let us stop stepping aside as if for "modesty". Everyone deserves to live fully.

Did a Rabbi Permit Self-Mutilation to Promote 'Modesty'?[9]

Self-harm is a very difficult topic to talk about and write about, as I know from having written about it in my book, Educating in the Divine Image *and faced difficult conversations about it. But here, the way self-harm is conflated with modesty is absolutely shocking. It took me two columns to get the story out completely. Nine years later, it is still horrifying beyond description.*

Ynet ran a troubling story about a high-profile rabbi in Israel who advised a young woman to cut her own legs to stay religious. The story, if it's true, conflates male religious authority, extreme body cover, and self-mutilation, and brings the discussions of the female body in Judaism to a whole new low. The problem is that this story may not be true, in which case instead of highlighting sexism in Orthodox Judaism; the story becomes an example of journalists' sometimes overzealousness in their desire to attack religion by pretending to care about women. Especially given the recent history of media attitudes towards France's burqa

[9] July 5, 2011. Originally published at the *Forward*. Reprinted with permission.
https://forward.com/sisterhood/139452/did-a-rabbi-permit-self-mutilation-to-promote-mode/

ban, the actions of certain journalists are no less troubling than those of religious leaders controlling the female body.

According to the article, written by a young Jerusalem journalist, Ari Galahar, for the *Yediot Ahranot* Hebrew news site, Rabbi Yizhak Silberstein was asked to respond to a strange query from a young woman who was accepted to a religious academy despite her family's non-religiousness. The young woman, struggling with the academy's strict dress code of long skirts, long sleeves, and covered collarbones because her secular parents were supposedly pressuring her to dress in a more revealing way, asked Silberstein whether she could cut her legs so that her parents would agree that she must wear a long skirt to cover the bruises. The rabbi reportedly responded, "She is permitted to cut herself in order to dress modestly, and thus to escape all sin." He reportedly added that "The blood from the bruise will redeem all of Israel like the blood of the ritual sacrifices."

Orthodox Judaism has issues with the female body, to put it mildly. In a culture defined by the degree to which women are kept silent and invisible, pressured to have as many babies and possible while maintaining the home and covering as much flesh as possible, this story could very well be true.

A community that promotes gender segregation in public and private to such an extreme that women who sit on the wrong side of the bus have been victims of violence is probably not immune to rabbinic recommendations that women inflict self-harm as well.

But when I went to verify this story and get commentary on it, some odd things happened. I spoke to two different Orthodox rabbis who are known for working professionally with Orthodox girls who suffer from body-issue problems, eating disorders, and the like. I expected to get from them explanations of why this kind of ruling is so damaging to girls' self-concept, some insights about why an Orthodox girl might be thinking about self-injury — maybe some statistics about how prevalent this is in the community. Both rabbis, unbeknownst to one another, replied that they did not believe that this story is true. Both said that they know Rabbi Silberstein well and that there is no way that he would make such a statement.

So I did what any good reporter would do. I went to try to verify the source. I tried several avenues to reach the rabbi or people who know him but was unable to gain access. Since Galahar is the only one who had this story, I went to him for some details. I asked him about the academy and the girl, but he said he could not share any details. I respect journalistic ethics, but I needed something, some information about how he knows this story. All he kept saying was, "Sorry, I can't help you."

His article, tellingly, does not contain any response from Rabbi Silberstein, anyone close to him, or anyone in the academy.

If the story is true — and it admittedly sounds like the kind of story you can't make up — then this is a shame. I would have liked to use this column as an opportunity to talk about body image among Orthodox women and girls, about how the issue of self-mutilation needs to be addressed and about how far Orthodox culture is from understanding the impact of body control on girls' inner lives. But instead, this story has made me wonder about the knee-jerk hatred of religion in the media.

So often, journalists jump on stories about the religious mistreatment of women without necessarily caring about the women themselves. This is particularly jarring given the brouhaha over France's burqa ban a few months ago, a ban that turned religious women into public spectacles and even criminals instead of punishing the male leaders who oppress them.

One can't help but wonder how many writers actually know what women go through, and how many care.

Post-script

This was the first of two essays I wrote on this topic, because even as I was keenly interested in writing about it, I was getting a lot of responses of "It can't be true". Today, I am a little bit wiser about how desperate communal leaders can be to cover up the truth about abuse. I also know more about how easily rabbis cover for one another.

Still, I am surprised to discover just how deferential I was to those who were saying, "I can't be true". Today, I would probably do it differently, be more suspicious, be less eager to hop on the "Everyone hates religious Jews" bandwagon.

But the experience I had with the reporter was also very confronting for me. The 23-year-old "rising star" so needed a story that he refused to engage with me honestly. It was a reminder that we as women, are objectified from all sides – even from people who claim to be on our side. Sometimes they are only on their own side. Sometimes men use women's experiences to gain street cred, especially as feminists.

But using women to boost your platform without giving women our own voice is not a feminist approach. Refusing to treat women with respect because you want to get an exclusive – that is not okay. This was a difficult experience for me, too, one of many.

I would also like to say something, in this little post-script, that I have never written about publicly. And that is, I also struggle with self-harm. I have struggled with it since I am a teenager.

And it is something that never truly goes away. Ever. And it has been very significant for me as well as others like me, that we tend to harm ourselves in areas where skin does not see the light of day. So the more we cover, the more area on our bodies we have to play with. It is so deeply clear to me that there is a connection between the rabbi telling her to cover her legs and her response that the legs are then a place where she can draw blood. Of course. "Harm yourself and cover up, and you're good to go." The layers of damage to girls are chilling.

And this brings me back to the issue that I keep circling back to: Shame. Just as my mother told us to cover our arms and our thighs because they were ugly, here, too, we have a rabbi teaching girls that their skin is something to be ashamed of, to the infuriating extent that we should self-harm in order to let the shame deepen. This language of "modesty" is so destructive to girls on so many levels. So many intersecting layers of control and shame. So many....

Keeping Young Women Hidden — at the Expense of Their Bodies[10]

Part two of the unbearable story about the rabbi who told a girl to cut her legs for the sake of "modesty". I think that the rabbi should be in prison, and that the justice system should find ways to severely punish this particular kind of cruelty.

Despite my earlier post, it now appears that Rabbi Yizhak Silberstein *did* support the idea that a girl whose mother refused to buy her "religious clothes" should cut her legs in order to force the mother's hand. An apparent recording of the rabbi's discussion of this topic surfaced on the Internet today, in which he says that girl deserves the "highest praise" for sanctifying God's name with her absolute dedication to Torah.

Contrary to the original publication in Ynet, Rabbi Silberstein did not receive the question from the girl about cutting her legs, but merely offered his opinion on

[10] July 7, 2011. Originally published at the *Forward*. Reprinted with permission.
https://forward.com/sisterhood/139602/keeping-young-women-hidden-at-the-expense-of-the/

the case, which was originally brought to Rabbi Eliezer Sorodskin, the leader of an organization called Lev La'Ahim, whose stated mission is to help secular Israelis become religious. (The organization is most recently renowned for bloating registration at Haredi educational institutions, as reported in *Haaretz*). The conversation took place at a conference of Lev La'Ahim held in May in Bnei Brak.

Sorodskin talked about the girl in positively ebullient terms. She apparently loves being religious, but her secular mother refuses to buy her "religious clothes" — i.e., long skirts. The girl's willingness to cut her legs to preserve the sanctity of her female body, according to both Sorodskin and Silberstein, is a model of self-sacrifice for the sake of Torah, an act worthy of emulation.

I don't know if these rabbis even realize how un-Jewish this entire discussion is. Not to mention cruel. And sick.

Aside from the obvious and ubiquitous Torah prohibitions about harming one's body, the imagery of a pure innocent young person bleeding for the sake of communal purity and righteousness is just so Jesus. I was about ready for someone to bring in a crucifix and shout Hallelujah.

Really, though, as I said in my previous post, this story brings the issue of Orthodoxy's treatment of the female body to a new nadir of horror. For those who still do not believe that Orthodox rhetoric leads to violence against women, here we have it — to the point of encouraging girls to act violently against themselves.

Self-mutilation, or self-injury, is a lesser-known of the body-image disorders but seems to be an increasing phenomenon in the Western world. Girls who cause themselves to bleed are expressing a profound self-hatred and disgust with their bodies. Moreover, the self-numbing that is required to self-injure effectively is clearly a response to enormous pain around body.

I contacted Adrienne Ressler Mott of the Renfrew Center for eating disorders, which has special programs for Orthodox girls, to find out how prevalent self-injury is in this population. She reported that between 2007 and 2010, 41.8% of the residential patients said that they intentionally self-harmed in the year leading up to treatment, and of those, 78.4% did so via cutting themselves. All told, out of the total residential population at Renfrew, 32.8% of the patients have cut themselves.

"There is the Jewish concept that all humans were created *B'Tzelem Elokim*," (in the image of God), Mott wrote to me, "that the human body is a holy vessel and a gift from God and as such, we are expected to care for our bodies and treat them preciously.... The rabbi's response can only lead to increased shame and lowered sense of worth."

Women's body shame, which is obviously a central component of self-mutilation, is a profoundly troubling outgrowth of Orthodox rhetoric. The girl in question has already internalized the message that her body is not meant to be cared for gently and tended to lovingly, but simply must be covered at all costs. She has completely detached from her body as her own; in fact, her body seems to have become the object of a tug of war between her family and her rabbis. Offering to cut her own legs — which should be a major red flag for social workers rather than a model of religiosity — signifies that she has completely disconnected from sensation in her body.

How will she approach her own sexuality when she sees her body as bleed-able rather than as worthy of care? How will she ever be able to feel her own contours? And how will she ever be able to be physically present anywhere without carrying that enormous weight of constant body-shame?

Moreover, I am incredibly concerned about the tendency within the Orthodox community to pretend that this issue is relegated to extremists. This disingenuous attempt to pretend that "mainstream" Orthodox rhetoric could not possibly lead to female body-shame not only sweeps these important issues under the communal rug but also completely silences any real reflection on Orthodoxy's approach to female body self-concept. Orthodoxy is not immune; it is part of the problem. The super-emphasis on female body cover in Orthodoxy — from pre-pubescent ages vociferously told to cover up and tighten the knees, to adult women who are placed in a far-off room for every possible occasion so as not to risk being seen or heard — has become the foremost marker of supposed Orthodox religiousness. Schools, shuls, and communities all across the Orthodox world are increasingly defined by how emphatically the girls and women cover their bodies and remain out of sight. This story is not an aberration but a natural outgrowth of today's Orthodoxy.

"Anyone who demands self-mutilation as the price/rationale for *tzniut* is out of the range of what I would ever consider a rabbinic authority," Rabbi Jacqueline Koch Ellenson, the director of the Women's Rabbinic Network, told me. "I find this beyond objectionable, a denial of women as human beings."

Mostly, I'm very worried about religious girls. I do not see how a girl can go through these kinds of rules and

47

regulations from the age of zero and emerge with her body-concept unharmed, not to mention her skin.

Post-script

This issue of self-harm is not well understood, especially not in the religious community. During my doctoral research on religious girls in school, I encountered girls who were self-harming, and I wrote a bit about it. I also tried to find someone in the girls' orbit to help them but was unsuccessful there as well. Today, I chide myself for not trying harder. And I am very worried about the emotional health of young women. It is one of the issues that keep me up at night – literally, as I spend much of my time chatting with girls and women who are self-harming or considering self-harm. And as I wrote following the previous post, this is one of the places where I am writing about myself, too. This issue of self-harm and its connection to "modesty" desperately needs more communal attention.

Hair

"*I got a problem*
Only a curl is gonna solve it
Man, I don't really care
Just get him out my hair, yeah"

- Little Mix

When I was a little girl, I had long hair. Very long. I used to show off that it came past my tush, and loved jokes about how to avoid getting pee on it when I went to the toilet. My older sisters and their fashion-conscious friends implored me to cut it, especially to fix the edges. But I stubbornly refused. Every morning, I spent a good ten minutes making my own hairstyles. I spent my allowance on barrettes and rubber bands so I could design it the way I liked. During my seventh-grade piano recital, in which I played Hooked on Classics to the entire elementary school, the part I was possibly most proud of was the French-ponytail that I had made for the occasion, which everyone could see from behind as I played the difficult piece. The truth is, it was both. Piano and hairstyles, two of my first loves.

But adolescence eventually beckoned, and the pressure had its effect. The day before I started high school, I cut my hair. Getting a short cut – the loss of my cherished locks – was the price of being a correct or acceptable teenage girl.

During college, I grew my hair a bit longer and enjoyed a wild wavy look. My father hated it and let me know at every opportunity. He liked his women neat and under control. For the most part, I ignored him, at least when it came to my hair.

Then, at the age of 21, I got married and began covering my hair. Even though my mother and grandmothers did not cover their hair, there was increasing social pressure in Orthodoxy for girls to cover our hair. In some kind of regression to an idealized old-school religiousness, covering your hair was a sign that you were more serious, more religious, and more devout. Ironically, I think for some women, it was also a signifier of more educated or fluent in religious law. It was like a religious declaration: We are going to follow the "true" dictates written down in books by men, rather than respect traditions practiced by our unschooled mothers. It was arguably a form of rebellion, part of the entire "frumming out" *trend in Orthodoxy in which children wanted to show that we were better than our parents.*

It is ironic and tragic, I think, that as religious girls became more formally educated and mastered rabbinic sources, we invariably adopted stricter rules on our bodies. This is despite the fact that the sources are far more ambiguous about the issue than rabbis and educators are willing to admit publicly. We even had rabbis who admitted how weak the legal argument for hair-covering was. But even as they admitted that, they would tell us that there is no other option.

As a young woman who was deeply attached to my religious identity, I had a hard time navigating all that. There were voices of reason screaming out in my head, but they competed with the voice of the Good Girl. I deeply wanted to do the right thing. And the rationales planted in our fertile minds included some alluring bits, like marital loyalty, avoiding being hit on by other men, and of course God's will. Your body is a Torah, your hair is holy, shit like that. It's hard to push back against all that, especially when you are all alone in that struggle.

I covered my hair for the first four years of my marriage, putting it up in tight clips under my hair, forgetting about how much I used to love my wild hair. It took me four years to reclaim my own relationship with my hair and have the guts to walk out of the house with my own hair. It should not be such an act of courage, but for many religious women, it is.

The process of covering my hair and then not covering my hair became a formative process for me. It was an exercise in learning to talk back to my culture. It helped me address the many ways in which Orthodox culture teaches people – especially women and girls – that we are not allowed to think for ourselves. Taking off my hat was a watershed decision and took me to many other places.

It also made me a fierce advocate for giving women permission to think and feel for ourselves, permission to want. And yet, that same advocacy sometimes gets me into trouble. Not everyone is interested in having a conversation about the many limits we accept as normal in our lives. I understand. It can be scary and very destabilizing. And, as I have mentioned, it comes up against all that God-language. It's as if, for some people, feminism is going to war against God.

But maybe that instability is a vital step on the path towards freedom.

On Hats and Hindrances[11]

I wrote this nearly ten years after I stopped covering my hair. Maybe it took me that long to appreciate what a huge moment that was for me.

The day I took off my hat, I felt liberated. After four years of marriage, during which time I accumulated an extensive array of berets, caps, scarves, snoods, and other popular designs for hair-hiding, I walked out of my apartment with my long brown mane completely exposed. I felt ten years younger. And I had the tingling sensation that I could actually feel who I was, once again – rediscovering that part of me, that fresh and vivacious young woman who had somehow gotten lost beneath layers of cloth – on the head, the arms, and the legs. I didn't even realize how missing I had been until I found myself again.

Obviously, this was a decision long in coming. The ambivalence I felt when I donned my first hat as I left my wedding stayed with me. Although my original reason for covering my hair was rooted in my commitment to full adherence to the religion – a desire to lead a more

[11] April 2004, From my blog, *A Jewish Feminist.*
http://jewfem.com/index.php?option=com_easyblog&view
=entry&id=23&Itemid=499

pious life – even back then, this particular act was one of the more difficult ones for me. I was not unfaltering, as I so tried to be. This ambivalence expressed itself in a continuous loosening of the act – first leaving out a fringe, then exposing the ponytail, then just putting a hat on my head with my thick, mid-back-length hair sticking out. Until finally, I decided, that's it.

It happened almost innocuously, though Jung would claim that nothing is by accident. When Shabbat guests arrived one Friday afternoon, I opened the door in a huff, wiping my hands on the dishtowel and juggling to try to make my friends comfortable while not burning the soup. It was only ten minutes later that I realized that I wasn't wearing a hat. And not only did my friends not seem to notice or care, neither did I. That's when I realized that the whole practice was something of a fiction.

We were taught in yeshiva, when I was an 18-year-old, somewhat independent-minded and good-hearted yeshiva girl, that the practice of hair-covering was a *chok*, an indisputable and inexplicable law, like the red heifer. Later on, other teachers gave other explanations. One said it was to "save" your most intimate parts for your husband. Another said that it was a symbol of woman as forbidden to other men. There was a notion floating around comparing hair to genitals and voice, those parts of woman's physicality that must be obscured from contact with weak and sexually uncontrollable Jewish men. With our hair out, we were told, we should feel as if we were standing naked. Others taught that this is simply the law as it has been passed down, that a man is allowed to divorce his wife for burning the soup and exposing her hair. Certainly, this rabbi said, we would not encourage our boys to do such a thing, but nonetheless, the law is law. We shouldn't seek to *understand*; we should just *do*.

Nobody told us that we had the option of not doing it. There wasn't even a discussion about how we might *feel* in this practice. In the places where I learned, person's experience was irrelevant – only obedience mattered.

Not only were experience and choice absent from the discourse, but the entire discussion of women's hair covering treated women and their bodies as objects. Whether our hair is somehow our husband's property, or simply another piece of our bodies that is subject to the male gaze so adored by Jewish sources, the discourse is of women objectified. But of course, I didn't fully understand that until after I took my hat off. Because when I did, I listened to my inner voice, and it was telling me that I wasn't naked after all.

I was reminded of the time at the airport on the way to making Aliyah – back during our first years of marriage when I was still idealistic about *halakha* and other things – when I was stopped at JFK security. Something was setting off the metal detector. I emptied my pockets, took off my belt. It still went off. Finally, the security guard said, "It's coming from under your hat." Torn between guilt, shame, and fear, I recalled the metal barrette that I used to hold up my long hair. The guard said, "Take off your hat." I meekly resisted, thinking about ways to explain to them how uncompromisingly important it was for me to keep that hat on. Yet, the guards were unyielding. And so, although there was a voice inside demanding religious freedom and insisting upon the importance of my modesty, the dominant voice at the time said, what's the big deal? Indeed, I took off the hat, took off the barrette, went through security, made Aliyah with my hat on, and didn't think about the incident again. Until that Friday afternoon years later, when the dominant voice truly took over, and I left the head covering for good.

One day, shortly after I had put my hats back in the closet, I was at a wedding where one of the bride's close friends, a young twenty-something woman wearing a long skirt and a hat covering every strand, was dancing wildly. As the music continued, she took off her shoes, arms flailing, kicking up, sweating, and smiling in love and friendship. And then it happened. Her hat fell off. Suddenly, the arms came down, she stopped dancing, a frowning blush replaced the smile, and she practically crawled to the edge of the circle to replace her hat. Sometime later, she returned to the circle, part of her vigor diminished, but she kept on dancing, anyway. Watching her, my heart ached.

Why must we feel shame, I thought, *seeing her hair*? She didn't feel shame at having her stockings exposed. So why her hair? This woman felt shame because she had been taught that she was *supposed* to feel shame when her hat was off. That shame reflected an acceptance of socially determined norms. Like Archer in Edith Wharton's *The Age of Innocence*, we live in societies that make determinations about right and wrong, and very few people have the courage and independence to challenge those norms without feeling that shame. For this poor woman, taking her shoes off was "okay," but taking off her hat wasn't. So it was not about some objective form of exposure or modesty. It was about what she understood as acceptable and what not.

I realized then how very socially constructed our practices are. We feel shame when we are told to feel shame, we feel pious when we are told we are acting piously, and we shake our heads in disapproval when we see people going against our societal conventions.

Taking off my hat was a watershed for me. Hat off, I found myself looking around and seeing Orthodox Judaism differently. Where once I bought into the whole way of thinking that women's status in Jewish law is a reflection of their more "spiritual" level and their greater moral responsibilities, I found myself doubting that whole line of thought. Instead, I looked around and saw a lot of women covering themselves up, hiding. I saw women who were expected to feel embarrassed to see their bodies. Like that famous story, we were once taught about a woman who merited extra rewards in the world to come because she even covered her hair even in bed. I began to look at this whole corps of Jewish texts that shape our view of ourselves. And I began to wonder, are these texts, indeed, making me more pious, more religious, and devout, or is there something else at work here?

That something else to me is human interpretation. So much of what we do in the name of religiousness or Orthodoxy seems to me less about Godliness and more about what men would like to think is Godliness. And that has a lot to do with how they would like to see their own society, particularly the women around them. If men have this picture of their world in which women are silent and invisible, so be it. The amorphous mass of Jewish legal texts we have come to call *halakha* is full of human assertions about right and wrong ways for women to be. But I have come to see all these claims not as Torah but as an instrument of male power over female beings.

Head covering has become a lens through which I see the way women are treated in Jewish law. Whether it's marriage and divorce laws, with the torment of *agunot*, the *mechitza*, rules of inheritance, exclusion of women from prayer and religious accreditation, or the notion that a woman's voice is sinful, they all become the same issue: what Jewish women are expected to be. For me, the oppression of women in Judaism – like in so many other societies throughout the ages – is not only a major failing of *halakha*, but as a mark of Cain, a stain on the garment which makes it entirely unwearable. How can I justify adherence to a set of codes that keeps women as secondary beings? And while the Orthodox community paints itself as somehow superior, immune to such mundane phenomena as "sexism," it remains mired in the swamps of these antiquated and anachronistic legal texts, so very reluctant to admit that it, too, oppresses women. All the apologetics in the world about women's "higher" spiritual level cannot change it.

In fact, I feel that language often used to convince women that their inferior status is "better" is merely another tactic for maintaining the status quo of gender relationships within Orthodoxy. If you say women are "better" when you mean "different" for the purposes of exclusion, the subjugation remains hidden. Say women are more "emotional" when you mean less intelligent, and women may not realize what is being done to them. There are so many ways to hold a person down. We experience these exchanges all the time. If we express anger and the listener says, "Oh, dear, you must not be feeling yourself today," we have just been silenced in a sweet voice – and convinced that our anger is forbidden. If a woman's husband says to her, "You don't want to drive, you don't want to shop, don't bother yourself with all that, and I'll do everything for you," her hands have been tied in the guise of supposed love that is really control.

HAIR

I almost feel lied to. During my 15 or so years in Orthodox yeshivot, I think I was being molded into a woman that doesn't exist. A woman who is so pious and self-yielding that she has no sensitivities, no needs, no desires, no voice. The quiet piety of this mythical figure bears the colossal burden of supposedly keeping the Jewish people alive. But this woman is not real, just a figment of the imagination.

Where are *we*? Where is the real-life thinking, feeling woman, who experiences herself, who is in touch with her own humanity and needs? Is there room for her within all this dictated behavior?

Our tradition, written and enacted by men, controls and manipulates us no less than other traditions. By telling us that it is our obligation to cover ourselves in the presence of men, it deprives us of self-knowledge by making our experience with our bodies about men, not about us. Women as sexual objects, women as responsible for others' actions, women as blamed and guilty, women as invisible. The messages tied in with head covering reflect an understanding of woman as different than man, a sexual object, subject to the male gaze, fulfilled only in marriage, whose body is designed for the fulfillment of male desires. Moreover, while the man has urgent, uncontrollable sexual needs, the woman's job is to suppress her own needs and cover her body lest she becomes the sinful temptress. Woman as ultimately responsible for man's transgressions. As if we didn't have enough guilt.

A recent shocking expression of this male-centered perspective on the female body was the resistance of religious councils in Israel to allow breast cancer detection information to be placed in the *mikveh*s out of concern for "modesty." Although the men finally relented, the struggle highlights the extent to which religious life takes this distorted male position.

This, then, is the message we get as religious women. In the religious educational system, the foremost institution for constructing social norms, women's appearance carries with it expectations of submission. Girls in yeshiva – as I once was and perhaps still struggle against – discuss with one another how they are going to cover their hair when they are married. In the delusion of choice, we would sit in classes and discuss the particular ins and out of how, why, and how much, but the choice to *not* cover is not really a choice. Sure, some students may privately articulate their own plans for not covering hair, but that is considered in the yeshiva world to be outside truly acceptable behavior. We, as girls, were *told* rather than heard. We were lectured to about how adherence to subservient forms of behavior represents God's will via *halakha*. Be good, be quiet, do for others – and of course, cover your body at all times, no matter what –and we will thus be serving God. A social construct presented as if it is couched in the unshakable unquestioned truths of the universe. A very powerful influence indeed.

I took off my hat so I could see myself. So I could *hear* myself. The more I have come to see and hear, the more I have been able to perceive what happens around me. It saddens me to see so many women silent, obedient, and covered. Jewish tradition ought to be full of life, energy, spirit, and women. Instead, women are busy serving others' needs, serving the needs of a society fixated on self-perpetuation and resistance to change. It is so very, very sad.

I have taken off my hat, and now I am looking for the Judaism that I once loved. So much of it seems covered in the ugliness of control and subjugation. I keep looking. I find comfort in Shabbat, in song, in friendship, and in study. More than anything, I want to help other women find themselves because I can no longer love a Judaism where women are absent. That is just not my Judaism anymore.

I would also like to see religious schools help girls take ownership of their bodies. It means running and sweating and doing yoga. It means having frank discussions about sex, allowing the girls to engage in what Michelle Fine calls "the missing discourse of desire," and acknowledging their own sensations and emotional flows of energy. It means opening up conversations about Jewish life that not only consist of the "how-to's" of *halakha* – how to cover your hair, how to prepare for the *mikveh*, how to serve your husband – but also encourage a discussion about the emotional impact of observance. How do these young women *experience* their behaviors, their expectations, their Jewishness, and their womanness? The notion that there is room for personal experience within practice is still relatively new to Orthodox Judaism. And yet it is so vitally important for the health of our daughters – and sons, as well.

Head covering is not just about hair. It's about a woman's relationship with the society around her. The time has come for us to begin to view women in relation to themselves, not just in relation to the men around them.

Post-script
I have come a long way in my thinking and writing about this topic since I first penned this essay in 2004. Even now, 25 years after I took off my hat, I still think of that decision as one of the most important in my life. It was without a doubt a watershed decision that brought on a whole wave of other

issues. It enabled me to begin asking myself what I felt, what I wanted, what I believed. It is what I think of as my first time talking back to my culture. That is the framework I often use when I speak to groups of women and girls – I encourage them to talk back to their cultures, whatever their cultures happen to be.

One interesting point that I think about when I read this essay has to do with my mother. Even though my mother was always very strict with us about sleeves, necklines, and hems, she was not in favor of me covering my hair. She was in fact very vocal about her displeasure in my head covering. She saw it as one of many signs that I was making bad decisions in my life, something she told me and anyone else willing to listen, at every opportunity. "You've made terrible decisions ever since you got married," she announced, often, with vagueness and determination. In the internal world of Orthodox politics in which everyone wants to see themselves as "moderate" and everyone else as "extreme", I think she saw the hair-covering as a betrayal of that entire posturing. So many religious women describe themselves as finding a kind of golden middle path – not too extreme, but not too secular; not too exposed but also not too covered. Everyone likes to see themselves as "normal", and those who veer to either direction are the extreme ones. But the truth is, I think about her anger at my hair-covering and wonder what she wanted from me exactly. Like, she wanted me to maintain her choices as my own, but gave me zero tools for independent thinking or fighting back against the entire Orthodox educational system that objectified women. I had no help and no support in navigating all this. Plus, the constant public shaming hardly helped. I was traumatized by the system and then retraumatized at home with a complex dynamic of being blamed for all of it.

But when I think about my mother and the way she treated my decision to cover my hair, I am reminded of Dr. Tova Hartman's article, "Maternal transmission of ambivalence," and how many religious women act as gatekeepers for a system that they are not sure they believe in themselves. Many women like my mother walk this fine line between cover and uncover, between religious obedience and living in a modern world.[12] *For the daughters, the objects of this confusing socialization, it can be hard to keep up and know what obedience looks like at any particular point. I was trying to find my path amid some confusing and hurtful messages.*

Even though my own sense of "normal" has shifted many times during the course of my adulthood, I am happy to report that I am no longer looking for normal. Or for obedience. I just want freedom. I want to answer to nobody else but me. I want to listen to what my body urges from me. That's where I am on this today. Although that may yet change.

---

[12] Tova Hartman Halbertal, "Maneuvering in a World of Law and Custom: Maternal Transmission of Ambivalence," *Nashim: A Journal of Jewish Women's Studies & Gender Issues,* Indiana University Press Number 3, Spring/Summer 5760/2000 pp. 139-163

The Case Against the *Sheitel*[13]

The sheitel, or the wig, worn by some Orthodox Jewish women to cover their hair, is fascinating. It is a response to the double gazes that religious women are subjected to – the rabbinic gaze that says, "Cover up" and the western gaze that says, "Be beautiful and sexy." The sheitel is a great little tool that enables women to adhere to both demands. Good for them. Still, I have some strong opinions on the issue. Warning: unpopular opinions ahead.

"Do you like the blond better? With or without the ponytail?"

Wig-shopping is the new initiation into religious life for women, writes Tali Farkash, a Haredi columnist for Ynet, who alternates between defending religious life and kvetching about it. If women used to accompany brides to the *mikveh* to welcome them ritualistically into

---

[13] March 2, 2011. Originally posted at the *Forward*. Reprinted with permission.
https://forward.com/sisterhood/135847/the-case-against-the-*sheitel*/

the club of married women, she says, today a trip to the *sheitel macher*, or wig-maker, is the thing to do. Farkash, who recently accompanied her friend to get a wig, is still recovering from the experience.

Her friend sat "right there on the seat of honor at the *sheitel macher's*," Farkash writes, "surrounded by relatives whose job it is to say, 'That looks so nice on you!' and to elegantly avoid the obvious questions about the net in front that presses on the forehead, or the sadistic job of the comber. There is something bittersweet about sitting on the waiting couch as support, witnessing the metamorphosis... from permitted hair to forbidden hair."

The *sheitel* is undoubtedly one of the strangest customs of modern Jewish life. No matter how many perky rebbetzins try to write funny or pedagogical blogs to rationalize this practice, there is no way to make this normal or sane. "Every attempt to take the discussion out of the religious-halachic loop is doomed to failure," Farkash writes.

The language of human morality has no way to make sense of this. That's not to say people don't try.

A glance through the online comments offers a glimpse into the wide range of thinking on matters in the religious world. One anonymous commenter writes that it's a "shame [Farkash] doesn't see the beauty in it." Meanwhile, a Haredi man calling himself *"gever gever"* ("man's man") writes, "The wig is even more sexually stimulating than your hair! I'm a Haredi man, and I implore you women, please shave your heads! I can't take the stimulation of a full head of hair!!" And Dana writes, "A wig is forbidden in the Torah ... Whoever thinks that a wig is the more religious (*mehudar*) head covering is really, really wrong because the wigs are nicer than the woman's own hair...."

The *sheitel* also creates a whole set of demands on women's bodies in which they have no say, regardless of the imposition on both physical and emotional comfort (just one more set of demands, perhaps), evokes many questions about women's freedom of movement in this culture. "There is no room to breathe in personal feelings," Farkash writes a bit enigmatically. "Those feelings remain to be whispered among close friends, the secret of married haredi women."

Wigs lack all moral, ethical, and rational value. After all, the concept that a woman's hair is too sensual — as offensive as that is, to begin with — is not alleviated when the hair is replaced by the permanently well-groomed hair of some other woman that just happens to be, technically speaking, detached from a scalp. The logic is completely flawed, and the moral argument is completely vacant.

But the problem is worse. Because when confronted about these paradoxes, the answer is "I'm following *halakha*." So following *halakha* means turning off one's own mind and heart and doing what everyone else is doing. It's about fitting in with the crowd even if it makes no sense and is a terrible imposition on women. If wearing a wig represents what the culture of *halakha* has become, then that culture has lost its basic value. It is no longer a moral guide, just a social one.

To me, the *sheitel* represents all that is wrong with Orthodoxy today. The emptiness of meaning, a disconnect from basic morality, following the herd, and the oppression of women. Doing all that, and then calling it *halakha*. As if.

These days, as I observe social trends in the Orthodox world, I'm not even sure what *halakha* means anymore. But I can say with all certainty that this, the *sheitel* and all that goes along with it, is not Torah. It is not beautiful, it is not spiritual, it is not inspiring, and it is not good. I'm waiting for some Haredi women to say this out loud, but I don't see it happening any time soon. The social pressure is just too great.

Post-script

Like my writing about pants and skirts, my writing about wigs gets a lot of people upset. And as cliché as it sounds, some of my best friends wear sheitels. It's true. Some women I love still do this. It's tricky – and in some of my essays below, I explore this challenge more.

Yet, even with all the pushback, I fully stand behind my belief that sheitels *are an absurd reflection of obedience and conformity, not of any kind of morality or spirituality. But this is a hard conversation to have with people who are in the system and following the rules. Very hard.*

But some of the worst exchanges have been with men, whose perspectives on this are less respectable than those of women living these experiences on their bodies. The following two essays are part of that reality.

Some Scholarly Looks at Women's Hair Coverings[14]

I don't know why I dedicated so much space over my career to the opinions of male rabbis about the female body – especially rabbis who promote themselves as being experts on the status of women. I find that entire stance particularly aggravating, men talking about women from a position of authority that women are mostly excluded from. I have also since stopped giving too much energy to people whose ideas are not worth it. Still, I've included here the series of exchanges I had about hair covering on the pages of the Forward with a particular rabbi not only because it's part of my history but also because it reflects a very difficult but common dynamic in which women have to grapple with men in positions of authority promoting obnoxious views on women.

---

[14] January 10, 2011. Originally published in the *Forward*. Reprinted with permission.
https://forward.com/sisterhood/134565/some-scholarly-looks-at-womens-hair-coverings/

HAIR

Jewish women's head covering is once again in the news, a heated topic among rabbinic men who are obviously not afraid of a little invective when it comes to women's bodies. The latest item is an incendiary letter by a Canadian Haredi rabbi named Shlomo Miller. Miller was responding to an article by Rabbi Michael Broyde in the journal *Tradition* that demonstrates that head covering is not a commandment written in stone, as it were, but "merely" a rabbinic prohibition that evolved over generations and therefore has room for interpretation and flexibility.

Miller, in response, said of Broyde's article that "all the lengthy diatribe therein is nothingness and an evil spirit," and proceeded to compare him to "Acher," a notorious heretic in Jewish history. So much for reasoned debate.

Broyde's article was actually written more than a year ago, making Miller's reaction a bit late in coming. Nevertheless, whether because Miller is a religious celebrity or because his language was so harsh, it seems that Miller's letter is buzzing in the Orthodox Jewish blogosphere.

The blogger DovBear is one of the few to take Miller to task. He writes, "Seems like a lot of anger for no reason." Well, it certainly is a lot of anger, but "no reason" ignores a fundamental dynamic among Orthodox rabbis. That is when it comes to women's bodies — particularly the increasing demands on Orthodox women to cover up more and more — there is a lot at stake. This is about the entire social identity and status of said rabbis and their followers that are at risk.

The Orthodox world over the past century has become a culture inside a culture in which men define their "level" of religiousness — and hence their own power and

69

standing in the community — based on the extent of cover on the bodies of the women associated with them. Religious identification — for men even more than for women — is measured along the woman's body, as if our bodies have a religious ruler running along our arms, our legs, our necks, our elbow. Degrees of cover mark degrees of approval and acceptance as women are observed and judged: leaves out fringe, leaves out the ponytail, goes without stockings, shows the knees, shows the elbows, shows *above* the elbows (gasp!) shows *above* the knees (double gasp!), shows two inches below the neck (choking!), wears jeans (help me I'm fainting!). The woman's body is a symbol for the entire community of men who surround her. For them to be respected by other men in their own world, the woman has to cover herself, and the more, the better.

Thus, for Broyde to suggest that perhaps women do not actually have to cover their hair according to the strict ruling of the law — well, this may have legal merit, but it is a huge threat to the societal conventions of religious life. He is messing up the social order.

Jewish feminist scholar and activist Susan Weiss takes this idea even further, reminding us that these laws are about owning women's sexuality. In an article in *Nashim* titled, *Under Cover: Demystification of women's head covering in Jewish law,* Weiss writes, "Head-covering, like the Jewish marriage ceremony, and like the Jewish laws of divorce, demarcates the exclusive and unilateral property rights that a Jewish husband has in his wife's sexuality." Weiss brings some compelling evidence from both sociological theory and women's explanations for covering their hair. Weiss also makes a strong case for the connection between women as chattel, and the ongoing struggle of Jewish women in divorce, particularly the problem of *agunot,* or women chained to unwanted marriages because their husbands refuse them a divorce decree:

> *[W]omen's head-covering obscures, legitimates, naturalizes, and thereby perpetuates the manner in which Jewish men retain proprietary interests in their wives' sexuality. So do the rituals of marriage and divorce. And so does the framing of the laws regarding the agunah and Israel's laws of marital property. Only by unmasking the many creative ways in which our customs, rituals, and laws act as mythical signifiers that protect the property interests of men will we be better able to protect the interests of women.*

Weiss speaks great truths but given the state of rhetorical debates among self-proclaimed Orthodox male leadership, I'm not sure that the Orthodox world has room for truth.

Post-script

Even though Broyde was the "lenient" or "progressive" in this exchange, the whole discourse makes me bristle. It is men talking over women about women and our bodies. Women try to have a say, but our voices often don't have any authority in Jewish law on the subject. That tells us everything we need to know.

On Purim Wigs, 'Modesty,' and Rabbi Broyde's Defense of the *Sheitel*[5]

Rabbi Brodye did not like my essay. And **The Forward** *published his response to me, in which he said that I don't understand why Orthodox women wear wigs, nor do I understand Jewish law or what he was trying to argue. Here is my response.*

I actually spent the past hour playing *sheitel macher* — combing out a long, blond wig, much the way Tali Farkash described in the article that sparked this blog-debate. I was doing it for my 7-year-old daughter because tomorrow is "wig day" in school. No, they are not training the girls to be good married women. It's just Purim.

It's quite funny, really. The wig is a fantastic tool for playing with identity, for stepping out of social norms

---

[5] March 16, 2011, originally published at the *Forward*. Reprinted with permission.
https://forward.com/sisterhood/136202/on-purim-wigs-modesty-and-rabbi-broydes-defense-of/

and boundaries and stretching one's reality and liberation. People use Purim to be who they are not "normally" allowed to be — *v'nahafoch hu* — and it is great fun. If society allowed us to play dress-up a little more, we might be a jollier people. But now that my daughter is finished giggling about her costume and gone to bed, I have returned here to this very serious debate about whether wigs somehow make women more religious. It's so funny that it makes me want to cry.

Michael J. Broyde opens his piece with an assertion that I am "mistaken in [my] critique of the wigs that many married Orthodox women choose to wear" — not that he disagrees with me, mind you, but rather that I am simply wrong. Rabbi Broyde then goes on to offer several assertions that, I believe, do nothing to rebut my basic argument. In fact, he perfectly demonstrates what I was trying to say.

First, he argues that "modesty" — i.e., the set of rules for excessive cover of the female body — is an antidote to belly-button rings, which in turn are an indicator of promiscuity and recreational sex. Really? This line of thinking is full of more leaps than an equestrian track. At the risk of stating the obvious, let me say that there are more than two choices for female attire. There is a whole series of gradations between the *sheitel* and the music video outfit. There is *a lot* of variation in between. Women who choose to wear jeans and a t-shirt, who play with ways to put their hair up in a scrunchy or let it flow naturally over their shoulders, who wear leggings to go bike riding in the park — these are women who, according to this reckoning, are immodest, likely to have sex as often as they eat, and dangerously on the fringe of acceptable social norms.

This black-and-white view (no pun intended) is particularly disturbing because it leaves out an entire range of female experience. It eliminates the practice of women freely choosing the way they exist in their bodies, because such practice would be outside of this dichotomy. It leaves out the very possibility that our clothing decisions are not based on the male libido but simply on our personal preferences.

And by the way, not all women who have belly-rings engage in recreational sex. One thing has nothing to do with the other. That is just a heterosexual male imagination at work.

Both the fervently Orthodox culture and the MTV culture involve a sexual objectification of women's bodies. Both expect women and girls to dress a certain way because we are objects of male desire. Both are dominated by men making determinations about what women should or should not wear based on their own inability to see us as more than a body. Orthodoxy, as opposed to MTV, says, *Okay, so cover up, and then maybe we'll respect be able to put aside our sexual desire and have a conversation with you.* But you know, the Taliban makes a similar argument. It's a no-win situation for women and leaves us completely passive and helpless.

Rabbi Broyde goes on to express exactly what I've been saying all along, "Women who desire to obey Jewish law while fully functioning in our open and valuable Western society found wearing a hat or a scarf to be a burden." Yes!! Head covering is a burden! Exactly! Women do not want to do it! "Hence, the *sheitel* became the perfect compromise because it promotes conformity with both Jewish law and Western culture." Indeed, the *sheitel* represents the worst of both worlds — conformity to two forms of the male gaze on the female body – the rabbinic gaze telling women to cover and the Western gaze telling women to be sensual and youthful. The *sheitel* is all about women's obedience to double sets of expectations on the female body; both of them inherently bad for women.

Moreover, the argument fully supports what I originally asserted, that the *sheitel* represents all that is wrong with Orthodoxy today. Meaningless conformity. I cannot even imagine what Moshe Rabeinu would think if he came down and saw these *sheitels*. Unrecognizable Torah.

But what makes this so painfully jarring right now is the world context of this conversation. Thousands of people lost their lives this week, and hundreds of thousands more are homeless, many of them elderly. We should be talking and writing about *that*. I mean, it is so distressing to me that I can blog about sexual abuse, violence against women, *agunot*, eating disorders, poverty, inequality, the social worker strike, and rape, and receive a small handful of comments. No rabbis writing in with great passion about what the Torah view is about the suffering of women. But as soon as I say something as horrifying as, say, "*sheitels* are dumb," suddenly the Orthodoxy community cares and is up in arms. It's upsetting. From my perspective, Orthodoxy has really lost the plot.

My friend Gal Lusky, dedicated founder of Israeli Flying Aid who goes wherever disaster strikes and sold her house to provide emergency rescue aid at Katrina, Haiti and elsewhere, has already dispatched a rescue team to Japan — even though she is $30,000 short of being able to provide the kind of disaster relief she needs to. "Do you know anyone who can donate $30,000?" she asked me. *I wish*. I can't help but think; maybe a few women can sell their wigs to raise the money. That is the sort of act that Moshe Rabeinu might possibly recognize as his Torah.

Post-script

The term "mansplaining," which was invented AFTER this series was published, would have been helpful. This exchange highlights not only how much Jewish religious life is defined by women's body-cover, but also by how much authority on the matter is given to men who deem themselves smarter and more knowledgeable than women – even on topics such as OUR bodies – but who often do not deserve even a fraction of the respect that the community affords them. And I believe that these issues are connected. Women are objectified because we are not considered to have knowledge or authority, and we are never allowed to stand on our authority because the culture is so used to seeing us as objects. It's a self-perpetuating cycle, and it is hard to break into. But I keep at it...

The Promises and Pitfalls of Discussing Hair-Covering with Women on Facebook[16]

Even though the act of uncovering my hair has been a source of empowerment for me, it has been very hard to share that with women who cover their hair. Here I share some painful experiences that explore why.

A woman recently announced on Facebook that she hates covering hair. The members of this online Orthodox women's forum initially responded with a fine dose of sympathy and commiserating – in some cases sharing their own struggles and changes with the issue. I contributed to the discussion, describing my own experience of stopping to cover my hair after a few years of marriage as one of the formative moments of my life, a turning point in relation to my body and to religion when I learned to start talking

---

[16] Unpublished, October 11, 2014. I wrote this essay in the context of a project in a Jewish leadership program.

back to my culture, and when I began to honestly face how my religious education left little if any space for women's lived experiences or passions or comfort or will. One woman responded that women who don't cover their hair obviously need to learn the halakhic sources, and a second woman called me "vain" and asked how I could possibly claim that taking off my hat gave me freedom – "Isn't halakhic life freeing?" I responded that you can say a lot of things about living a halakhic life but "freeing" isn't one of them.

Upon reflection, I'm particularly troubled by the comment that living a halakhic life is "freeing" – as if the prospect of making one's own choices about things like what to eat and what to wear is SOOOOOOO burdensome that having someone else decide every life detail of your life for you is freeing. It frees you from having to, you know, live your own life. It reminds me of the conversation my husband had once with a haredi colleague in the days before a national election. My husband asked him who he was voting for and he replied nonchalantly, "Whoever my rabbi tells me to." He was very happy. *Free*. Free from the trouble of having to think for himself, yes.

Still, on the thread, many of the responses were honest and empathetic. I found the discussion enriching and perhaps even exciting. We were engaging in an important conversation.

At least at first. The next day, a woman posted a new status: "I love covering my hair." There came a whole string of women saying things like, "Me too!" and "Thank you for posting that" and "Gee, I was beginning to think that only negativity was allowed here."

On the surface, this sounds like an open and balanced exchange of multiple viewpoints, where there is room for all sides. But that image, borrowed perhaps from presidential debates or courtrooms with two tables, belies something a bit more sinister in the online dynamic. The idea that the debating-team image was the wrong template for this discussion emerged when the woman who posted the first status ("I hate covering my hair") joined the second discussion ("I love covering my hair.") She said she felt hurt and dismissed and delegitimized, that her entire discussion was undermined and minimized. The second woman, the hair-covering-lover, was flabbergasted and insulted in turn. She didn't understand why the first woman was so upset, and she herself felt stifled in the discussion. "I guess there really is no room for people like me in this group," she huffed, adding that this is not a forum for a marketplace of ideas, and then the promptly left the group.

If you view women's forums like this from that "marketplace of ideas" or "debate team" model, something doesn't work. The second woman seems justified in her accusation that there is "thought policing" going on, that only "certain" opinions are allowed in a discussion. I get accused of this from time to time in my own Facebook group because I have been known to remove people who do not respect feminism or feminist women. The purpose of my group is to create a feminist forum, so this seems like a no-brainer to me. Still, every once in a while, I get someone angrily slamming a virtual door because the group is not particularly open to anti-feminist sentiments. This other group had the same tension. If one woman is allowed to say that she *hates* covering her hair, then civil discourse seems to dictate that another should be allowed to say that she *loves* it – and yet, there was something wrong with that second post, and it can be hard to explain.

One way to understand why is to consider the debating team versus the consciousness-raising group. Many online forums, especially feminist forums or women's forums are not necessarily for cold debate over rules, regulations, and practices but rather for finding support for one's experiences – especially when those experiences are challenging in real life. This is especially true in forums that take place within patriarchal cultures. Orthodox Jewish women trying to unpack their feminist ideas with religious culture are not necessarily looking for a cold rational Talmudic debate but rather for support in understanding their own experiences. Women's ideas, even about our own bodies, are so absent from the formal Orthodox discourse – women aren't even allowed to be rabbis or judges or witnesses in Orthodoxy, so our views and experiences are often completely marginal – that some women can be desperate for a place where their ideas are both legitimized and empowered. Not debated against the same anti-feminism that saturates their everyday life.

Online forums are often places where women need to process all that. These are spaces to get away from the dynamic of rabbinic authority and approval, where they can be free to fully express and explore who they are and what they are actually going through. The woman posting that she hates covering her hair was not asking to be taught religious "sources." She was asking for help and support. To hear "I love covering my hair" as a response was completely unhelpful and, in a way, hurtful. She had finally had the courage to come out and say how she felt, and some of her sisters did not understand that and instead sought to mark their own territory. The last thing she wants to hear is, "Oh, I don't have that problem at all." It's like someone writing a very personal post about a struggle with suicide, for example, and someone else responding, "I have never had such thoughts." That is just unhelpful. Undermining. I might even say it's toxic. It is a comment intended to dismiss a person's struggle under the misguided rationale of "I have a right to speak, too!" *Toxic.*

Another issue is the role of secondary observers versus those with lived experiences. When men – even Orthodox men, even rabbis – enter feminist conversations, the result can be very painful for women. Certainly, many men are caring and compassionate. But that's not always the case. And when a man, such as an Orthodox rabbi, responds to a woman's experience with Talmudic debates about permissibility versus violation, the result is often an unwanted authoritative injection of judgment in the middle of women's processing. The last thing a woman needs when she is finally finding the courage to speak out is to hear from some man that what she is doing is against Jewish law, something which only men are allowed to have authoritative voices about.

Orthodox rabbis are probably used to discussing the lives of people who are removed from their own personal experience. A group of male Orthodox rabbis discussing women's hair covering women, a practice that, by definition, is not their own, can have a dispassionate discussion of all angles and all rhetorical arguments. They're not affected by it in any way, so there are no personal issues at stake. It's just a fun debate. But a group of Orthodox women discussing this topic are exposing their lives, their bodies, their own visceral experiences. Posting something to the effect of "I'm struggling; I'm hurting; I'm suffering" is *not* an invitation to spar. It is a cry for help. That is someone reaching out into the virtual community and saying, "Someone, please save me." In that case, the last thing that person wants to hear is, "Your view is outside the norm of religious practice; You're not really Orthodox." Orthodox rabbis who talk this way to a woman – and there are way too many to count, especially on Facebook – are living examples of why so many Orthodox women have had enough of rabbis.

People really need to understand these dynamics before getting all huffy about what goes on in some online forums. There is a message here for men and a message for women. The message for men is this: *Respect women.* I know that sounds obvious, but unfortunately, it's not. There are many online feminist discussions where men take over, and women end up not speaking. This happens because men will, at times, take discussions about women into very abstract and irrelevant places. I have been attacked by Orthodox rabbis online too many times to count, where they take my sharing as an opportunity to use me for target practice.

For women, feminist issues are ALL personal. They are lived and suffered and pained. And these discussions are places to acknowledge that lived experience first and foremost. Men don't have the same need. (Well, the truth is, that they do; my first book *The Men's Section* was all about what feminism can do for men in unpacking their own lived experiences. But that is not the discussion that I'm referring to. When those discussions take place, which they do on occasion, men have every right to dominate.) And so, men need to understand their place in feminist discussions, or in any debate about women's lived experiences. You can be an observer, a supporter, and a commentator. But whatever it is that you have to say is secondary to women's discussion of their lives.

And there is a message for women as well: *Listen* to other women. This practice of women who respond to other women's experiences with the reaction of, "Well, I didn't experience that so it must not be true," is really quite undermining and painful. I hear it unfortunately, too often. Like the time I heard a woman from Beit Shemesh say, "I don't mind sitting in the back of the bus." What I said to her was that even though *she* doesn't mind, she should try to listen to all the other women who say that they *do* mind. She didn't hear me.

Women go beyond your own experiences. Don't formulate grandiose views based exclusively on your own okayness. Allow yourself to hear the pain of other women, even if the pain isn't your own. The world needs more empathy, and particularly the empathy of women towards women. That is the starting point of social change. We need to practice truly listening to each other and allowing ourselves to feel the other person's pain.

Post-script
I'm imagining the hair-covering-lover reading this and getting a bit huffy. After all, I seem to be prioritizing the hair-covering-hater's needs over hers. What about empathy for her!

The response isn't as complicated as it so often becomes. The first poster was in pain and asking for care, not the second. And in general, when someone else is asking for help, we should try to avoid centering ourselves in that process, especially if our experiences undermine the act of listening and validation.

But these nuances of care and compassion are hard to convey in our toxic world. And we know that social media is a terrible place for emotionally-charged discussions. And yet that is where so much of the consciousness-raising is taking place. So I continue to grapple and try to express ideas that help people get support that they need when they are struggling. I'm not an expert, but these exchanges are spaces where I dwell and I'm trying to make it work.

This essay is just a small piece of a larger discussion about how to manage this reality in which some important conversations are taking place in unhelpful settings. It is also one of my first attempts to sort through this quagmire by writing from my own experiences. There is a lot more to say on the subject and important research to share.

The Feminist Debate Over France's Burqa Ban[17]

I weighed in on the France burqa ban. Secular men controlling women's bodies are no better than religious men controlling women's bodies. They are the same – and women objectified lose out either way.

The burqa ban went into effect in France this week, and feminists are torn about what this means for women, religion, and freedom.

On the one hand is the oppressiveness of enforced, excessive female body cover in the name of religion. Islamic custom, not unlike Jewish custom, has historically placed supreme emphasis on covering the female body as a sign of piety. Whether or not layers upon layers of fabric bring about closeness to God is less of an issue than the extreme gender disparities involved. The picture of Muslim couples walking down the street in the Middle East heat, for example, in which the men are wearing whatever they please — jeans, shorts, tank-

[17] April 13, 2011. Originally published in the *Forward*. Reprinted with permission.
https://forward.com/sisterhood/136982/the-feminist-debate-over-frances-burqa-ban/

tops, flip-flops, whatever — while the women with them are in long black robes (often walking paces behind), is a living, visceral illustration of absolute gender discrimination. Add to this the fact that men are making all the rules, and female powerlessness becomes readily apparent. And add to all this the underlying rationales, which are filled with rhetoric of wife-ownership, distrust of women and outright misogyny, and it becomes abundantly clear why the burqa and all other Muslim customs of women's body cover are bad for women.

As Islam scholar and pundit Mona Eltahawy said, "I ... detest the niqab, and I detest the face veil. And I say this as a Muslim woman. I think that it represents an ideology that does not believe in Muslim women's rights to do anything but choose to cover her face.... I believe that the niqab dangerously equates piety with the disappearance of women and so I support banning it everywhere...It's not in the Koran, it's not an obligation for a Muslim woman to cover her face, and.... I believe that the human face is central to communication."

On the other hand, even agreeing with Eltahawy, the question is, does the government of France have the right or obligation to put this idea into law? At first glance, the burqa law seems to pit freedom of religion against the protection of women. Presumably, the French law is protecting women from religious oppression, something that democracies are supposed to do. But in practice, when the women themselves become criminals instead of the men oppressing them, the law misses the point.

This week, women who defied the law by wearing a face-covering niqab in public were arrested. The law, rather than providing women with freedom and choice, is punishing women. And ironically, these arrested women are in some ways expressing a freedom and acting in defiance — even if the defiance is against French law instead of religious law. This law, then, ends up forcing women to choose between disobedience at home or disobedience on the street — making them, to an extent, equally as empowered whether they wear the niqab or not. Moreover, it has created a completely twisted situation in which women are out demonstrating for their right to adhere to misogynistic practices, which is not exactly the goal of feminist awakening.

Opponents of the burqa ban include some religious Muslims as well as some non-Muslim feminists. Religious Muslim activist Hebah Ahmed said, "I think that it's a bad idea because I think it's yet another example of men telling women how to dress, how to live their life. It's another way to try to control women. And to take it to a government level and to try to legislate the way that a woman dresses is not just wrong and against human rights, but it really violates the whole basis [of] democracy... This is a free choice." Some liberal feminists agree with Ahmed, such as feminist scholar Martha Nussbaum who has surprisingly come out against the ban. This bizarre alignment between Muslim fundamentalists and liberal feminists really begs the question: Who is looking out for women's interests?

Moreover, there is something deeply disturbing about the fact that all this is taking place in France. As anthropologist Prof. Tamar El-Or, my doctoral advisor, said to me in one of our many conversations on gender and religion, it's as if the French are offended by the burqa because it flies in the face — literally — of French ideals of femininity. It's not so much about protecting women as it is taking back ownership of the female body — French and Muslim men fighting over the correct appearance of their women.

To me, it seems abundantly clear that burqas are oppressive to women. And I take issue with the idea that the ban threatens women's choice and freedom of religion because women in specific communities have no more choice about whether to wear the veil than women in Meah Shearim have about whether to wear sleeves. This isn't about protecting women's rights but about protecting the rights of men to make absolute determinations about the way the women in their communities must dress. The opponents of the ban are co-opting the language of post-modernism and democracy to enable misogynistic practices in the name of religion, and we need to be careful of that. I think that democracies have obligations to protect women from oppression and abuse and that certain practices – like those that cause harm to people – are not be protected by democracy.

That said, I'm not entirely sure that the ban is the way to go, and it's looking like the ban is doomed to failure, buttressing Islamic fundamentalism, and placing Muslim women in some challenging predicaments. If Muslim women are being oppressed, punishing them by law and making it hard for them to leave their homes are not the answer. Education, empowerment, intervention, and even the education of Muslim men are much better approaches. But secular, liberal non-Muslims cannot do education and empowerment unless they adopt a stance of respect for Islam. Empowering religious Muslim women in a way that is respectful of their traditions, their needs, and their real lives seem to me the most important – and perhaps most difficult – task ahead.

Post-script
Today, I would conclude much more emphatically that the burqa ban is not the way to go, that a GOVERNMENT

banning certain types of women's clothing is no different than RELIGIOUS LEADERS banning women's clothing. Neither patriarchal authority should be allowed to have that kind of control over women's bodies, period. I think that at the time I was writing this, I was still grappling with my own recovery from Orthodox clothing issues for women, and therefore that position felt more important to me. But today, I see many more sources of women's oppression beyond religious ones.

I also think that, upon reflection, it's clear that releasing one form of body-oppression is not the end of the journey towards freedom. We as women confront patriarchal practices at every turn. And sometimes what seems like an alliance is merely patriarchy in a different suit. I see this often in Israel, where secular political leaders can be heard condemning religious practices of excluding women without bothering to look inside their own camps. The difference between religious patriarchy and secular patriarchy is that in religion it is explicit and official while in secular circles it just is. Neither group has a monopoly on the issue, and neither has done the real work of eradicating its own misogynistic cultures.

In fact, I would say that at times, the patriarchy emerging from so-called progressive circles can be the hardest to confront. Men who talk about the importance of including women while ignoring their own subconscious bias and the absence of women in room – they can be particularly resistant to hearing that there is a problem. The latest iteration of this is French legislators acting as if they are "protecting" women from religious patriarchy, armed with liberal language, effectively making religious women criminals are just one iteration of that phenomenon. But we have many examples in our own community. And encounters with self-described progressive-feminist sources of misogyny can be just as infuriating and intractable as religious ones.

Why Jewish Women Are Wearing Burqas[18]

As I unpack my own history with body cover within religion, I find a lot of connection with Muslim women who have had similar experiences. Yet, when I make these parallels, I get a lot of pushback from religious Jews who want to believe that we are not the same as Muslims. Well, it may be hard to hear, but it's true. Women's body oppression in the name of religion cuts across cultures. We are far more alike that many of the religious authority figures around us would like to admit.

Fundamentalist Muslim women and fundamentalist Jewish women have a lot in common. Both groups live under the forced rules of ancient, male-controlled religious legal systems that place extreme emphasis on women's body cover as the supreme symbol of righteousness and community purity. In conversations I have had with Muslim

---

[18] April 7, 2010. Originally published at the *Forward*. Reprinted with permission.
https://forward.com/sisterhood/127114/why-jewish-women-are-wearing-burqas/

feminists over the years, the similarities between their work and the work of Orthodox feminists have been astounding. "I'm the first woman in my family to stop covering my hair," one Muslim feminist told me, with unmistakable echoes of religious Jewish women discovering personal empowerment.

The parallel issues between Jewish and Muslim women found a startling expression this week, as a *haredi* woman wearing excessive body cover was shot by Israeli police who assumed her to be an Arab terrorist.

She was dressed in all black robes, and in addition to covering her hair with a black scarf, she also covered her face, with what looked like a Muslim burqa. The 43-year-old Jerusalem native was riding a bus in Kfar Saba on her way to the ultra-Orthodox community of Tel Mond, and apparently believed that her outfit was either necessary or appropriate for such a visit. Some people call this "modesty," but that word, I believe, is a misnomer. Police asked the woman to stop, but she ran, so they shot her and detained her. She was not hurt and was later released from custody.

This story is reminiscent of the recent, highly publicized child-abuse case of Bruria Keren, the so-called "Taliban Mother." Keren, a 54-year-old Beit Shemesh mother of 12 who regularly wore layers and layers of clothing, including gloves on her hands even in the heat of summer, and also refuses to speak in the presence of a man, was convicted of severe child abuse. In keeping with her extreme views about religious women's behavior, she habitually punished her children by pouring water on them, locking them outside, and restraining them in the storage shed. Her children were so confounded by her fanaticism that her son and daughter had incestuous sex in that shed. So much for modesty.

It seems that even in the Orthodox community, where female body cover from the ankles to the neck to the wrists is already the norm, there is currently a process of further radicalization around women's bodies. Keren was apparently famous for the classes she delivered on this topic. According to The Awareness Center, which tracks sexual abuse in the religious Jewish community, Keren led a sect of some 50 women who regularly flocked to her like a guru expert on how best to achieve purity by being completely unseen and unheard. According to the *Forward*'s Daniel Treiman, this trend has spread to Brooklyn, as well. This week's arrest is the latest anecdotal evidence of the radicalization of women's body cover in Orthodoxy.

What is fascinating to me is how some members of the Orthodox community try to disassociate themselves from this radicalization. Shmuel Poppenheim, a spokesperson for the Eda Haredit, has said that the women of the cult are "crazy," as if his own haredi culture bears no resemblance to the women's behavior as if one can easily distinguish between extreme body cover that is "normal" and that which is somehow extreme.

"Even the strictest rabbis who require women to wear black head coverings and black stockings understand that a woman must allow herself to be a woman," he added.

In other words, "normal" body cover makes women "womanly," but some unspecified amount of cover transforms a woman from "womanly" to "insane." As if women – bombarded with radical messages of body cover supposedly in the name of God that claim the purity of the entire Jewish nation dependent on women's invisibility – are somehow supposed to be able to know the difference between body cover that is "womanly" and that which is "crazy." Given the predominance of this rhetoric in the Orthodox community, it was only a matter of time before women internalized the messages to the extreme.

What is really infuriating is that none of the male "leaders" in Orthodoxy who rant and rave about women's body cover now claim responsibility for the current extremism. It's not their fault. Women have merely taken it "too far." Right.

Here is some feminist wisdom on the subject of excessive body cover in the name of religion:

> *We should not be debating the clothing itself but what it stands for, the sexual morality and based on morality that says men cannot restrain themselves sexually. They are like wild dogs ... and we women are like pieces of tempting meat, and if we do not want to put society into chaos, then we should ideally stay behind closed doors, and if it's necessary for us to go outside of the house, then we need to veil ourselves. ... [A] woman who veils herself of her own free will, is actually wearing a banner telling every man that he is a potential rapist. He is incapable of sexual restraint, and I would like to know what men think of this and a woman who covers herself freely is also telling every woman who does not that she's a whore.*

The speaker is not Jewish, but Muslim feminist Ayaan Hirsi Ali — a woman whose ideas and courage should inform discussions of Orthodoxy, gender, and women's body. If Orthodox Judaism, like Islam, ultimately assumes women to be primarily objects of male sexual desire, it is hardly surprising that Orthodox women have started to take up the veil.

This week's arrest of the burqa-clad Jewish woman is a wake-up call. It is time for the religious Jewish community to confront the similarities between Orthodoxy and other fundamentalisms to rid our community of practices that harm women — practices that have nothing to do with the Torah or God but everything to do with men and power.

Post-script

Since writing this essay, I have had many conversations with haredi men and women disassociating from the Jewish women in full body cover. There reflects a deeply-rooted human tendency to see ourselves as "normal" or "middle-of-the-road", while everyone else is extreme. In Orthodox Judaism, there are many variations of women's body cover – from baseball caps to wigs to this Taliban-style; from heavy tights and long skirts to short denim skirts and sandals to jeans. Yet every sub-group considers itself moderate and normal, and tries to distinguish itself as different from "extreme" groups. Yet, on some level it is all the same. If all-male religious authorities are making determinations about women's bodies that are based exclusively on their own readings of both law and life, then the culture is fundamentally flawed, even cruel. The differences are nothing more than details.

As for Ayaan Hirsi Ali, I wrote this essay shortly after having read two of her books. I loved her writing, was inspired by her courage and wisdom, and found many points of identification with her. Since then, she has become a star of the religious right in America. I find that unfortunate. I think she may consider it unfortunate as well. Politics makes strange bedfellows.

Still, she has every right to work in places that value her and give her the status and compensation that she rightly deserves. And perhaps, considering her arduous journey to freedom, it is not our place to judge where she chooses to hang her hat.

Rav Yosef's Wife Shows Some (Gasp!) Hair[19]

Some anecdotal history of hair covering in Orthodoxy. Just for fun. Stirring the pot.

T he portrait of Rav Ovadia Yosef's family that hit the web this week was surprising not only because it is a rare example of the rabbi without his characteristic dark glasses and long dress. Most surprising

is his wife's apparel, her hair, neck, and collarbone are all exposed.

There has been some speculating as to why the rabbi "allowed" his wife to dress this way, some six decades ago when he was chief rabbi of Egypt. However, according to the Jewish Women's Archives, Yosef has

---

[19] February 15, 2012. Originally published at the *Forward*. Reprinted with permission.
https://forward.com/sisterhood/151383/rav-yosefs-wife-shows-some-gasp-hair/

always had something of a mixed record on women's issues from an Orthodox perspective. On the permissive side, he ruled that women should have a bat mitzvah ceremony, can be radio broadcasters, and can even wear pants under certain circumstances. On the restrictive side, he has also made some outrageous statements, especially on the hair-covering issue, having announced several years ago that women who wear hair-like wigs instead of scarves and hats will burn in Hell — or at least in the world to come — along with their *sheitel*s.

Still, I think that this mixed record is not as interesting as the evidence of historical evolution. It is clear that the way his wife covered her hair back then is considered unacceptable today by his family and followers. In other words, times have changed, as tends to happen.

This point – that rules of body cover have gotten more restrictive over the years – should sound obvious to most of the American Orthodox community. A browse through the photo archives of any Orthodox synagogue in America will undoubtedly reveal bare-headed rebbetzins — even in sleeveless tops and short skirts. The Young Israel congregation in which I grew up used to line the lobby hallway with such photos. Today the neighborhood is dominated by black hats and wigs.

Indeed, the social evolution of Orthodox dress codes — a process that happens in every culture that has ever existed — would not be such a surprising finding had it not been for the accompanying narrative of divine imperative. It's because rabbis try to tell us that women's head covering is God's will. It's also the entire deceptive discourse shrouded in the fallacious idea that this is somehow an immutable expression of divine law. As if. Clothing changes as do social sensibilities and the Orthodox community ought to recognize that.

96

It's not just that female body cover in Orthodoxy has evolved, but it has actually become more and more extreme to the point of obsessiveness and even violence (see: *Beit Shemesh*). What we are witnessing in the Orthodox community is not the process of more people becoming more devout but rather more and more people becoming a bit crazy about the issue of female body cover.

All this raises the critical question of why? Why is female body cover seen as the be-all-and-end-all of Jewish observance in so many circles?

I have some theories. One is that these are external identity markers, like a university sweatshirt, a way to identify one's belonging to a group easily. It's very comforting for people to have such a strong sense of allegiance. It helps people avert the insecurity that comes with having to walk through life on one's own. In some ways, it is the antithesis of loneliness and aimlessness, two excruciating human conditions. So by putting on a particular uniform and living among people who all wear the same uniform and live by the same codes, one can live with a certain social comfort, the ability to wake up in the morning, and know where one belongs.

There is also a particularly competitive dynamic in Orthodoxy that places a role. In my book, *The Men's Section,* I wrote extensively about the "man-on-man gaze," about the ways in which members of the Orthodox community watch and judge one another based on external markers like dress codes and time of arrival at shul. Clothing gives people an easy way to judge one another, and to judge where they are in relation to one another, even on such esoteric and seemingly personal issues as religiousness.

Finally, there is an obvious gender factor. There is an enormous desire in the community to control women's sexuality and overall behavior. This is not all that different from dynamics in some other religions (Islam and the American Christian right come to mind). This is about men creating cultural rules for themselves based on how much control over they have over women to retain their own power and status quo. Perhaps it's a response to women's liberation. As Ahasverus said in the Book of Esther, the wrath of the King whose wife refused to obey him must be known throughout the land, "so that every man dominates in his household and speaks according to the language of his nationality."

When I think about Orthodoxy's trend toward restrictiveness, I cannot help but worry about women's lives. I just hope that images like this one of Ovadia Yosef's wife showing some hair and skin will remind some people that the path to righteousness does not include controlling women.

Post-script

I am once again reminded that my mother and grandmothers did not cover their hair. History is not a linear progression. Interestingly, though, many of my contemporaries started out in marriage covering their hair and then stopped, like I did. So that is happening, too.

Voice

"It took me quite a long time to develop a voice, and now that I have it, I am not going to be silent."
- Madeleine Albright

"I raise up my voice — not so that I can shout, but so that those without a voice can be heard. … We cannot all succeed when half of us are held back."
- Malala Yousafzai

"The world is trying to kill you by stealing your voice. Kill it back."
- Melissa Newman-Evans

When I was in elementary school, I sang in a girls' choir. It was a source of pride, especially for my father. His father was a cantor in Brooklyn in the 1940s/50s, and in my father's world, leading the community in song is a sign of valor and worth. At least for men.

Of course, doing this as a girl was misleading. Yes, it was fun and exciting to sing. But there was no real notion that I would go anywhere with it, especially after I became a Bat Mitzvah. Then my status would change. In my world, women did not actually lead – not services nor anything else. What my father truly wanted was for me to marry a guy who could sing like him: Lead services, speak from the pulpit, be a Leader. Sure, they let me sing, I enjoyed singing, and I enjoyed speaking, but there was a brick wall ahead. It was a trap.

I still love singing, although I don't do it often and I'm not particularly good at it. I can hold a tune and do a decent harmony – mostly as an alto though I used to be a soprano – thanks not only to my choir experience but also to singing zemirot around the Shabbat table. But just as we outgrew singing zemirot, I also outgrew being a girl, and evolved into a woman, whose status is different. I'm not a leader of the service. And actually, when I do sing, I unconsciously hold back. I never let my full voice out.

I'm working on some of this, though. In fact, I recently began taking singing lessons with the enormously talented Rabbi Dr. Minna Bromberg. She has not only helped me release my voice, but has also pointed out other forms of patriarchy in women's singing. For instance, she taught me that people's discomfort with women's head voice, which is often considered "fake", is internalized sexism. Discomfort with women's loud voices – as Lindy West explores with her book Shrill – is also a way to keep us in down. And generally, I have very distinct memories *of gossipy conversations in school and at home about girls who liked to sing. Like, a girl who sings is perceived as arrogant. As taking up space. As too much. As not "modest". It's all connected.*

I also have some very distinct, painful memories about my voice. In my family, I was always the one who talked too much, who talked too loud, who didn't know when to stop or to be quiet. It was embarrassing, and I received many eyerolls when I wanted to say something. My father frequently and emphatically shut me down at the Shabbat table. One of my sisters would always say, "Elana doesn't know how to do anything softly," like that's a bad thing. The only one who I remember experiencing a similar fate was my Grandma Bea, a brilliant and fiercely independent-minded woman who was not interested in gossip or small talk but could talk for hours about sociology, history, and philosophy. She was also deemed embarrassing, subject to those same eyerolls when she opened her mouth, and frequently shut up with force. I am sad that I did not appreciate the dynamic during my teens, before she got Alzheimers and lost much of her personality. I am also deeply ashamed that I participated in her boxing-up, even as I was to endure a very similar position for much of my life.

Over the years I've experimented with my voice, both musically and in other ways. In my late twenties I joined women's-only prayer groups and learned to chant from the Torah. Later, I joined and helped form "partnership minyanim", Orthodox services where women are given select roles for leading. I embraced every opportunity to chant from the Torah or lead a prayer service – even when men around me were less than enthusiastic. I wrote about many of these painful experiences in my book, The Men's Section: Orthodox Jewish Men in an Egalitarian World. *I wrote about the man who eagerly admitted that his buddies cringe when certain women get up to lead, including me. I wrote about the man who confessed that when a woman leads, he stands very close to the* bima *with a few of his mates in order to overpower her because he doesn't trust that women ever know the correct nusach, or liturgical melodies.*

At a certain point I tried out Reform rabbinical school thinking that was where I would be able to enter my whole self and where the singing me would be celebrated. At first, I was excited about the possibilities. I was eager to lead and chant Torah and even play piano at services. But there, too, patriarchy reared its ugly head and found other ways to silence me. When a teacher did not like what I had to say, he had no problem mocking and shaming me, which has a definite, emphatic silencing effect. When I shared feminist insights on the Talmudic passage we were studying, I was quickly shunned with the assertion that feminist thought is not "rigorous", my PhD be damned. When the heads of the college did not like what I blogged about or posted about, I was told that I needed to be silent and just listen. I realized that my desire was not just to sing but to actually be heard, in my own voice, on my own terms, with my own thoughts and ideas. Turns out, rabbinical school is not necessarily the place for that.

Ultimately, the Jewish traditional view that singing and leading are for men is a position not merely about the perceived sexuality of women's singing voices. It's also about something deeper. Voice evokes speaking, sharing views, and expressing a vision for oneself and for the world. Restrictions on women's singing are just one small part of this. Limiting voice is about stunting women's power in the world.

To wit, in my house growing up, girls sang. At the Shabbat table, we sang in harmonies and our singing was welcome – except for my mother, who was firm in her role as passive observer of this and so much else. Still, it would be a mistake to interpret the fact that we sang as an indication that we were being empowered – and not just because we could only do it at home and not during the synagogue service. It was more than that. At our table, my father was the only one who was allowed to think. His opinions were the only ones that mattered, and our job as his children was to accept his rhetorical displays as fact. Whenever I would dare question or disagree, I would be summarily punished. My mother was the gatekeeper of this rule. My father, for his part, sometimes tolerated my speaking with a certain amusement, occasionally commenting that I was the closest thing he had to a son. But my mother would inevitably shut me down and remind me that it is not my place to speak against my father. His voice was gold. Mine was a disruption.

That is the message of women's voice. Even in places where we as girls sang, we were socialized to understand that thought leadership and all other kinds of powerful participation in society were not for us.

There's more. Voice is also about passion, creativity, personal expression, and public performance. And it's about being fully seen in one's whole self and body. In that sense, the struggles of being the person who does not sing in public continue to trigger other side effects. I still struggle with the injunction in my head to be quiet. Don't be too loud. Don't take up too much space. Don't yell. Don't get angry. *These things are all connected in my consciousness and in the way I walk through the world.*

Interestingly, an essay that I wrote about women's voice ended up having a very painful consequence in which I was publicly shamed by a family member. That experience in turn birthed a story of fiction that I include in this section, "The Story of a Boy and his Witch-Aunt," which I originally published under a pseudonym out of a combination of shame and protecting my family of origin. That was a watershed moment in my life, a clarification about the world from which I emerged. I'm glad to report that today, I am no longer ashamed, and I am learning to sound my voice fully. But some days, the truth still hurts.

Bnei Akiva, and the Efforts to Silence Women[20]

This was one of my first essays about the growing religious pressure to ban women from singing in Israel. The problem has gotten worse, not better, and I wrote about it extensively in my 2014 book, The War on Women in Israel.

Women can solve the world's problems by just being a little quieter. That is the message emerging from the resolution of a little fracas in the Religious Zionist world recently. The conflict revolved around the traditional IDF event memorializing the "Lamed-Heh," the 35 men from the Haganah convoy who gave their lives to protect Gush Etzion in 1948. Bnei Akiva announced their withdrawal from the event because there are to be women singing in the choir. After some hemming and hawing and a few angry responses even from within the Bnei Akiva constituency — including condemnation of the boycott from Bnei Akiva World head Daniel

---

[20] January 31, 2010. Originally published on my blog, *A Jewish Feminist*.
http://jewfem.com/index.php?option=com_easyblog&view=entry&id=95&Itemid=622

Goldman, as well as Kibbutz Hadati youth, Kolech, and others — the groups reached a "compromise" in which women would not sing at the event, but would sing after the event (once all of the Bnei Akiva kids have left).

Actually, this event is just the latest in a series of national religious boycotts of women's artistic expression — boycotts that, for the most part, have resulted in public capitulation to demands of religious men, amounting to victories for anti-woman rabbis at the expense of women's well-being.

In 2008, for example, a leading dance troupe set to perform at the gala opening of the Jerusalem Bridge of Strings was forced cover up "Taliban-style" in order to placate haredi men (some of whom are on the city council). Similarly, a group of religious paratroopers walked out of an IDF event in which a woman was singing. According to Haaretz, there have been several similar incidences over the past two years: One army brigade canceled a female singer's performance at a program for commanders after two religious commanders refused to attend. A year earlier, a group of men walked out in the middle of a woman's singing, and there have been similar tensions at several other events.

It is important to note that these events are taking place in public spaces. We are not talking about a private party run by some religious group. We are talking about the IDF, the Jerusalem Municipality, and programs aimed at the entire population of Israel. For these groups to capitulate to religious demands sets a frightening precedent — and I don't think that the Taliban analogy is unwarranted. This is how it starts.

There are a few issues here. One is the effect on women. I cannot help but wonder how the women singers feel about this. Yesterday, they were equal members of a mixed choir; today, they are the ones that are not meant to be heard. Their "leaders" basically offered the women as sacrifices in the name of peace between brothers. I would feel completely betrayed, with nobody covering my back.

Moreover, the decision turns women's singing into a sexual act. Men can sing freely without ever being accused of being provocative. Yet women, singing the same songs and with the same passions and motivations, are told that their voices are a turn-on to religious men. Let's parse this out for a minute: I want to know which men, sitting in a memorial service for the Lamed Heh, are going to be getting an erection because women are singing. I would like to know who educated those men to be able to ignore all serious content and turn everything into sex. Frankly, I think these men should all be kicked out of the army. I mean, how are they supposed to fight a war if they can't keep it in their pants for a five-minute mournful choir performance?

But of course, there's a less visceral and more symbolic reason for this fanaticism. (Let's face it: I doubt they're all Don Juan.) It's an attempt to appear more "religious." As Assaf Wohl writes in *Ynet*: this is "merely an example of a much broader phenomenon taking place within the national-religious camp; a process that is mistakenly being referred to as 'going haredi'."

Indeed, religious men are systematically taught that to be more religious means to look more haredi. And to "look" more haredi ultimately means to cover women up. The more silent and invisible women are, the more men can congratulate themselves on being increasingly religious. That is the narrative playing out here.

One can only wonder what God thinks about this religious flock supposedly representing His will. Divinely inspired? Spiritually uplifting? Living out His words? I don't think so. It's just men proving their manhood by demeaning women. It has nothing to do with being a good Jew.

Post-script

I would have hoped that there would be more resistance to these practices, but unfortunately that does not seem to be the case. The problem seems to be getting worse, not better.

Women are Jews, too[21]

I covered the Women of the Wall extensively for several years, and even have a chapter about the group in my book, The War on Women in Israel. *Here is one essay on the subject, which tackles the many sources of misguided misogynistic attitudes in Israel. It explains what the ban on women's voices can lead to: a complete lock-down, incarcerating women who dare to use their voices.*

When a woman is arrested, shackled, strip-searched, and held in a cell, one might expect to learn that she committed a horrific crime of some sort, like a terrorist attack or breaking into the White House. The fact that Anat Hoffman's crime for which she received this treatment was singing at the Western Wall has left many people reeling – but apparently not David Landau. In an opinion piece here, Landau tried to justify the police's attitude, dismissing women's prayer at the Kotel as a "cynical charade" and nothing more than a "stunt" to make Israel

---

[21] Oct. 26, 2012, Originally published in *Ha'aretz*. Reprinted with permission.
https://www.haaretz.com/opinion/.premium-elana-sztokman-women-are-jews-too-1.5194791

look bad. Landau's entire essay, which is based on flawed thinking that dismisses women's religious experience and ignores the sentiments of most of American Jewry and of modern Orthodoxy, not only failed to convince but also actually works to justify institutional hostility towards women.

In trying to argue that women's prayer groups are offensive and should be banned at one of Israel's holiest sites, Landau likens women's singing to "a few Armenians encroaching onto one minute of the prayer-time demarcated by ancient accords for the Greek Orthodox," and adds, "Wars were launched for less." He might as well have said that women's singing in prayer is akin to serving pork to the Chief Rabbi. The portrait he tries to paint is one in which the female voice is a mortal enemy of Judaism, that a female presence when "Jews" – read, men – are in prayer is enough to start a war.

There are a few things wrong with Landau's troubling analogies. For one thing, his unfortunate analysis places women completely outside of Judaism, beings whose presence is damaging to Jewish men, who are seen as the normative ones in terms of religious practice. Landau's androcentrism is used to justify the notion that the police apparatus should have the right to do whatever it takes to ensure to protect Jewish men from encroaching, interfering, offensive women. If the sound of women's voices is experienced as an offense this grave, then women's very presence becomes the opposite of "authentic" Judaism, a presence that can never be remedied other than making women completely silent and invisible.

At the risk of stating the obvious, I would like to note that women are Jews, too.

Second, Landau makes the outrageous claim that Orthodoxy is the state's religion and that everyone in the world just has to accept that. The primary defect in this assertion is that this issue is not about Orthodoxy but about a radical fringe of Orthodoxy that believes that women should not be seen or heard anywhere. Landau would be wise to remember that many Orthodox communities around the world embrace women's prayer groups and have been for the past forty years. What he seems to be saying is that radical anti-women Orthodoxy, a phenomenon that unfortunately seems to be gaining influence in some places, should guide all of life in Israel.

Moreover, Landau forgets that there is tremendous opposition in Israel and throughout the Jewish world to the idea that this radical Orthodoxy should determine everything that has to do with Judaism in Israel. It has taken a generation or two for Jews in Israel and around the world to realize that giving religious parties these powers to determine how the state guards Judaism was one of David Ben Gurion's greatest mistakes.

Ripples from that mistake are felt in every area of life in Israel, by every demographic sector – including by ultra-Orthodox women and men, who are often stuck in lifestyles that they have no say in controlling. So Landau may scream and shout that the entire Jewish world should just listen to the radicals and shut up about it, but that idea is out of step with the overwhelming sentiments of Israelis and the Jewish people at large.

We need to be asking ourselves a straightforward question. *What side of history do we want to be on?* Generations from now, our descendants will be looking back at these events and asking how people could hold such prejudiced views about other human beings. What we will be able to answer our great-grandchildren when they ask us, where were we when women were crying out for the right to sing to God - without being arrested for it.

Post-script

These stories raise a critical question: What is so threatening about women's voices? I think the answer, again, is this: singing is not just about singing. It's about free-thinking, free-expression, and women seeking our own freedom and independence. It's about our power. And all these are connected.

Unlikely Orthodox Superstar Finds Her Voice[22]

Apropos women seeking independence via singing, this story about Shayna Rehberg broke my heart – and also left me inspired. It has a happy ending for the singer, who has found her voice and a new life. But it had a less happy ending for me.

Shayna Rehberg is an unlikely superstar. A 30-year-old religious mother of four originally from Texas and now living in Safed, Shayna walked onto the stage of Israel's popular singing competition show, Kochav Haba [Next Star], donning her headscarf and long skirt, and made it to the next round following a rendition of Alanis Morisette's "Ironic." She impressed the judges perhaps less with her singing — which at times was lilting and commanding and, at other times, withdrawn and fragile — and more with her life story. She told the judges, and thousands of viewers, that she had stopped singing for ten years because of religion.

---

[22] January 8, 2015. Originally published in the *Forward*. Reprinted with permission.
https://forward.com/sisterhood/212318/unlikely-Orthodox-superstar-finds-her-voice/

"This is like coming out of the closet," Judge Harel Skaat sympathetically told her, adding that it was no different from his own experience of coming out as gay. "You're coming out of a cage, even if it's a self-imposed one."

This exchange with Harel Skaat was beautifully empathetic as well as incredibly revealing and insightful about the dynamics of being an Orthodox Jewish woman.

The powerful idea that emerged from this exchange is that the custom of women not singing hurts women. It's a restriction, like Ariel's curse in *The Little Mermaid*, of silencing not only voice but also passion and even personality. Singing is a vital expression of life. Music has profound spiritual and emotional meanings. A life without singing can be a deeply painful one, especially for a person who has a special voice. Orthodox Judaism would never consider imposing such a rule on men. It would never enter anyone's mind to say that a man who loves singing should stop singing. And yet, this is what Orthodoxy does to women all the time.

In her interview, Shayna said, "I decided that *kol isha* is not *erva*" — that is, that the halakhic description of women's voices as causing sin is wrong. This was such an inspiring model of empowerment. It is a close-up view of what it means for women to talk back to their culture. I don't know if the audience realized how hard this is. To be hearing for years — for your whole life, perhaps — about what women's bodies and voices are or aren't, and then to wake up and decide that your culture is wrong, well, that's an incredible moment of awakening.

There are a few more interesting points to this performance worth harping on; one is about her marriage. When one of the judges asked her what she had to overcome to be able to sing, her response was a shocking, "I filed for divorce." The implication here, even though not stated explicitly, is that her husband was not letting her sing. This was not surprising for me to learn, even if the public admission had some of the audience booing. But this was also a massive admission of truth. I belong to several different online forums for religious women, and there are constant posts in the style of, "I would like to do X, but my husband says that it's not okay." I find these kinds of posts chilling, and often suspect abuse. Let's be clear about this: a man who controls his wife's behavior, even if he is using religion as a justification, is abusing her. This may be abuse in the name of religion, and it is still abuse. Shayna gave a face to this kind of abuse, and I do not doubt that there are many religious women at home watching and listening carefully.

I also think that there is a broader implication for religious women about other practices that are emotionally confining — what Harel Skaat called a form of prison. For some women, forced clothing choices may fit into this category. Little girls wearing only skirts effectively are unable to engage in fun childhood activities like climbing a tree or going swimming with the family. So often, I see religious families on the beach where the men and boys are frolicking, and the women and girls are sitting still. As someone who used to do this, I can attest that this socialization into a complete stance of passivity in the face of life's beauty and the earth's invitation to play is painful and even tragic.

For other women, head covering is the prison. (I used to do this too). I've been speaking with religious women who stopped covering their hair – as I did many years ago – and many women describe the process as liberating. Our hair can be such a huge part of our identity. When you start to put that scarf or hat on, your whole face looks different. Your personality may change too. You become the covered, married woman, owned and unavailable. Maybe some women like that feeling of not being able to be hit on by men. But it can also be a stance of self-restriction and containment.

There is so much for women to learn from Shayna. When the judges said, "She has so much light emerging from her," I totally saw that. The process of talking back to your culture, taking ownership, and finding your own voice — in this case literally — is a beautifully spiritual and empowering process. I hope Shayna can find her power again, as Skaat said, and really belt out her music on this show. I wish her well and hope that she continues to shine her powerful light on women and all of humanity.

Post-script

My blog post, which offered compassion for women and would have come as no surprise to anyone who has ever read anything I wrote, generated some ugly pushback within Orthodox social media. A particularly obnoxious troll, who happened to be teaching at the Yeshivah of Flatbush and for some reason has a following, posted my essay in a supposedly "liberal" Orthodox Facebook group with some 10,000 members, along with his own brutal commentary about how this essay is an example of why the Orthodox community hates [me] so much. He wrote this opinion as fact, not his own opinion. What's worse, his post generated over 200 comments at last count before I exited the group and blocked him. Tellingly, very few of the comments were about the issue of whether women should be allowed to sing, and most of them about me and my apparently terrible personality.

To my surprise, one of the comments was from my then 25-year-old nephew, who wrote. "This woman is my aunt. She is brilliant but all emotion. Don't listen to a word she says."

Ouch.

It wasn't so much that he said this himself but rather that this is obviously the driving opinion in my family of origin. I mean, he hadn't seen me or had a conversation with me in probably 7 or 8 years, so he was not judging me for himself. He was reflecting the consensus around him.

Well, I blocked him and some other people, and then crawled under the covers for a while. When I emerged, I decided to process this experience in a different way: through fiction.

The following short story, "The Story of a Boy and his Witch-Aunt," is what came out of me. I submitted it to Jewish Fiction.net and the beautiful editor there, Nora Gold, let me publish it under my pseudonym, Mia Martos. I was too ashamed to publish something so close to my real life, witches and all. I also hid my identity out of a misplaced concern for the feelings of my family of origin, as if I should protect them from knowing the truth about my experiences.

Recently, however, I decided that I have nothing to be ashamed about, and it's time to own this, even if it means exposing the story to sunlight. I also learned that it is not my job to protect others from facing the truth of their own actions. My story is mine to tell. And in this book, I am, for the first time, not protecting anyone. I am just sharing my experiences. This is my story.

I posted this on Facebook in 2019, dropping the need for the pseudonym. I also shared the backstory about my nephew's attack and received some very supportive feedback. The experience was freeing, and my wounds have mostly healed. But the scars remain.

The Story of a Boy and His Witch-Aunt[23]

As I described above, this story came out of me after an experience in which my 20-something nephew publicly sided with my trolls. I was too ashamed of all of it to publish this under my own name. But today, I have let go of a lot of that shame and have taken ownership. Still, it is a reminder of the cost of being a woman with a voice in Orthodox Judaism. I paid a steep price for speaking out, but I would do it again without a doubt.

Shimshona remembers well when the boy was born. It was a warm summer day, and all the women of the family were hot, practically dripping in pools of their own sweat. That's how the sisters were back then: whatever one of them went through, the others experienced as if it was happening to them. When Shimshona's sister, Diane, screamed in labor, her sisters all clutched their stomachs. When Diane's baby arrived,

[23] 2016. Originally published at Jewish Fiction.net. Reprinted with permission.
https://www.jewishfiction.net/index.php/publisher/article view/frmArticleID/449

the women's shouts filled the corridors of every house in their family, of every room in the synagogue. But the women's celebration was nothing compared to that of the men. The sisters' father, who had been waiting for a whole generation for a boy, was pouring *schnapps* at his morning *minyan*.

"*Baruch hashem*, we did it," he said. Finally, after four daughters, he could make a *bris*, even if it was for a grandson. The boy was given the name Daniel.

The sisters did what aunts do. They brought cakes and balloons and blue outfits and chickpeas and witch hazel. They commented on how beautiful he was, how smart he would be, how perfect the world was now. When the boy Daniel slept in the house, everyone removed their shoes and spoke only in whispers. When the boy Daniel recited his *divrei Torah* homework at the Passover Seder, everyone listened in rapt attention. When he received his first A, the paper was framed and hung in the vestibule. Although Daniel's mother would deliver six girls after him, none would ever be greeted with quite the same fanfare as the boy.

On the day he was born, Shimshona closed her eyes and took a breath before she blessed her nephew. *What will become of you, little Daniel?* she wondered. She summoned all the angels, asking them to bestow special protections on the boy. He was, after all, a special gift to her father and to the other males of the family, who, she reasoned, were right to welcome one of their own. It was an opportunity for her father to reproduce himself, so to speak, like on a photocopy machine. All the effort her father exerted in his life to be a Good Jewish Man — all the praying, all the waking up early to practice his *laying*, all those shul meetings, all those business lunches — he now had someone to teach it all to. At one time in her life,

Shimshona had thought that he would teach *her* to be a Good Jewish Man. He used to joke that she was so smart she was the closest thing he had to a real son. But that stage passed. Shimshona could not exactly recall when he stopped doing that — maybe when she started developing hips. Or something else. She opened her eyes and walked away from the boy.

Shimshona did not know when she became a witch. For most of her life, she'd never really thought of herself as a witch. She was, well, just a feminist. A religious feminist, actually. That's what she called herself. She put her energy into helping women find their power, using whatever spiritual tools she had at her disposal. Like Shimshon, her namesake, she had an affinity for fire and playing with animals, and she sported thick locks of hair flowing down her spine. Also, like her namesake, she spent many years trying to run away from her superpowers. She did not at first know what to do with them. At times she was startled to discover what she was capable of. She found she could speak to people with impact and persuade them of all sorts of things. But she didn't always like doing that. It seemed to make people uncomfortable - including herself. These days, she tended to speak selectively. Mostly, she preferred to use her special gift for helping women hear their *own* voices.

It was one of her brothers-in-law, she believed, who first used the word "witch" to describe Shimshona. At first, she was startled, but then she liked it. And the man didn't even know half of her powers.

Of course, it wasn't long from the time she received the label until her first experience of hate. Yes, the haters were swift to come. After all, once she accepted her title as witch, she inherited a history of pain and persecution to go with it. The attacks took many strange and new forms that her witch ancestresses may have recognized. Sermons were dedicated to eviscerating the witches. Shabbat lunches became opportunities to spread the mission of "destroying the evil witches from our midst." Children, especially religious boys, hung on every word.

Daniel grew to be "a fine boy," as his grandfather would say. "A beautiful boy," his grandmother would say. "Girls will be fawning all over him," the aunts would say. He was, in fact, very popular in school, although more among the teachers than among the girls.

Daniel was also a precocious boy. He read encyclopedias for fun and loved to study the weather. He and his grandfather would sit every Shabbat and study the Torah portion, but not before spending fifteen minutes analyzing atmospheric pressure, cold fronts, and wind directions. The grandfather would eat chocolate babka that the grandmother served and marvel at the boy's genius. "It must be in the genes," he would say, laughing, though not actually joking.

One of Daniel's teachers, a man named Pesach, who was beloved by many parents for his special way with the boys, was especially impressed with Daniel and took Daniel under his wing. Pesach had a trim black beard and tucked his black side curls behind his ears. (He didn't want people to get too intimidated by how religious he really was, he told Daniel in secret.) Pesach spent long hours studying and was considered — at least by himself — a master of *halakha*, Jewish law. However, when he was not studying, he was hanging out with his students, listening to Jewish rap music. Still in his mid-20s, he was not much older than his students, and they were attracted to his youthful energy — and his ability to talk.

Boy, could Pesach talk! He would give lessons that awed his students. They would laugh, nod, raise their hands with fervor, and chat about Pesach for days afterward. A regular Pied Piper! He talked to his boys about all the topics that they wanted to hear about most: girls, dating, and sex. He taught boys about what girls liked and wanted to hear. Of course, he told them that it's forbidden to touch girls before marriage. But he did it in a way that was cool and funny.

"He keeps the boys engaged," Daniel's grandfather would say. "He has that special quality of charisma."

His gifts also included writing. Thousands, including Shimshona herself, read his blog. It was called *True Torah* and covered not only standard topics like the rules of Shabbat and keeping kosher, but also some taboo topics like sex, which made him especially popular. His boys believed that he was *the* expert on girls. "Treat girls gently," he was fond of saying. "They are like delicate flowers, like princesses. They are not designed to handle excess power." The fact that he was still single and dating gave him even more credibility. They loved him.

Shimshona encountered him once by chance. She'd gone to the yeshiva to meet her friend Sophia for lunch. (A fellow witch, actually, who was working as a guidance counselor in the yeshivah). She peeked into a classroom and saw her nephew listening intently to his teacher. She tried to get his attention, but he was too focused Pesach — Rabbi Winter, his door said. She opened the door just a crack to hear more, and then all the boys heard the noise and turned to look at her. Rabbi Winter looked irritated at the interruption, and Daniel looked mortified. Shimshona apologized profusely and closed the door. After that, she tried not to think about Rabbi Winter, since she did not want to pry into her nephew's life and relationships. But she had a flash of an image of him standing on a soapbox. She smiled briefly and then got a chill, but quickly put it out of her mind. This person was none of her business. After that, she did not read his blogs or follow his activity. She just kept doing her own things.

The family was proud of Daniel and believed that he, like Pesach, was destined for greatness. "He's a born leader," Shimshona's father would say about the boy to those around the Shabbat table, "Just like me." Daniel glowed with the pride of being Chosen.

"And isn't he handsome?" Shimshona's mother would say, bringing out the brisket. Shimshona had her eyes closed. She did not eat meat.

Anyway, she was busy with her own work. Women needed her. Although people called her a witch, she saw herself as more of a healer. She found that many women in her community needed that. She liked to think of her work as a kind of *feminist* healing. She helped women heal by showing them their own power. She had quite a following of her own. But it was not the kind of following that her father would ever have discussed at the Shabbat table or that the rabbi would have commended from the pulpit. Even as more and more women were healing and finding their power, the men in the community who were writing the sermons did not approve.

Meanwhile, as Shimshona embraced her work, her relationships with her sisters faltered. They stopped being as close as they once were. Diane and the others did not like Shimshona's work and called it witchcraft. Their husbands liked it even less. "Does she think she's better than us?" her sister Rose asked.

"It's like suddenly she hates the family," Cheryl added.

Shabbat meals became uncomfortable for Shimshona. Her sisters and their husbands stared strangely at her. They commented on her wild hair, on her hippie clothes, on her lack of make-up, on her unflat stomach.

"She's out of control," her mother would say.

"What do you expect?" her brothers-in-law would say.

"It's so embarrassing," her mother would complain. And the sisters drew apart.

But Shimshona still loved her nieces and nephews. She did not see them often, but they were always in her thoughts. She lit candles for them and prayed for them and summoned special angelic protections for all of them, especially for Daniel. He was, after all, *special*.

By the time one of Shimshon's friends warned her of the threat of Pesach's current blogs, it was too late. *The feminist witches are evil and need to be removed from our midst*, was the title of one entry, the one that got 35,000 "likes" in three days. *And their leader must be removed. Start at the top. Her name is Shimshona.*

Shimshona was devastated. Why was Pesach writing about her? She did not understand. Why was he mentioning her by name? When did he even start noticing her? She had had no idea that all this was going on. And why did he think of her as so dangerous? Why was he so scared of her?

She scrolled down the comments. *The feminist witches are ruining society*, someone named "MysteriousMark52" wrote. *They are turning women against their husbands, making mothers leave their children.*

It's unnatural, wrote someone named "Leibel the Wolfhearted." (Who are these people? Shimshona wondered.) *They are distorting Torah. They must be stopped.*

Shimshona kept reading, not heeding her witch-sisters' warnings never to read the comments, until she came to this one. *Shimshona is my aunt.* Daniel had written it. *She is brilliant but dangerous.*

Daniel! She couldn't believe it. Was this real? Did he just write that? Why was he doing this to her? She did not understand.

Nothing made sense. She needed help. So she did what she knew best; she gathered the other "witches." Together they read Pesach's words. She did not tell them that her nephew was in agreement and prayed that they would not see his comment.

"This man is declaring war on us!" her friend Erin said.

"We must act," Sophia added, as she lit candles.

Together the women prayed. They called on the angels and the Shechina for help. They incanted, summoned their powers, and drank their special teas. They cooked for each other a kosher, vegan organic feast to get the energy they needed for the task at hand. And then they blogged. They blogged and blogged and blogged, drawing on words and powers to reach women and men far and wide with the singular message: *Save the religious feminist "witches."* They believed that their keyboards were their most powerful tools.

But their actions were fruitless. Getting power to work requires a true heart. And Shimshona's heart was not entirely true. She had not been honest with her "witch" sisters. She did not tell them that her nephew was the blogger's protégé. After all, how does one go about sharing such a thing with one's closest friends? "My family members think we are all evil and should die!" She couldn't do it.

In fact, she could barely even feel her own powers anymore. She felt her energies draining from her as the whirlwind surrounded her heart. How does one wish one's nephew ill? She just could not do it. So while her witch-sisters were toiling over their save-the-witches campaign, she was inadvertently blocking their power. She didn't mean to. It just happened that way.

Which just goes to show, a woman whose family members hate her is destined for a life of torment.

Shimshona thought about calling her sister Diane to whom she had not spoken for some time — not since Diane had confronted Shimshona over one of her incantations. Shimshona had been trying to save Raziel, a former classmate, from her kitchen. Raziel felt trapped there all the time, cooking and feeding and cleaning up after all her children. To enable her to escape the stifling energy that perpetually engulfed her in her home, Shimshona had taken the unusual step of inviting Raziel to her own house in order to do a healing. As she was shaking sagebrush and lavender leaves over Raziel to calm her and singing some *techinot* written by one of her ancestors, Diane walked through Shimshona's unlocked door, took in the scene, and let out a wild yelp that sent the birds flying out of the eucalyptus tree in the front yard.

When Shimshona tried to explain what was happening, Diane screamed, "What is wrong with you? Bringing all that *avodah zara* idol worship into her Jewish home? Don't you know that she is doing holy work in her kitchen? Who do you think you are? Sullying her with your stupid ideas! You're crazy!"

125

Diane stormed out. Shimshona immediately stopped her work and ran after Diane. She begged for her forgiveness, but Diane just kept screaming. "We don't need you or your feminism! Stay away from us!" Shimshona called her several times over the next two days to apologize, but Diane would not forgive her. That was seven years ago.

Now Shimshona picked up the phone and dialed Diane's number. Her husband picked up. "Hello?" Shimshona tried to find her voice, but she couldn't speak. "Hello? Hello?" he asked. She wanted to beg for help. She wanted to say, "Help me! Tell your son to stop doing this to me!" But the words wouldn't come. She couldn't even say, "May I please speak to Diane?" It was as if the Angel of Death had dried up Shimshona's voice. "Who *is* this?" the man on the other end asked. Eventually, he hung up.

Next, Shimshona thought of her father. He was the one she really wanted to talk to. She closed her eyes and took a deep breath. She hesitated. Should she tell him what was happening? Would he care? Firestorms exploded in her heart until, like a volcano, she erupted and called him. "Look what is happening in your family!" she yelled finally, unable to contain her feelings. "You did this! You taught your grandson to hate me! You taught everyone that it's okay to hate me!"

He listened for a moment before responding. "You're obviously very upset," he said calmly. "When you're ready to stop being so angry, when you're ready to grow up and stop acting like an adolescent and attacking everyone, call me." He hung up. What was left of her heart tore into shreds.

There was nothing in her arsenal of prayers and incantations, no secret powers or potions that could stop what was to happen next.

It was not until two blogs later that they came for her. On the night that the blog with the title: *Kill the witches!* went live, the mob arrived at her house. They dragged her from her bed and beat her with what seemed like rolling pins. As she lay there on the floor, she saw that these were not rolling pins; they were Scrolls of Esther.

Then she saw him. Daniel looked down at her, lying on the ground in a pool of her own blood. He was holding the scissors in one hand and her chopped-off hair in the other – oh, her beautiful locks of hair. She knew what that meant. After all, it was foretold in her name.

Pesach, standing next to him, put his arm around Daniel in brotherhood. "*Baruch hashem*," he said. "We did it." They turned and walked away.

"So this is what has become of you," Shimshona said. She closed her eyes and took her last breath.

Post-script
Ah, the ending. That heart-breaking ending. I can't believe I wrote that. Tragedy.

Well, it reflects how I felt at the time I wrote it, and many other times in my life. When all I wanted to do was lay down and die. This is, indeed, a life of torment. I am no longer in contact with my family of origin, and that is the right thing, tragic as it is.

Still, today, I would write a different ending.

Maybe Shimshona would move to Hawaii and live in her commune of witches that was so powerful it could affect events all around the world. They would live on the beach, spend most of their days in the water and dancing the hula, eat pineapples and papayas, and write music when they weren't using their powers to save the world.

Or maybe the witches would out Pesach as a sexual predator, send him to prison, and rescue dozens of boys and girls who would love them forever and start a brand-new religion, one in which everyone is loved and embraced exactly as they are.

Or maybe Shimshona would study martial arts and summon her warrior sisters to find their physical strength, and when Pesach's army came at them with pitchforks, they would all know what to do. She would hang Pesach for all to see. Then the entire community would realize that the witches are the true leaders, and they would rebuild the community according to the values of non-violence and compassion, and nothing like that would ever happen again.

Or maybe Shimshona would become a rabbi, build her own synagogue and pulpit, cultivate a beautiful community, and stop holding back her voice, once and for all.

Maybe I'm still figuring out what my own ending is. When I do that, I'll write a new story.

Sexuality

"Constant craving is all I know."
— KD Lang

"When a woman has lost her chastity she will shrink from nothing."
— Tacitus

*A*ll of these discussions about body, hair, voice, and modesty disguise an obsession with one underlying connecting issue: sexuality.

When rabbis, teachers, or politicians rant about the importance of girls covering their bodies, or stand at the entrance to their schools measuring girls' knees and necks, what they are really doing is controlling girls' sexuality.

The fact that so-called modesty is for girls and not for boys speaks to a lot of hidden messages about sexuality: that boys are free to be sexual beings, but girls are not; that boys have a desire, but girls are merely objects of others' desire; that girls are being watched all the time, and boys are merely the watchers; that boys' natural sexual desire is animalistic and uncontrollable but girls' nature is to be controlled and contained; that girls have responsibility for men's and boys' sexual morality while boys don't have any responsibility at all; that sexual control of girls and women is the most urgent aspect of religious morality.

I often think about a little thing that always irritated me growing up, and I could never figure out why. In our synagogue, the men's section was in the center of the sanctuary and contained all important aspects of the service – the podium, the Torah, the ark, the rabbi's seat, and even the special seats for the president and treasurer. The women's sections flanked the sides, as women were the gallery, the audience. The only important communal component that existed in the women's section was the windows. Every once in a while, when some men decided the room was too hot, men would come into our section and open the windows. It always felt odd to me, how easily they could come in. Because I knew that there wasn't a single circumstance that I could envision the reverse – that is, where it would be okay for a woman to casually walk into the men's section. It just wouldn't happen. And only recently have I realized what the message of this was: Women have no desire. That is, if a woman walks in front of a group of men – even a well-covered woman in front of men engaged in prayer – her very presence would excite the men so much that all hell would break loose. But men can come and go in front of women and nothing happens because women are simply not thinking about sex the way men are. We are rendered asexual beings.

It's such a little thing, but I think it reflects the whole culture.

What happens to girls growing up in this culture? It took me decades to unpack the answer to that question.

I remember well my experience going to the mikveh, the ritual bath a few days before my wedding, to make myself "pure" for sex with my soon-to-be husband. It was a secret, hidden experience enshrined in body shame, a ritual quietly passed down from women over the generations, revealed only when a girl was about to enter the marital bedroom. It was the equivalent of sex education, as if going to the mikveh was everything a woman needed to know about her own sexuality. Scrub, pluck, and cleanse inch of skin. And then stand naked in front of a strange woman, the mikveh lady, who will determine whether your immersion is "kosher," like a piece of meat. If you're kosher, your husband can consume you after your wedding.

One of the most striking memories from that experience was how completely wrong it felt to me to get undressed in front of someone. My entire life until that point had been a practice in exactly the opposite – never letting anyone see you naked. I was so completely socialized into feeling shame in my body that the entire experience became traumatic for me. For 21 years, I was taught how to be invisible, and suddenly to be able to have sex, I needed to undress – not in front of my husband, but in front of a stranger who would judge my religious observance based entirely on my excessive cleanliness, a particular grooming for sexual OCD.

Another memory from that moment is how ashamed I was of showing my skin, as well as how ugly I felt. There is a very powerful overlap between the body shame that comes from "modesty" language and the body shame that comes from the obsession with thinness. In my experience, these two forces often felt like one. I covered myself – my thighs, my stomach, my breasts, my chin – because men were watching me sexually, and because I was fat. Or at least I thought I was. Even when neither of those was true in reality, I believed I was, all of this gaze so deeply embedded in me. And it left scars of shame that stayed with me for decades.

In this section, I share some of my writings on sexuality. This is only the tip of the iceberg. Or the tip of something. Something. I am still processing. It is not easy for me to share this way, but it is part of the process of releasing the shame.

And perhaps other people who have had similar experiences will benefit from it. After all, as they say, sunlight is the best disinfectant. Maybe opening the windows truly is the beginning of something.

Sex and Women's Pleasure Debated in the Orthodox Sphere[24]

This essay marked a very important period in my life. For the first time, I was meeting with other Orthodox women and chatting about sex. I learned a lot about my friends, and we shared our struggles – and our triumphs. It was a major turning point for me in reclaiming ownership of my body, my feelings, my sensations, my desire. And of letting go of secrecy and shame.

It seems that sex is on everyone's minds this week. ("Just this week?" The cynic replied.) It's not just on The Sisterhood that sexuality in Jewish life became a focus, but also elsewhere on the Jewish Web.

Asimon, "Israel's Women's Site," for example, announced that in honor of "May is Masturbation Month," they are holding a raffle to give away a free vibrator. Meanwhile, on Unpious.com, a rather funny post about financial pressures and family planning turned into a talkback debate about women's sexual pleasure.

---

[24] May 7, 2010, originally published at the *Forward*. Reprinted with permission.

"Isn't 'the mitzvah' about making sure that she is satisfactorily pleasured?" a commenter named Gigi wrote.

"I'm not sure the mitzvah has much to do with her having an orgasm," Hassidic Rebel replied. "The entire concept of Judaism placing so much emphasis on pleasing a woman sexually is more or less the invention of apologists and *kiruv* [outreach] professionals. And you can be certain no *chosson* [groom] teacher in the chasidish world ever mentions orgasm to his charges, let alone emphasize it as an inherent part of the mitzvah."

Kafhakela disagreed. "HR – You are clearly wrong on this... [I]t is clearly defined in Shulchan Aruch...the sexual responsibilities that a husband has to his wife. The Shulchan Aruch doesn't mention orgasm specifically, but from the context, there is no room for doubt that the husband has to please his wife in bed, just as she has the same requirement to him. The chassidishe which don't teach these things, are probably hoping that the couple will figure it out on their own, as most do."

Finally, someone named Laura, chimed in. "Ancient texts were only able to be as modern as was possible at the time, and the Bible and biblical texts *were* pretty modern by those standards. Obviously, the Talmud is not going to speak about orgasm because documents of that time — or people of that time — did not speak about orgasms. But if the texts mention satisfying a woman ... why is that a form of apologia?"

This entire discussion reminds me of my friend Jackie, who often counsels women — mainly Orthodox women — to reclaim their sexuality and develop what she calls "sexual literacy." She teaches women to sense and experience their own bodies, and to become open and explorative in their partnerships. She also runs "toy parties," teaching women how to use sex toys. Jackie, like Hassidic Rebel, is very critical of the way sexuality is taught in the religious world.

"When I openly discuss sex with Orthodox women," said Jackie, who asked that her last name not be used in print, "and they tell me 'I could take it or leave it,' I think that it is a cause of concern. These women are not enjoying themselves the way they should. God made sexual pleasure, and many women need to learn to enjoy themselves and use the gift that God gave us."

Teaching Orthodox women to explore sexual pleasure can be a challenge in the religious world, where sex revolves around the woman's menstrual cycle, in which couples are forbidden from all forms of touching for two weeks of every month. As Viva Hammer, a popular Orthodox writer-blogger, wrote this week in a post titled, "What *Mikveh* Means to Me – Sex in an Orthodox Jewish Marriage:"

> *[T]he discipline required to follow the Code of Jewish Law on nidda [menstruation] is almost unendurable.... Every single day of the woman's cycle has to be counted, to determine the monthly anniversary of the beginning of her last period, when she either has to do some more internal examinations or temporarily stay away from her husband. It was like being in a whirlwind, with a constantly changing status having dramatic consequences. Checking, measuring, withdrawing, responding. None of it was on my cue, all imposed by this massive external book of law.... Apologeticists for the nidda laws claimed that each time a woman returns to her husband after the period of separation is like a honeymoon, all fresh and new again. Nonsense! I didn't need the separation of nidda to come*

back to my husband with refreshed interest; I enjoyed the constant company of his body.

These conversations are an essential element of women's empowerment, and it is encouraging that they are taking place within Orthodoxy. It's one more vital way in which religious women are waking themselves up.

Post-script

I enjoyed Jackie's sex-toy parties and listening to other women share their experiences and insights. I had never done anything like that before, and it was comforting, validating, and educational. I think that the changes I experienced personally were reflected in surrounding cultures that were also experiencing shifts and evolutions on this topic.

Well, mostly. When this essay came out, I received a message from a former teacher of mine who said, "I saw your mother. She wants to know when you are going to stop writing all that stuff." So there's that.

Meanwhile, I now have many friends who work on the issue of women's sexuality, both in and out of Orthodox settings. There is so much pain and dysfunction all around. But I think that writing about it helps advance the conversation – not only for my readers but also for me. It's about releasing myself from the need to hide, and hopefully helping others do the same along the way.

It's Time to Tell the Truth about Kallah Teachers[25]

In the spirit of letting go of the shame and letting the light come in, here is a blog I wrote about how I learned about sex in religious marriage. I wrote this essay shortly after I finished my job working at JOFA, the Jewish Orthodox Feminist Alliance; around the time that I decided I was leaving Orthodoxy for good. Writing this was hugely cathartic for me. I felt like I was finally telling the truth about something that I had been hiding for way too long. Or at least starting to tell the truth.

Whenever I hear the term *"kallah* (bride) teacher," I cringe.

Maybe it's the result of my own experience meeting with the *kallah* teacher of my community before I got married 22 years ago. The sexless, humorous rebbetzin taught us all the religious laws involved in going to the *mikveh* before having sex. There was nothing in the entire experience that actually

---

[25] April 29, 2014. Published on my blog, *A Jewish Feminist.*
http://jewfem.com/index.php?option=com_easyblog&view=entry
&id=424&Itemid=513

suggested that sex was going to be a wonderful, enjoyable experience for women. It was more like, this is what *halakha* tells you to do to get clean (excuse me, "pure," as rabbis like to insist, as if there is actually a difference). There was nothing in the classes that taught us about intimacy, sexuality, or our own sensuality.

Maybe it's how *kallah* teachers tend to morph *halakha* and OCD. Preparing a woman for marital intimacy by teaching her to obsessively count, internally check, and scrub, pluck, and rub your skin until its raw, before dunking naked in front of the strange woman who declares your body "*Kasher.*" (Very romantic.)

Maybe it's the whole notion that all you need to do in order to be happy in marriage and in life is to follow the rules. Don't think, don't feel, don't experience. Just go through the handbook, and everything will fall into place. Maybe that's the big lie here, passed down from generation to generation of women, like a recipe for gefilte fish. Just do what you're supposed to do, be like everyone else, and everyone will be happy. That's how it works, right?

Maybe it's the fact that in many places we're still doing "*kallah*" teachers rather than courses for men and women together. I mean, sure, my now-husband had a class for grooms in the living room with the rabbi while the brides sat in the kitchen with the rebbetzin (symbolic?). But then men are pretty much learning a watered-down, kind of passive version of what the women are learning. It's kind of like, "Hey guys, your wife is going to be doing all this internal-cleaning-purity stuff that you don't really want to know the details about. Just humor her and buy her flowers, and everything will be fine. She'll let you know if she needs you to show her undies to the rabbi."

It's preparing women for a gendered life starting in the bedroom and continuing everywhere else.

It's possible that *kallah* classes have gotten better since I got married; after all, there are all sorts of programs out there that supposedly train women to be a different kind of *kallah* teacher. And then some women are "trained" to look at the stained undies instead of men. Whoo-hoo... Can't wait to ask a WOMAN these questions instead of a man... Um, no.

Pardon me if I'm skeptical about all of this.

First, just because a *kallah* teacher is sweeter, younger, nicer, or more "trained" than my uninspiring rebbetzin, the fundamentals of what she is teaching have not changed. It's all still a very bad version of sex-ed.

Second, many of the "newer" *kallah* teachers are themselves products of a very Orthodox approach to marriage, relationships, and sex, living the life of "OCD as sexuality," so how can they possibly be teaching anything that different? I know for sure of one popular *kallah* teacher, "*yoetzet*", who has never had an orgasm herself, so how can she possibly be preparing young women for a healthy sexual life? All of this talk of *niddah* counselors as models of women's empowerment doesn't work for me. If you're still teaching and practicing the same stuff, I don't care how glossy your brochure is or how pretty your earrings are or how much Talmud you can quote. You're part of the problem and not part of the solution.

Let's face it. Orthodox women are socialized into really unhealthy sexuality, and it's possible that the practice of using *kallah* teachers makes it worse, not better. According to one recent study, Orthodox women are nearly four times as likely as women from the general public to be unhappy in their intimate lives. From 7% in the general population to 25% among Orthodox women – that's how many women admitted that they are not happy. Many women in the study talked about the *mikveh* experience as being traumatic. Others talked about being socialized into so-called "modesty" and then being expected to be able to be sexually free in the bedroom suddenly. It doesn't work like that.

Orthodox women are socialized into constant, excessive pressure to cover and comport our bodies. We learn from the time we are in preschool that we must cover, cover, cover, because men of all ages and sizes are looking at us. Religious educators take every opportunity to discuss how and why we should cover our bodies. Women's bodies are analyzed to death at every religious or educational encounter. The boys we know are taught that touching our bodies is considered a terrible thing that can lead to the worst sins in the world. There is no such thing as affection or hugging that is not sexual, we are taught. Boys can't possibly hold our hands without thinking of sex or listen to us talk without thinking of sex. Our bodies are a thing to be feared and covered and talked about. Our bodies are owned by the collective – by the male-dominated collective – not by ourselves.

And then, *whoosh*, one day suddenly you're supposed to get married young and fast, and suddenly everything is supposed to change just like that. All that obsessive cover is magically transformed into the secret *kallah* classes, where you learn that you're going to be getting naked in front of your new husband and having sex. You go from one extreme to the other without anything in between. You weren't supposed to touch, but now you're going to have sex. Plus, there are lots of rules about it. You learn that times for sex are completely regimented around your period, that you have two weeks to prepare

141

for that prescheduled and inflexible night, and once again that there is no such thing as affection which is not sexual – a man is not even supposed to pass the salt to his wife during the two weeks he can't have sex with her because you never know where passing the salt can lead to! Meanwhile, you learn that the most important prerequisite to a sexual encounter is your own body's extreme cleanliness, to be determined by the *mikveh* lady. Of course, the man has no prerequisites for sex. How does it feel spending a week scrubbing and checking and getting naked for a strange lady, when all your husband has to do is show up? I mean, technically he doesn't even have to shower.

So, no matter how much a *kallah* teacher tries to finesse this story, it's still the same. This is the Orthodox version of sex-ed. No matter how it's packaged, it's still awful. The whole thing is warped and twisted, and many Orthodox women are still suffering in privacy and silence.

I've been talking to Orthodox women about their sex lives for a few years now. So many women I've spoken to are tragically unsatisfied. Many have no idea how to have an orgasm or how even to fulfill their own sexual needs. One woman spent 15 years being completely unfulfilled, going through the motions like a machine. Another admitted to me that she was not even attracted to her husband. Another woman told me she was just "resigned" to the fact that she will never have an orgasm – she thought her body just doesn't know-how.

As I think about real solutions to this problem – not another program for *kallah* teachers or *yoatzot niddah*, not another hotline teaching women how to check themselves, but rather a real solution to completely reform the way Orthodox women are socialized into sexuality and intimacy – I would really like to hear from women out there.

Post-script

This was my most shared and commented post of all time on my Jewfem blog, with over 50,000 hits and 10,000 words of comments. Is it because it was about sex? Or did I hit a nerve?

Some people thanked me. One woman wrote, "entering religious marriage with all the unromantic practices that goes with it can really set you back and clam you up. It took me years to return to the prior 'normal' where pleasure and enjoyment were the focus instead of fulfilling a mitzvah." Another man wrote a very long complaint about the sex education that his wife received:

> *I couldn't agree with you more.... My wife has not been taught ANYTHING useful about her body and her sexuality!!! You ask what I would like to be done differently? my answer is: EVERYTHING. They should be taught that "sex" is not just a "Mitzvah", another thing on the to-do list. Sex is enjoyable and should be viewed that way. They should teach them that they possess a clitoris and other sensual organs that could give them immense pleasure! They don't teach them to participate in the act, they just teach them to lay there dutifully like a log (no matter how painful it is) so your guy can finish up what he needs to do! And not only that.... they teach them that during penetration they should pray to Hashem to give them Erliche children!!! Are they insane?? Are they completely ignorant of their bodies? Don't they derive any pleasure of sex, or is this a way of keeping them in the dark?? They need to revise the whole system from A-Z. They need to throw out those outdated useless Rebbetzins and the teachers that don't begin to understand what "sex" is all about. Let them have educated teachers teach those girls about sex and how they can "learn" to enjoy it.... Let*

them explore their bodies on their own, figure out where the like to be touched, so they can both be ready for it, and enjoy the experience together. And i truly believe that if the men in our community would be properly satisfied with their wives they wouldn't have to look for their sexual needs somewhere else, and it would also solve so many of their problems with "shalom bayis."

Yeah, I clearly hit a nerve. I wonder how many stories like this are out there.

Some commenters were a bit more defensive – especially kallah teachers and their supporters. One wrote that what I experienced is not the "norm" – a very hurtful tactic for dismissing someone's experience, by adding that they are not "normal." Some said that I am describing something "old", that maybe there were problems in the past, but "progress" is being made. One Orthodox feminist activist wrote in a more nuanced way:

> *Elana makes some excellent points regarding the lack of sex education and the unrealistic expectations placed on young Orthodox women. She is right that as a result many young Orthodox women have a less satisfying sex life and more hurdles to cross when they get married. But it seems to me that progress is being made in this area, albeit slow and frustrating. [Our organization] has sponsored a number of on-site learning programs for kallah teachers. Our goal is to teach Kallah teachers a broader perspective on halakha as well as educate them as to how to approach the women they are teaching with issues of intimacy and sex.*

The good news is that some organizations are aware of the problems I raised. The bad news is that I'm not sure their initiatives are all doing the work of repair the way they claim to be. The jury is still out on that.

144

And then there were the angry critics. Some commenters did not mince words in their opinions of my ideas and my words. One wrote, "This article makes me sick - it's so interesting how being critical of Orthodox Jews is so accepted, yet if any other minority were depicted in this way, the author would be quickly shunned," as if I'm motivated by some irrational prejudice instead of, say, my life. Others tried to educate me, as if I haven't studied any of this in the traditional way. "Taharas hamishpacha *is intrinsically deeper than just a set of rules that are 'unromantic.'"* Others were less gentle. "At the end of the day, it's always the same crap... complain, yell scream and fight. You will never be happy," *wrote one man. He sounded a lot like my mother. I wonder.*

Finally, there was this gem:

> *SHAME on the writer of this article, to think in generations gone by our holy Jewish mothers put their lives in danger, dipping in ice cold water making hidden underground mikveh just to sanctify themselves and bring themselves closer to their creator and here this woman belittles it all!!! I am a very proud Jewish woman and have a very clear understanding that men and woman were created very differently and forever will be different not matter how must western ideology tries to challenge it. what do I care that my husband just' shows up after I do all the work' it's MY mitzvah and a way I get to connect to hashem and my husband, it's my gift to him.*

When all else fails, there's always guilt. Like, maybe if they remind me that speaking out makes me a bad wife, a bad mother, a bad daughter, and a bad Jew, I'll just stop. I wonder what Shimshona would have to say here.

These comments indeed demonstrate that progress and regression coexist, which can be hard to wrap one's head around. The women talking about a new generation of kallah teachers are describing real trends in the field. And yet, the retrograde anti-feminists defending all kinds of bizarre things are still here and still powerful. It is a paradoxical reality.

While writing the article was somewhat cathartic for me, I don't think that I would write this kind of article today. I'm no longer trying to fix a system that is broken. I have left it behind.

I also know that today, I would not allow myself to stay for over 20 years in a practice that I knew was wrong and unhealthy. That is the biggest change. Today, I give myself permission to feel and think for myself and to follow my own heart, my ideas, my needs, and my desires.

One last comment: I recognize that a lot of women have different experiences, that some women love the practices and many never experienced the kinds of traumas that I did. I would like to acknowledge that this is not the only possible view of things. I know that a lot of women take offense at my writing for the tone that I sometimes sound like I speak for all women. I don't mean that. I write in order to offer a perspective, one that goes against what is perceived as the correct version of the culture. I am simply trying to give voice to my lived experience, and open up the possibility for other women to share their lived experiences as well. But if women love and enjoy the practice, I'm happy for them.

After all, my dear friend Rabbi Haviva Ner-David has dedicated her entire life to mikveh. She runs the Shmaya mikveh in her village of Hannaton in the Galilee. She does the whole thing differently – no prerequisites, no imposing gaze, no judgment, and no necessary dates, times, or body clocks. The ritual isn't even necessarily connected to menstruation or sex. She has adapted mikveh as an inclusive water-focused personal, spiritual transformation. I applaud Haviva and celebrate what she does.

Change is possible.

How the Freundel story triggered me[26]

At a certain point, I began to push back against the entire mikveh *practice, and against all the messages that Orthodoxy gave about sexuality. But this process hit a particularly low point when it was discovered that Barry Freundel, a high-profile Orthodox rabbi with a powerful seat in the Rabbinical Council of America in charge of deciding issues of conversion, is a sexual predator. He was placing hidden cameras in the mikveh – which is used not only by married women before sex but also by converts – and would direct his congregants on where to stand in the mikveh, using a pretense of following Jewish law when all he wanted was a good view of their naked bodies. This story sent me into an emotional tailspin, as it did many other women. I wrote about it for months afterward. Here is one of my essays. This is my first time publishing it.*

A psychologist friend tells me that mental illness is over-diagnosed, especially in women, because it's much easier to call someone, say, "bipolar" than it is to admit that the person is merely recovering from pain and abuse. She has a lot at stake in this discussion. She was sexually molested by her

[26] December 2014. Unpublished

brother when she was a teenager and has spent most of her adult life going through the healing process while resisting labels and meds. She is one of the most beautiful women I know, and her wisdom has stayed with me, especially as I observe patterns in my own adulthood.

When I think objectively about how many periods I have had in my life when I have been unable to get up off the couch or out of bed for weeks at a time, it occurs to me that I should probably say about myself that I battle with depression. But I don't. In fact, I don't see myself that way at all. Each of those periods followed a particular event or series of events that I simply needed to recover from.

Like the time I took my daughter to New York to be with my mother and found out that my mother spent much of the time talking to my daughter – or talking to others in earshot of her – about how "embarrassing" I am to the "entire family", whether because of my body, my writing, my life choices, whatever. My daughter said to me frankly, "Your mother doesn't love you." I suppose I knew that intuitively, but to hear it that directly – from my 11-year-old child, no less, in whom I was trying with all my might to inculcate the immutability of her mother's love – was completely upending.

When I came back from that trip, I was unable to breathe, move or function normally for quite some time. There have been too many encounters like that over the past 25 years, and I have been in several workplaces where I simply faded for a few weeks and did not explain to anyone why. But when I look back at these episodes, I don't think of myself as battling depression. I think of myself as using restful withdrawal to allow myself to recover from abuse. My body knew what it needed, and

I allowed it to happen. That's all. It may look like depression, but I think it was just healing.

Sometimes I think that perhaps if I had a better handle on the language of abuse in my own life a decade or more ago, I might have saved myself some agony, but I'm not sure. I think that my body sometimes just collapses under the weight of pain, and it just knows that this is what it has to do to heal itself and survive. I have some tools at my disposal, like yoga, meditation, reiki, Chi Kong, and journaling. But ultimately, I think that I just have to accept the fact that I carry a certain weight on my shoulders, one that many women share – as well as some men – and these things affect me. I can often feel the breath of my grandmothers and great-grandmothers whispering in my ear, "Hang in there. We are with you." They smile at me and dance with me and in circles around me in my dreams, and I know that it is because of them that I am able to resume living.

As strange as it is for me to admit this, I am going to share that I had an episode like this following the emergence of the Barry Freundel scandal. It was slow to set in – after all, the initial fragments came to light right before the holiday of Simchat Torah, and more details emerged only after the three-day holiday, in fits and starts, like bursts of red paint on a canvas, until the full portrait of his transgression formed like a slow-motion scene of slaughtering a lamb. I found myself obsessively following the stories emerging, my life punctuated by Facebook conversations and updates about it, sometimes conducting half a dozen chats at once all about this story, often with victims or members of the community. Soon, I was lying in bed with my laptop next to me, doing nothing but following the story and sleeping in between. Everything else just got pushed aside as I felt the energy and life-force drain from my body, a feeling that was familiar in its warped deformity.

I couldn't immediately explain why the story was having this effect on me. I am not from Washington, DC, I only met Freundel twice, I have never been to the Kesher Israel *mikveh*, and in short, I'm not one of his victims. So why did I feel so nauseatingly violated by the whole thing? Was I over-identifying with the victims, blurring personal boundaries in a clearly unhealthy way? Or was there something else going on?

It was after I shared the details of my emotional state with my beautiful friend Dr. Chaya Gorsetman – one of the few people to whom I know I can turn when I'm at my worst, who will always provide wisdom with love and care – that I started to genuinely understand what I was experiencing. What I came to understand is that for me, and possibly many other women, the entire *mikveh* experience is one of sexual trauma, even without having been peeped on by a perverted rabbi.

No matter how many ways religious leaders – men and women – try to explain the *mikveh* practice or reclaim it in a zillion new-age ways, there is something sickeningly off about the whole thing. The idea that, for the sake of one's marriage, or for the sake of one's "purity" whatever the hell that even means, or for the sake of being "Jewish," that a woman has to stand naked for inspection and then dunk in this water while being watched and being called *"kasher"*– it is a complete and utter violation of one's body. It doesn't matter if the person watching you and plucking the hairs off your back is a woman. It just doesn't matter. There should be no eyes on your body at all. So many of us do this regularly, accepting as "normal" that which is just so completely not normal, and we pretend that we don't feel the violation. Maybe some women don't. I'll be hearing, I'm sure, from all the women who love *mikveh*, pushing back about that.

I am confident that some women have a perfect relationship with their naked bodies and with the eyes of someone presuming to represent God in their intimate spaces. Sure, there are women like that. Some women have 12 babies and have no medical issues or financial issues or emotional issues and are skinny and strong and able to get out of bed to pee ten minutes after giving birth and run the marathon a month later. We all know women who don't let anything get to them. More power to them; I'm not one of them. When I am hurt, I struggle, and I need time to heal.

And here is what I know for sure. I've been keeping these *mikveh* rules for so long, and I hate it. My entire body and soul utterly despise all of it and know it is all wrong. And the Freundel story brought all of that out and reminded me to listen to my own inner voice when it tells me that I'm feeling violated.

There is a terrible and quite revolting irony to the way *mikveh* traditions are passed to Orthodox women getting married. Orthodox girls spend their first two decades, on average, being told to cover their bodies at all costs. Sure, the details may vary between communities, whether an elbow or collarbone can show, whether shorts to the knee are okay, whether girls are allowed to speak publicly or sing in a group, or even those activities are limited. We were taught to hide our bodies – and although the word "shame" is not used, the fact is that girls are easily able to interpret the rules as representing body shame. In fact, there is an active and lively thread on one of my Facebook groups right now about the intersection of so-called "modesty" and body shame.

Like in my house, where we were not allowed to wear sleeveless clothes not only because of modesty but also because my mother told us that women's arms are ugly. Or how we only wore long shorts not only because those were camp rules but also to hide the cellulite in our thighs. We used to gawk at women in the Loehmann's dressing room or in the Brighton Beach Baths locker room, the ones who walked around stark naked while we expertly manipulated ourselves to get in and out of outfits without baring too much skin. We found other women's absence of self-consciousness strange and amusing, like something that only people from outer space might do. Women's nakedness, even other women's and not our own, was weird and embarrassing.

While you're being given this message in every corner of your life, you're also being prepped for marriage. And preparation for marriage, which took place in the "*kallah* class," (literally the "bride class"), was all about one thing: *mikveh*. So you go from having this obsessive need to cover your body to suddenly being told that for you to be sexually permitted to your husband, you must stick your finger inside your vagina twice a day for a week, then scrub and pluck your skin like you're prepping an operating room, and then allow yourself to be gawked and further plucked by a strange woman. At the same time, you stand naked in front of her – and you're supposed to do this all without flinching, without being anxious, without allowing any of that body-shame that has been so ingrained to get in the way. AND all this is in preparation for sex. In fact, all you're really taught about preparation for sex is to do all this before you go to the *mikveh*.

And by the way, this is all God's will. And if you don't do it, your punishment will be that you are your children will be cut off from the Jewish people. *karet*. The worst punishment. Completely cut off. That is what "family impurity" does to you and your offspring. It's all on you. You. Not your husband. *You.*

It may have taken me 25 years for my body to finally have the proper response to all this. But it's not too surprising that at a certain point, just thinking about all this made me unable to get out of bed.

I have spent much of my adult professional life writing about this subject as an observer. I've studied and documented the socialization of Orthodox women and girls with the skills, training, and perspective of an anthropologist and academic. I've interviewed literally hundreds of women and girls about their experiences and ideas, as well as a few dozen men. In other words, I have been writing about others while avoiding writing about myself, but I think that really all my work has been about this, an attempt to find a way to explain what I have felt and experienced myself as a product of this culture.

I feel like my entire adult life has been a process of trying to recover from all of this, trying to reclaim my body, trying to let go of constant shame, trying to take ownership of my own sexuality, trying to release all the twisted messages about self that have gotten so tangled into my own self-concept that I don't always know where the Orthodox chatter in my head ends, and my own true self begins. I've spent all these years trying to allow myself to be true to myself, learning to heed my own voice and trust my own inner promptings with love and care. Despite all that work, I'm not there at all. In fact, all it takes is a sick story like that of Barry Freundel to enter my world and trigger mountains of pain. I haven't even shared all that it triggered for me, barely a fraction. This is my first time really writing about myself in my own name about the intensity of my body-shame experiences, and I'm not really ready to share all of it quite yet.

I am, however, deeply interested in hearing about whether anyone else has had similar experiences. I ask not only for curiosity and research but also because I know that the most powerful healing comes from connection when women share experiences and provide support and validation and love.

Post-script

Well, I never did publish this, not even on my blog. Too personal. Too scary. Too raw and real.

But something about my decision to publish this book, the decision to frame all my writing as intertwined with my actual life, has given me the courage to publish it here. Even though, the truth is that even as I type these words, I'm terrified.

What am I terrified of, you ask? Excellent question. I'm asking myself the same thing.

Don't Blame *Mikveh* Attendants for a Broken System Created by Men[27]

Many of the kallah teachers and mikveh ladies I know are angry at me for the things I write. It's nothing personal. I'm just unpacking my own experiences. I have nothing against the women in those positions. But the system is broken.

I'm not big on manicures. My life is filled with things like typing and piano, so manicures make my hands feel pretty but useless – good for appearances and bad for actually creating stuff.

One advantage of infrequent manicures is at the *mikveh*, the ritual bath, where the polish is considered an "obstacle." Immersing Jewish women are taught to remove every potential speck of every possible obstacle between our bodies and the water before immersing, giving *mikveh* attendants the thankless job of checking bodies for tiny minutiae, like a spot of eyeliner on the eye

[27] June 27, 2016. Originally published in the *Forward*. Reprinted with permission.
https://forward.com/sisterhood/343682/dont-blame-*mikveh*-attendants-for-a-broken-system-created-by-men/

rim, an unattached hair on the torso, or a remnant of nail polish.

The *mikveh* attendant is like a cross between pot-scrubber and a religious cosmetologist, searching skin for dots of dirt and plucking away unwanted microbes to declare women's bodies perfectly pure before God and husbands.

Of course, this perception of God as one who needs women's bodies bleach-scrubbed clean came to us through the writings of Jewish men over the ages, which explains a lot about what the rabbis really thought about women's bodies. In any case, avoiding nail polish altogether ought to make this experience a little less dramatic.

Still, this is not a foolproof plan. I will never forget the time a *mikveh* attendant took umbrage at my clean cuticles. She had already interrogated me about my body parts like I was a machine on an assembly line – "Eyes, ears, navel…" – but then decided, upon close inspection, that there was something wrong with my hands.

She magically whipped out cuticle scissors and started pulling away at my skin. She didn't ask me or inform me, but simply began cutting away at "obstacles" that were actually still attached to my body. I protested – pointing out that she was making me bleed – but she did not stop until I started yelling, which naturally turned me into the crazy one in the situation. I didn't care. I eventually screamed at her and said that if I never go to the *mivkeh* again, that will be on her conscience, and she will have to explain that to God. She stared at me and let me go.

The problem with *mikveh* attendants, who were the source of several agitating Knesset and Supreme Court events in the past few weeks, is not that they have an innate desire to pluck, scrub, and kosherize women's naked bodies. (Yes, they really say "kosher" when women dunk correctly, ignoring the implication that our bodies are like meat.)

The problem here is not the attendants but rather the attendants' bosses who make the rules that the attendants enforce. Attendants who go rogue and allow immersions that the rabbinate consider wrong – such as single women immersing or non-Orthodox conversions – are at threat of losing their jobs. Attendants are instructed to call the rabbi with any doubt. So, earlier this year, when a woman came to a *mikveh* asking to be allowed to immerse alone without being checked by an attendant, the attendant called the police on her. I am pretty sure that this is the first time in history that a Jewish woman was threatened with arrest for using the *mikveh*. And it happened in Israel, of all places.

The results of the recent governmental discussions on *mikveh* have been a mixed bag. The Knesset Interior Committee voted to send through a bill that would continue to make Reform and Conservative dunking illegal but would allow women to dunk without an attendant. In a Supreme Court petition this week, the state agreed that women would be able to request dunking without an attendant – so that hopefully, the police-calling scenario will be a thing of the past. (I say "hopefully" only because the rabbinate has a history of non-compliance with orders from the State.)

In any case, these events are good news for Orthodox women who want to dunk alone – which also includes many women who have experienced body trauma, sexual abuse, or body-image issues. In the Orthodox world especially, where girls are groomed to obsessively cover their bodies from the age of five, the practice of suddenly standing naked in front of a stranger who is checking every inch of your skin can be excruciating. And all this is supposed to be preparation for sex, so we can imagine what the real impact on women's intimate lives might be. The Knesset and Supreme Court discussions did not go into much detail about women's trauma, but I am sure that many religious women heaved a sigh of relief.

But the impact on the *mikveh* attendants is less clear. In good news, the women finally received a salary hike of 17% that was promised to them two years ago. The position of *mikveh* attendant, one of the few jobs in Israel's Religious Ministry that can go to a woman, is on the lowest possible pay grade in the government.

Women working several nightshifts a week will take home less than 2000 NIS ($500) per month. And yet, when the Finance Committee chair discovered that the Religious Ministry had failed to give the *mikveh* attendants their promised raise, and he asked the ministry representatives why, they shrugged and said, effectively, "We didn't feel like it." (Hat tip: Rachel Stomel who live-tweeted the event).

At least now, the women will get their due, though I doubt it will be retroactive, and it is still not a salary that will get them a vacation in Eilat.

Post-script
This is a tricky stance. It is nuanced. I do not like the work that mikveh *attendants do. I have had many experiences with* mikveh *ladies who were invasive, gawking, commenting, and inappropriate. And overall, I think that if the mikveh practice took place without any attendants at all, then the whole thing might be a totally different experience.*

Still, even if I have felt somewhat abused by mikveh ladies, it is not necessarily because they are bad people but rather because they are socialized into a patriarchal culture that they are agents of. And even if I would prefer to see them resist some of that socialization, in the meantime they still deserve to be paid for their time and work. And on top of all that, they still face sexism, as a group.

This is my stance. Protect women who face gendered discrimination. Even women who protect the patriarchy. It sounds a bit odd or even crazy for me to say that, but it's where I am on the matter.

On Teaching Talmud and Sex Toys[28]

So a whole new cohort of religious women are talking about sexuality. Some are even professionally trained. Dr. Jennie Rosenfeld was one of the first to write and speak professionally about this topic for an Orthodox audience. I interviewed her shortly after her first book came out.

D r. Jennie Rosenfeld is equally at home teaching a page of Talmud and showing women how to use a vibrator. Dr. Rosenfeld, 31, who co-authored the book *The Newlywed's Guide to Physical Intimacy*, is also an Orthodox Jew, and her expertise in sex education is aimed at an Orthodox audience. The book, which the Jerusalem resident wrote with sex therapist David Ribner of Bar-Ilan University, explores the most intimate topics with no restraint, topics such as female orgasm, masturbation, and varieties of sexual positions. She spoke recently with The Sisterhood.

Elana: Sztokman: Why did you decide to write this book?

[28] January 16, 2012. Originally published at the *Forward*. Reprinted with permission.
https://forward.com/sisterhood/149054/on-teaching-talmud-and-sex-toys/

Jennie Rosenfeld: My work at The Tzelem Project, which I co-founded in 2005 with Koby Frances to address sexual education in the Orthodox community, convinced me of the need for such a book. Running training conferences for *chatan* and *kallah* [grooms- and brides-to-be] teachers and rabbis, hearing the questions that were asked, I saw the need first-hand – seeing the outpouring of people that came to our conferences, wanting to learn from medical and mental health professionals so that they could do a better job at preparing their students, seeing the way that often the teachers don't know anything about sex beyond their own experiences, and speaking to young couples who simply weren't given enough information or accurate information about how to begin their sexual relationship. This was the real tragedy for me.

What were the greatest challenges in writing about sex for the Orthodox community?

We didn't want to write something that would alienate those to the "right," but we also didn't want it to sound inane to those on the "left." That created a major challenge for us both in terms of content and how to word things — not to mention drawings.

What has been the response so far?

We've had lots of people telling us, "I wish this would have been around when I got married," and how much easier it would have made their first months/years of marriage. But there have certainly been people who felt that the book was too explicit. When I spoke in England, there were a few women who said that though everything we wrote was true, they wouldn't want their daughters reading it before their wedding. Having seen the fallout of what happens when things aren't stated

ELANA SZTOKMAN

explicitly, and having seen the tragedies, such as unconsummated marriages, which could be prevented by speaking more frankly.

What do you think of that now-famous YU Beacon story about the girl having premarital sex and the university's response?

I think that the fact that the girl chose to write about it and felt the need to share her experience so much that she was willing even to publish it anonymously was powerful. It's as if she couldn't bear being alone with her story and needed someone just to listen. It should serve as a wake-up call to provide some form of support for students like her, or even just a cathartic outlet to share their feelings.

Do you think premarital sex is common in Orthodoxy?

That I really don't know. But I definitely think that violation of *"shomer negi'ah"* [the prohibition against touching] is common in Orthodoxy — but whether people are having premarital sex or are engaging in other forms of sexual expressions, such as mutual masturbation and oral sex, to preserve the woman's virginity, of that, I'm not sure. Either way, many singles feel isolated and alienated from the mainstream Orthodox community because of issues of sexuality and *halachic* violations in the sexual realm.

What is the main message that you want to send to the Orthodox community?

That it's vital to talk about sexuality, at the very least between spouses, but also more broadly as a community: parents educating their kids, day schools educating their students, and people feeling that it's legitimate to ask questions about whatever sexual issue they are facing throughout the lifespan.

Post-script

I would also like to give a shout-out to some other women who are doing this holy work. Dr. Talli Rosenbaum is a wonderful psychotherapist counseling religious couples about sexuality, and also has a great podcast. My dear friend Dr. Rabbi Melanie Landau is an exquisite teacher, healer, and spiritual sojourner with a very special voice on sexuality and self. Paula Mills in Haifa is a wonderful sex educator. And many others. I'm so glad that over the past few years, there has been some growing, healthy attention to this issue, not only in Orthodox communities but everywhere.

Amy Coney Barret and Me: Women who protect the patriarchy[29]

I wrote this essay after watching the confirmation hearings of Supreme Court Justice Amy Coney Barret. I thought to myself, she is a walking paradox – a woman who has risen so high in her career, only to use her power to control other women's bodies, lives, and sexuality. And yet, I know so many women like her. In fact, I could have been her myself. I was groomed for that life. This is also the first time I published about cutting off ties with my family of origin. It was just one more aspect of my life story that I had been hiding. But I am not hiding anymore.

As the world watched Amy Coney Barret on display in the Senate judiciary hearings, I practically heard the sound of bewilderment erupting in viewer's heads. It's like the noise that your Waze makes when you make a wrong turn and then she has to adjust her entire plan. It's that scratchy sound of reconfiguring.

The disconnect has to do with the realization that Coney Barret has two sides. She is on the one hand a smart,

---

[29] Winter 2020, *Lilith Magazine*, Reprinted with Permission
https://lilith.org/articles/amy-coney-barrett-and-me/

competent career woman, and on the other hand also a voice for repressive patriarchal ideas.

But she is hardly alone. We don't need to go all the way back to Phyllis Schlafly to find examples of Women Who Protect the Patriarchy (I call them WHIPPs for short. We have plenty of examples of WHIPPs today. I'm not just talking about the women on the public stage like Sarah Huckabee Sanders, Kimberly Guilfoyle, or KellyAnne Conway, women who have dedicated their public-facing careers to being mouthpieces for patriarchal power.

No, I am referring to a different dynamic. I am talking about women for whom the patriarchy is personal. Women who live it while defending it. An Orthodox Jewish woman, for instance, may be the head of the brain surgery department at a hospital but accept that she doesn't count in a minyan and her voice can never be heard in public. She may be a brilliant musician while accepting the reality that she cannot sing in front of men, or an outstanding athlete who would never run in anything other than long sleeves and a skirt.

I know this stance well, because I lived it. I was expanding my horizons beyond what my female ancestors did – getting an education, working, earning money, speaking out – while at the same time finding my place in the women's section behind the partition. Keeping my shoulders covered. Participating in ritual practices where I did not count, and my voice could not be heard. My head was making that reconfiguring noise, but it took me a while to notice the sound, or to figure out what it was saying to me.

It makes sense: Pushing back against your community and everything you've ever known often comes at great personal cost. And women everywhere pick and choose our battles. Plus, you might say that all women are in some kind of negotiation with the patriarchy, some more painfully than others. None of us has truly fixed our worlds yet, so we all choose to shut out the noise.

The issue that Coney Barrett's hearings evoked, though, is when women who are protecting the patriarchy enter leadership. Then, the contradiction can take a sinister turn. Religious women can use their newly acquired power to keep other women in their place.

Coney Barrett especially reminded me of learned women *like yoatzot halakha*, women halakhic advisers, who are breaking barriers while using their platforms to protect patriarchal Jewish practices. *Yoatzot* have been among the first women allowed to take a role that for generations was the domain of male rabbis – advising religious women on ritual immersion and halakhic menstrual 'purity'. No matter how you try to parse these laws or how many books are written about the "benefits" of these practices, there is no way to escape the fact that they are based on ideas that are terrible for women: that the purpose of our sexual lives is to procreate, that our menstruation makes us "impure," that there is no such thing as non-sexual physical contact between men and women, that men cannot look at their wives without wanting sex, and that women's most intimate body care is under the purview of rabbis. For generations, women have been showing their stained underwear to rabbis to rule about whether they could have sex with their husbands. The *yoetzet* position brought a welcome change: women with questions about their "purity" could at least show their underwear to a woman instead of a man.

On a closer look, though, you will often hear learned women insisting that they are not making actual rulings but merely acting as vehicles for men, the genuine voices of Jewish authority. Like Coney Barrett, they are exercising "judgment," and "power" but only to support a sexist structure.

I grew up with female gatekeepers. The Rebbetzin in my post-high school seminary who taught us that head covering was a law brought down from Moses at Sinai. The teachers who monitored the lengths of our skirts, who reminded us that we were not 'obligated' to pray *mincha* because we were just girls. The nice young teachers who, in twelfth grade, took us on an exclusive and exciting field trip to the local *mikveh*, to school us in getting ready for sex in marriage. As if ritual immersion is all you need to know about sex. And then years later, the local Rebbetzin who gave me "*kallah* classes" that traumatized me in ways I could not articulate.

It is hard to break away from the patriarchy, but even harder when you've been indoctrinated by women, women who appear warm, and speak about meaning, connection, tradition, and of course God. I call this *Indoctrination with a Pretty Face*.

But female gatekeepers can also indoctrinate with force. My mother aggressively groomed us – my three sisters and me – for a life of servitude as wife and mother, and as an object that was pleasing to men. It wasn't just my clothing, my body, my face, and my food that were managed and monitored. It was also my words, my behavior, my demeanor. A girl who ate too much, who spoke too much, or who stayed seated at the Shabbat table instead of serving, was bad. A girl who challenged her father's ideas, who ate before her father ate, or who dared get up from the table before the father declared it done, was worthy of disdain. Embarrassing.

All this was to prepare us for marriage. "Behind every successful man is a woman" were words that we lived by. And yet, even though we were taught that women's open ambition was ugly, we were encouraged to get an education. The same way we were told we must get a driver's license, as a kind of protection, but we were never expected to drive. Women's driving was considered unnatural! My father mocked women drivers, including his daughters, and would never get into the passenger seat when a woman was driving. Nevertheless, my mother ensured that we got licenses, just as she wanted to make sure that we all got a Bachelor's degree, and even a part-time job if we insisted. It was a back-up plan, not to be confused with a career. I mean, the idea of one of the daughters becoming an independent woman was almost as appalling as becoming fat.

Somewhere in the back of my brain, hearing all this, there were those screechy sounds trying to get my attention, but they were blocked by messages that we had the secret to women's success. Plus, once you pay attention to the screechy sound, once you start to question the premise of your way of life, well, the whole thing can come down like a house of cards.

That is what happened to me, though the process took 30 years.

For a very long time, the idea that this whole identity was in conflict with itself was too hard to unpack. So I took down little pieces, one at a time. Took off my hat. Started sharing roles at home. Pursued a doctorate. Made *kiddush*. Sat down while my husband vacuumed. Fought for *agunot*. Added Miriam to the Seder. Drove while my husband sat in the passenger seat.

But the thing is – and here is where it gets tricky – even while I was sorting it all out internally, externally I was still acting as a megaphone for the patriarchy. I taught religious high school girls, spitting out the same language that today I find intolerable, rhetoric about the beauty of women's modesty, the wisdom of the halakhic system. Once when a friend of mine shared with me that she had stopped going to the *mikveh*, I reacted with horror. She still reminds me of that, just for fun.

One day in my sophomore year at Barnard, I was in a lecture hall listening to a class about gender and politics. In a discussion about the evolution of ideas about women and child care, I raised my hand and said, "But everyone knows that a child who grows up in daycare is going to be messed up."

You can imagine the uproar. People who know me today probably don't even believe the story. But I came from a very different place. I could have continued on my path. Perhaps had things been smoother for me, I would still be there. I think that it is very possible that I could have been an Orthodox version of Coney Barrett. One of my sisters is a *yoetzet halakha*. Another sister wanted to be a doctor, but did not go to medical school because she kept saying (as I did that day in Barnard) that a woman cannot be a doctor and a good mother. Sometimes I would say to her, "Just do it, just go to medical school." And she would yell back at me, "I don't need any of your feminism!" Our conversations never ended well.

Today, we are no longer on speaking terms. It was my choice. And yet my sister's story is also my own. The messages she got are the same ones that I got. Marry early. Have lots of kids. Be a good mother. Dedicate yourself to everyone else. Oh, and do all that while being thin, pretty, perky, happy, smiling, and servile.

Had I not been unhappy with my life, I would have stayed in that world. I challenged what I was living with not because it didn't make sense but because I was being emotionally and sexually abused. And even despite that, I tried to make it work for a long time.

It is not hard for me to imagine how a woman can be both a career-go-getter and also a defender of her religious patriarchy. In fact, these personality traits may even go together well. Religious women are often good students – smart, diligent, hard workers. And not even just religious girls. It takes a lot to manage the kinds of lives that working mothers of big families manage. It's a lot of organizing and thinking ahead, attention to detail, multi-tasking, and problem-solving. To wit, in Israel, Haredi women are considered outstanding employees. They tend to be efficient and punctual, they get a lot done in a small space of time, they do not stand around drinking at happy hour, and they are reliable.

Maybe it's no wonder women like Coney Barrett go far. In places where diligence is rewarded, religious women are well suited. You don't always need to be creative to get ahead. You sometimes need to do what is expected. That quality fits in quite well with being an obedient religious woman. Her behavior at her confirmation hearings reinforced that impression – she articulated no independent thought, and maintained a resolve that enabled her to get through the grueling process without getting her hands dirty or ever sharing a single personal belief.

At the end of the day, Coney Barret was well-rewarded for her performance as the perfect patriarchal woman. She demonstrated a powerful reason why women – even smart, thinking, self-driven women – sometimes become the great protectors of the patriarchy. And that has to do with what they get out of it. For them, the system works. Not only does it work, but it offers compelling rewards.

For the obedient WHIPPs, life can be very good. You know where to go and what to do all the time. And while a house full of kids is a LOT of work, it is also at times comforting in its busyness. Predictable trips to worship are vital for so many people – less because of prayer and more because of community. Coney Barrett may love her "People of Praise" group where her highest position as a woman might be "handmaiden" as opposed to "leader" because it gives her all the same kinds of benefits that women get in Orthodoxy – community, belonging, identity, friends, structure. Succeeding in the patriarchy offers what Viktor Frankel argued may even be more powerful than love: purpose. Gender equality is a nice idea. But then there is what really drives us.

I think many of us fall into this trap, too, even feminist women. Working within the patriarchal system is simpler and at times easier than trying to change the world to adapt to our needs. So not all of our choices are consistent. As we all negotiate with the patriarchy, this can be annoying or even infuriating. I hear accusations like this in feminist circles all the time. *You cannot be both a feminist and a mother of lots of children.* Or a feminist and financially dependent on a husband. Or a feminist who gets plastic surgery. Or a feminist and mother of soldiers. Or a feminist and a Zionist. Perhaps all of us, in some way, are gatekeepers for parts of the patriarchy. Maybe it's unavoidable. After all, the patriarchy is the very water we swim in.

But in that water, we still have choices. Coney Barrett made choices. My mother made choices. And I made choices. Maybe we are all complicit.

Still, there is something else going on with WHIPPs in power. If our personal choices are private, there is limited impact on others. However, a WHIPP stance taken in a location of public power is a whole different game. If Coney Barrett chooses to embrace patriarchal lifestyles – such as her participation in "People of Praise" – she has every right to be in that place. But once she is a Supreme Court Justice, then she is not just a woman in conflict. She has ironically broken a glass ceiling, but only to use her position to inflict some great harm on other women. If the Supreme Court knocks down Roe v Wade or cancels birth control coverage, then Coney Barrett becomes a damaging agent of the patriarchy. It doesn't matter that she happens to be a woman.

Post-script

I think a lot about choice. I think about the choices my mother makes, the choices my father makes, the choices that I have made. At the end of the day, no matter how abused or oppressed we are, we have choices. Every day, my mother chooses her status in the patriarchy over a connection with her daughter. Every single day.

What do I choose? I choose freedom. I choose independence. I choose putting myself first. And I choose love and compassion. Not the kind of love that comes from getting approval and status. But rather I choose the love that comes from accepting people exactly as they are. Including myself.

A Nice Jewish Girl Falls in Love with Beyoncé [30]

In another Covid-era essay, I rethink my entire approach to women's body un-cover. Perhaps I'm finally releasing the last vestiges of the male gaze on my sexuality. I'm rethinking all of it. All of it.

Last week, around the same time that Beyoncé released her documentary "Homecoming" on Netflix, a storm raged in Israel – and on my Facebook page – about girls' legs and behinds. At issue was an event that sparked a high-profile protest. A school principal had sent home 15 ninth-grade girls for wearing shorts that he deemed too short – despite the 110 degrees Fahrenheit weather, the eagerness of families to get their kids back to school after the Covid lockdown, and perhaps most importantly, the lack of similar disciplinary measures against boys for the length of their shorts. As a result, some forty girls showed up the next day in short shorts, took a photo of themselves from behind that quickly went viral, and ignited a national conversation about girls' bodies.

---

[30] May 2020. Unpublished.

I fully support the girls and their protest, and emphatically expressed that on my social media. After all, I have been writing about the policing of girls' bodies for a long time. In my doctoral dissertation about the identity formation of girls in religious schools in Israel, I described the "double gaze" that many girls are subjected to – that is, one set of cultural "eyes," so to speak, admonishing them to be covered and saintly, and the other set of cultural "eyes" often coming from Hollywood, fashion, advertising, and the music industry, urging girls to be alluring and exposed.

Although the double gaze I studied took place in religious and traditional cultures, it is also spreading to non-religious cultures as well. Having grown up in Orthodox Jewish Brooklyn, I know well the traumatizing impact of having rabbis and teachers standing at the front door of your school checking your knees and necklines. However, the school that sent the girls home for the length of their shorts is *not* a religious school. This event represents an expansion of conservative-religious female-body policing in secular society and even in state schools. In my 2014 book, *The War on Women in Israel*, I documented many locations in which religious ideas about covering women's bodies have become normalized in Israel – from buses to municipalities to streets to cemeteries. And now, schools. *State* schools.

Still, in my Facebook feed, I received a lot of pushback, even from self-described Jewish feminist friends. Some said that the girls were wrong to disrespect "proper school attire" – an idea that I disagree with because I find teachers' "clothing-discipline" to be unhealthy and oppressive. However, the comment might have had legitimacy had boys' bodies been similarly policed. Some complained, correctly, that it's nearly impossible to find longer shorts for girls, a dynamic of objectifying girls' bodies that starts outrageously young, as Peggy Orenstein documents in her important book, *Cinderella Ate My Daughter*. Yes, girls are trapped between two sets of extreme demands on their bodies – cover/uncover.

Several commenters, though, openly attacked the girls, metaphorically clutching their pearls with the horror that girls should dare dress this way. "I hate the idea that girl power means the right to show off your tits and ass," wrote one particularly adamant commenter.

I found these comments particularly jarring – especially as I would never talk about girls' bodies using language such as "tits and ass," which reflects the violent internalized patriarchal gaze. It is bad enough for men to talk about girls' bodies this way. But when women adopt the worst language, acting as gatekeepers of the patriarchy – while calling themselves feminists – it poses a particularly confounding threat to girls' well-being.

That said, I am familiar with the underlying point. Does women's empowerment necessarily entail maximum exposure? Isn't that too extreme?

For most of my career in writing about gender, culture, and education, I have been sympathetic to the idea that the opposite of body policing is *not* full body exposure but rather something else: that is, women's choice, women's desire, and women's comfort. As Harvard researcher Michelle Fine wrote so many years ago, there is a "missing discourse of desire" in all these conversations about girls' bodies.[31] The opposite of

---

[31] Fine, Michelle. "Sexuality, schooling, and adolescent females: The missing discourse of desire." *Harvard educational review* 58.1 (1988): 29-54.

objectification is self-ownership. It is about learning to feel for myself what my body is. We should be encouraging girls to make their own decisions about their bodies, free from *both* sets of gazes – the one telling them to cover up and the one telling them to expose themselves. That doesn't mean walking around half-naked, I often told myself. It means making choices for one's own comfort and desire.

"I wish people would stop looking at girls' behinds," is what I ultimately wrote. Honestly, I wanted the entire conversation to stop. It all feels so, well, *creepy*.

Then I watched Beyoncé's enthralling "Homecoming" Coachella concert in which she struts around in shorts that are much shorter than the ones that got the girls into trouble at school. The contrast is explosive for me. While I'm trying to get my friends to stop looking at girls from behind, Beyoncé is saying, "PLEASE look at my behind." It was hard for me to wrap my nice-Jewish-girl brain around that.

Is this what we want? Do we want people to STOP looking at us as sex objects? Or maybe some of us want exactly that – to be wooed and worshipped for our sexual power?

In the past, I have been ambivalent about the kind of feminism that Beyoncé brings – or Madonna, for example, who I also love watching and thinking about. Isn't Beyoncé encouraging girls to believe that the only way for us to have power is by objectifying ourselves? Doesn't her relentless sexuality participate in the patriarchal gaze? It has been confusing for me. You know, "Why does she have to dress like *that*?" I thought, wouldn't she be doing women a favor by encouraging her audience to love her music and not just her exposed body?

I think I finally understand my conflicted reactions. I think that perhaps I, too, am still looking at girls' and women's bodies with an internalized patriarchal gaze – the pearl-clutching thing. I thought about it when I read Michelle Obama's memoir, *Becoming*, in which she describes how sex in her house was always considered something "fun." That was pretty surprising to me. I don't think I knew anyone growing up who received a message like that, at least not that I knew of. The relentless message was that sexuality is scary, dangerous, bad, or sinful. Showing your body is slutty, distracting, inappropriate, impure, vulgar, wrong – in short, "immodest." The word "immodest" is simply a euphemism for "a girl or woman who has sexuality." These messages have not gone away – in fact, what we are seeing is that they are alive and well and being spread even in non-religious settings.

For years, while embracing women's freedom of choice, I have maintained my own limitations. Although I have rejected a lot of the Orthodox norms I grew up with, I still have never in my life worn short shorts, or even a mini-skirt, and certainly not a bikini. Sure, I will support every single girls' protest for the right to dress for their own comfort and desire. Secretly, I would not embrace it for myself. I don't strut or swagger or announce my sexuality in any way. Maybe deep down, I'm still an affected Orthodox Jewish girl who has internalized the idea that my body should be "modest" – read, asexual, and invisible.

As I watch Beyoncé, whose power comes from being fully herself, in all her beauty and sexuality, I think I've been changing my mind about this. I look at Beyoncé now, and I think, *I want some of what she's having.* Here is a woman who owns her sexuality. I barely know what that means for myself. I have spent so much of my life recovering from my traumas around all this that I have had a hard time embracing that kind of Beyoncé stance on my own.

I am finding Beyoncé healing and empowering. I think she has an important message for girls and women – even those of us who come from different cultures but may still struggle with patriarchal body messages. I think she has a lot to teach me, and many women I know, about learning to love our bodies and own our power, even our sexual power.

So, what am I going to do with this newfound realization? Well, writing this essay is a start. It may the first time I'm writing about this issue not just as an outside researcher but also as someone affected. Just writing this involves letting go of a certain kind of sexual shame – being willing to say out loud that I *want*…. That I *desire*…. That is the first step.

And we'll see where that takes me. I may just go do some clothing shopping and put on something new. Really new.

Post-script
In another Covid-lockdown project, I created some new playlists. Feminist playlists. I love Beyoncé, Madonna, Lizzo, Mary J. Blige, Christina Aguilera, and so many other female artists who celebrate women's body and sexuality. The music is helping me awaken my own passions. And also, I've been singing. Out loud. It's all connected.

Sex Cultures and the "Chosen" People[32]

After revisiting my own experiences around women's sexuality, I'm going back to unpacking the entire Jewish faith around the topic of sex. Maybe the problem with how we approach sexuality is deep-rooted and has been going on for a long time.

D r. Lea Mazor packs a powerful punch into a tiny frame. This brilliant retired professor of Bible and walking encyclopedia of ancient Israel is teaching us a course in Gender in the Bible, one of my favorite topics. And every week, she blows me away all over again with her knowledge, scholarship, and verve. There isn't an issue that she hasn't already thought about at length, and there isn't a verse that she doesn't have a fabulous personal anecdote about. The first week of class, when she interrupted her main thesis to share a story about that time she wrote a personal note to Professor Uriel Simon to tell him about the errors he had in his book, I made that mistake of saying – my pen furiously glued to my notebook – "Wait, can you please

---

[32] November 19, 2017, originally published on my blog, *A Jewish Feminist*.
http://jewfem.com/index.php?option=com_easyblog&view=entry&id=590&Itemid=499

finish your sentence?" She responded, "Of course not!" (Actually, what she said, was, *"Ma pit'om,"* which literally means "What, suddenly," but has the effect of a mix between, "No way!" and "Are you kidding me!?") She did actually finish her sentence eventually, and we have all learned to follow her along her effervescent stream of consciousness, which tends to lead to mind-blowing places. This is a woman with a lot to share, and I don't want to miss a beat.

Last week, we were exploring the issue of sexuality in Genesis. Big topic, I know. She has a particular idea that she is demonstrating to us, and it is riveting.

The Israelites – that is, the twelve clans that derived from the family of Jacob – were a relatively small bunch of shepherds surrounded by some big empires of ancient Mesopotamia. The Egyptians, the Sumerians, and the Assyrians were among the massive neighboring cultures that were advancing in areas of technology, engineering, medicine, art, and writing, among other things. Modern-day scholars are still in awe about the things that the Egyptians were able to do. (To this day, nobody knows how they built the pyramids.) And so, these little Israelites needed a way to preserve their identity and to maintain their own uniqueness and singularity. They needed to create a narrative for themselves to remind themselves of how different they were. Special. Chosen.

The way the Tanach chooses to relay the Israelites' distinction from the Other Nations is along one particular issue: Sexuality. If you read the text carefully, even from the beginning of Genesis, the main point is that the Israelites stood out from the pack due to their "purer" sexual behaviors.

This narrative, Dr. Mazor tells us, is apparent from many texts. For instance, the story of Noah after the flood, in which his son, Ham, and grandson, Canaan, "saw his nakedness" – a euphemism either for rape or castration according to Rav and Shmuel in the Talmud (BT Sanhedrin 70a) – aims to justify a future reality in which Canaan, grandson of Ham (Africans) would become servile to the descendants of Shem (Jews and ultimately Christians). The sexual sin was used to demonstrate that Israelites were destined to conquer Ham and Canaan in order to vanquish this evil sexual deviance.

The story of Lot and his daughters is another instance of sexual deviance that begets evil nations that will become the mortal enemies of Israel. Lot's daughters rape him in a misguided effort to save the planet, and as a result, give birth to the nations of Moab and Ammon who Israelites are commanded to reject and repel.

In fact, throughout the rest of the Bible, these nations are viewed as the antithesis of Israeli culture. The section about forbidden sexual relationships, for example – the text that is viewed as so sacred that we read it on Yom Kippur – frames these sexual rules around the idea that we are not supposed to be like the other nations, "You must not do as they do in Egypt, where you used to live, and you must not do as they do in the land of Canaan, where I am bringing you. Do not follow their practices." (Leviticus 18:3) Dr. Mazor says that their "practices" refer primarily to sexual practices. (I would like to point out that these sexual dictates do not ban rape or sexual violence, just forbidden relationships such as incest.)

Another interesting iteration of this theme is in the book of Joshua, where the Israelites enter the land of Canaan. Who is the first person that the Israelites encounter in Canaan? Rahab, the prostitute. Even though she surprisingly ends up saving the Jews, she represents the notion that Canaan is a land of sluts and whores who constitute a danger to Israelite culture because of their incorrect sexuality.

The laws of forbidden sexual relations are, of course, told to men and not to women. (As such, for example, lesbianism is not forbidden according to the Bible, as opposed to male homosexuality, because almost nothing in the Torah speaks to women.) The Bible also warns that men who violate these laws will be "expelled" from the land. The land, interestingly, is often cast as female. So is Jerusalem, in later years. Men who sin with women bring expulsion from that female land, as well as other forms of suffering, to the poor Israelite men.

Thus, in the book of Lamentations (*Eichah*), for example, which mourns the actual expulsion of the Jews from the land, Jerusalem is called an "impure woman," and is blamed for the suffering of the Israelite (men). The narrator of *Eichah*, a man, blames the female Jerusalem for causing this pain. *"Al ken laniddah hayta"* – that is, Jerusalem became an impure menstruant female, dirty and outcast. We know that being a menstruant is not something that women can change about ourselves; we just are. And yet, that very natural state is framed as the evil impurity that causes men to suffer. In other words, the default "Israelite" is a man, the object of sexual experience is woman, and the purity of their sexual interaction is what will determine the fate of the Israelites, whether they will live up to their destiny and become a special nation, or whether they will be sexually perverted like all the other nations and cause themselves to be expelled from the land. That is a core message of the bible, as explained by Dr. Mazor.

I think it's brilliant. And it explains so much of how Judaism evolved as well as what is happening today in contemporary, Western society. Perceptions of women's correct behavior and sexuality are at the core of Orthodox identity-building (in particular male identity) as well as Judeo-Christian-drenched American political discourse – sometimes in ways that are hard to understand. America's obsession with birth control, abortion, and women's dress as hallmarks of pro-Christian politics can only be understood by going all the way back to these biblical messages. Controlling women's sexuality has been the preferred way for men to assert their superiority over others for millennia, apparently.

One more fascinating tidbit: Dr. Mazor has reminded us that the 24 books (or "scrolls") that were ultimately included in the bible are chosen from among 600 books that were found in the Dead Sea Scrolls. They were chosen to promote a particular agenda, or set of agendas, that scholars are only now fully understanding.

I learned about one of the interesting findings a few years ago from the Dead Sea Scrolls in a lecture by Professor Rachel Elior, one of the primary scholars investigating these topics. She found that some of the alternative texts of Genesis discovered in the caves record the names of the daughters and not only the sons. Generally, in the Biblical canon, lineages are recorded from father to son with only rare exceptional references to daughters. We take this for granted as the "culture of the time." But apparently that is wrong. Professor Elior says that archaeologists found alternative scrolls from the biblical period that do, in fact, list the names of daughters – even the daughters of Adam and Eve. So much for the "culture of the times." Even back then, there were different degrees of patriarchy.

The reason that these scrolls weren't included in the Bible, Professor Elior says, is obvious: they infer incest. Think about it. How did Adam and Eve's children create the next generation? There is only one way. And it violates the rules that have since been passed down.

Professor Elior argues, as does Dr. Mazor, that the bible does not include these scrolls in order not to highlight the fact that we are all descendants of forbidden relationships. So un-Jewish.

Not only would that reality make us all feel a little gross, it would also interfere with the narrative about how special and pure the Israelites are. Maybe none of us are really that pure after all.

Post-script

Although this is the only essay in this book that looks at biblical interpretation, I consider it a crucial aspect of understanding Jewish patriarchy and attitudes towards women's bodies. In my many essays and talks on the Torah portion over the years, I frequently establish links between bible-speak and contemporary practices. I believe that there is a deep connection between the way Torah is taught in many circles and what people accept as ultimate truths. The culture goes deep, it's old, and it's rooted in a lot of God language. Dr. Mazor's lecture pulled some of this together for me in a way that resonated deeply.

Perhaps I will one day publish an anthology of my Torah essays on gender. I think we need as much feminist revisiting of these texts as possible.

Why Israel's *Mikveh* Bill Is About More Than How Orthodox Women Immerse[33]

Even as I empower myself, the problem goes much deeper: The mikveh *has been adopted by the State of Israel. Every married Jewish woman and convert have to immerse – naked, in front of a state employee, and in the case of converts, in front of three male rabbis. When religion, state, and the patriarchy collaborate to control women's bodies, it can't be good for any of us.*

This has been a tough week for women in Israel. While the Knesset was debating how much power the rabbinate should have over women immersing in the ritual bath, or *mikveh*, Women of the Wall Executive Director Leslie Sachs was being arrested at the Western Wall for carrying a Torah.

All this reminds us that Israel is the only Western country where the following happens: Jewish women cannot get married without proving that they dunked

[33] June 13, 2016, originally published in the *Forward*. Reprinted with permission.
https://forward.com/sisterhood/342595/why-israels-mikveh-bill-is-about-more-than-how-Orthodox-women-immerse/

naked in front of a stranger; non-Orthodox Jews cannot legally get married; non-Orthodox converts are not legally considered Jews; and a Jewish woman can get arrested for wearing a *tallit* or holding a Torah scroll.

Welcome to Israel 2016, the scary version.

On the upside, all of this provides a real, powerful illustration of why Israel desperately needs a separation of religion and state. The idea that all-male, ultra-Orthodox deciders of religion should have legal means to control the movements and religious expressions of an entire nation is medieval and frightening in its implications.

The tension over women and religion emerged with particular force at this week's Knesset hearing to discuss Knesset member Moshe Gafni's *"mivkeh* bill," which would give the rabbinate absolute authority in determining who, how, and why people are allowed to use state *mikvehs.*

The bill is an attempt by religious politicos to co-opt power from non-religious arms of government, completely evading and neutralizing the Supreme Court, which ruled in February that Reform and Conservative converts must be allowed to use state *mikvehs,* and in 2014 that attendants may not interrogate women using the *mikveh.*

Signs that the Religious Ministry was having trouble adhering to the Supreme Court ruling came earlier this year when the police were called to arrest a woman who had been asking to immerse alone.

Yes, that really happened — adding to the list that Israel is the only country where a Jewish woman might be arrested for using the *mikveh.* The Knesset meeting erupted with objections of women – such as religious feminist Knesset members Rachel Azaria and Aliza Lavie — as well as those promoting religious tolerance and pluralism in Israel. But the bill has not been shelved yet.

One of the most outrageous and perhaps surprising moments in the meeting came when Gafni told the committee, "This doesn't have anything to do with women." Considering that married, religious women (and not men) are expected to use the *mikveh* monthly, and that an estimated 80% of converts are women, his comment was preposterous.

But it revealed another element of his targets here: Reform and Conservative Jews. The *mikveh* bill is not only aimed at limiting the ways Orthodox women use the *mikveh* but also at the way Reform and Conservative rabbis use the *mikveh* to convert people.

I would posit that on some level this is the same thing. In my research about Orthodox perceptions of Jewish masculinities that I described in my book, *The Men's Section*, I found that the reason why Reform and Conservative Judaism is seen as so threatening in Orthodoxy is because it is seen as destroying Jewish masculinity. Women encroaching on the activities deemed as "male" has a kind of emasculating effect, and threatens to leave Orthodox men powerless. So when Gafni says, "It's not about women", what he means is that he is out to punish Reform and Conservative *men* who are threatening *his* masculinity with their own versions of too-soft and too-effeminate masculinities. It's about messing with gender hierarchies and power. It threatens the established order of things.

But I doubt Gafni or anyone else in his orbit will admit that this is what is going on. They may not have ever articulated it in quite these terms, although the sentiment abounds in Orthodox culture.

His statement also makes women's lives and experiences invisible. The fact that he doesn't consider the women converts of Reform and Conservative Jews to be women would be funny if it weren't so reflective of the Jewish condition. In the battle over who gets to determine who is Jewish, there is a perception that is a discussion among men alone — men talking to men about genderless and personless "converts," having nothing to do with women. The patriarchal notion that Jewish leadership and authority are a men's thing is far from dead.

One take-away from this is that there is cross-denominational invisibility of Jewish women that desperately needs to be repaired.

Another takeaway is that denominational divides were invented by men and are maintained by men, eager to be gatekeepers of entry into the Jewish people, in a Kafkaesque position as holder of The Law. And these divides are so often gendered – which denomination uses partitions, which count women in a quorum, which allow women to speak or lead. Gender is so ubiquitous as the definer of Jewish identity.

Orthodox and non-Orthodox feminists should be seeking ways to join forces in opposition to patriarchy rather than retreating into corners. Even if Gafni bows to Orthodox feminists with a concession that women can immerse alone, that is not satisfactory enough. Orthodox women need to stay in the battle on behalf of all the other women who are still in Gafni's crosshairs. This is about more than women being "allowed" to immerse themselves alone. This is about ensuring that the government stays out of women's bodily experiences, and about separating religion and state altogether.

The third takeaway, given the confluence with events at the Western Wall, is that Israel has reached a critical moment in the tension between women and religion in Israel. Women's basic rights are being challenged on so many fronts in Israel — in the army, in public spaces, in work, in economics. Religious demands for women's invisibility and passivity continue to be met with acquiescence — whether by the police in the Old City of Jerusalem or by coalition partners seeking to make a deal. If the women of Israel don't find a powerful and effective way to fight back, the very nature of Israel as a democracy will be at risk, if it isn't already.

Women have lots of tools at our disposal. We have our voices, our minds, and our bodies — as well as our pocketbooks and our votes. Women in Israel need to unite, to drop denominational and political differences, and to launch a widespread campaign for change. Some women have been proposing a "Lysistrata" solution where women stop going to the *mikveh*, but that is only one of several strong possibilities. There are many ways for us to have an influence, and we need to use them all. We need to take back the *mikveh*, take back the streets, take back Judaism, and take back democracy. As Hillel said, if not now, when? Soon it may be too late.

Post-script
These explorations about sexuality and power reflect one of the most potent intersections of the personal and political. I'm fighting for my own right to live in my own skin, as my own, to allow myself to feel, to want, to desire. But that struggle comes up against religion, community, and even state laws in Israel. It should not be this hard for a woman to own her own sexual life. But here we are. Here I am.

ELANA SZTOKMAN

The messages about women and our bodies come at us from everywhere – from families, communities, religious leaders, pop culture, fashion, Hollywood, history, politics. And the messages live in our heads – live in my head.

It is so hard to navigate all these issues from all these angles. And at the end of the day, this is about our real lives and experiences and the many ways in which we walk through the world and build relationships – with others and with ourselves and with our bodies. The patriarchy inserts itself into our intimate selves and releases its poison inside of us, sometimes impregnating us with its evil.

For most of my adult life, I have been reluctant to delve into the impact of all this on my own relationship with my body. I have pursued academic, political, communal, religious, and non-profit work in order to raise awareness and make change on behalf of women generally. But the truth is, the most important work – and possibly the hardest – has been making the change in private, in my own relationship with myself. The task of clearing out the manifold texts from my brain and body continues to challenge me.

But rereading the collections of essays here – which run the gamut from biblical analysis to political work to personal explorations – has helped me clarify the connections between all these messages. I have had to admit that I am not just an observer in all these things but also an object in them. And this has had an impact. Shedding light is crucial for healing, both personally and collectively.

190

Food and Fat

"For much of the female half of the world, food is the first signal of our inferiority. It lets us know that our own families may consider female bodies to be less deserving, less needy, less valuable."
– Gloria Steinem

"No, I'm not a snack at all. Look, baby, I'm the whole damn meal."
– Lizzo

*F*atness – or rather the fear of fatness – has dominated my life since I was small. And when I say "small", I don't just mean young. I mean, when I was 14 years old, weighed 98 pounds and wore a size four dress, I was as weight-obsessed then as I was when I was 40 years old and, well, much bigger. I was taught this fat-fear early and emphatically, often as the most important aspect of my being. Even when I was the star of the school play, my cheeks and double chin were more fodder for commentary than my actual performance. When I went clothing shopping with my mother and sisters, the issues at hand were invariably (a) whether we were covered enough and (b) whether we were thin enough. When I was pregnant, I was constantly warned by the people who were supposed to love me that there is nothing worse than gaining too much weight during pregnancy. "Women who get fat during pregnancy never get back to themselves," my father cautioned me with authority, in a broad-brush blaming of mothers for their own unacceptability in his visual landscape, an expulsion of incorrectly outlined female forms as evidence that their bodies must belong to unworthy women.

And then, of course, there was the food. Every time we sat down to eat, the alarms sounded. "It's fattening," or "No, no, too many carbs," or "I can't, it goes straight to my hips," or the worst, "You don't need that." These were constant reminders that you are always being watched when you eat, and that food is dangerous. It threatens your body appearance, and thus your standing and your worth in society. Eating was about keeping to the bare minimum of what your body may need, never about what you may want or desire. And the messages stuck. Like, forever. I am fairly certain that there hasn't been a single day in my adult life when I wasn't trying to be thinner.

In my house, there was often a particularly Jewish angle to these warnings. This is not only because of how connected food *is to the Jewish experience. I mean, can we even imagine a Jewish event without food? It is also because these exchanges were a mainstay of our Jewish-centric gatherings, especially our weekly Shabbat table. We would come home from synagogue and spend the meal analyzing in great detail how everyone in shul "looked" – and by "looked," we meant, how thin they were. And by "everyone" I mean women and girls. Those who were thin looked "good," and therefore they must be doing well in life – even if they got that way, say, by getting cancer or being anorexic. It didn't matter as long as they were skinny. Those who gained weight were obviously having trouble in life – money, marriage, bad personality, whatever. There must be something very, very wrong with them.*

To confirm our okayness, my sisters and I had a regular routine at the Shabbat table. As my father sat at the head of the table, we would bring him copious amounts of food and ask him how we looked. He would look us up and down, check out our stomachs, our legs, and our chins, and tell us whether we look like we gained or lost weight that week. "You look like you could lose five pounds" was the usual response as we desperately endeavored to suck ourselves in.

What I really wanted and needed – and spent most of my life seeking out – was to hear, "You are beautiful exactly as you are. Perfect and loved." Those words never came. At least not from anyone in my family of origin. I spent much of the rest of my life trying to create those words for myself. I'm still trying.

Although I rarely write publicly about these very personal struggles with body and food, I realize that the reluctance to share still comes from a place of shame. I'm writing it here because I think it's time for me to let go of that shame and allow myself to be as I am. My tense relationship with my body is a significant part of who I have been for the past 25 years. And even when I have not written about it explicitly, it is always there.

Passover: Freedom for Women NOW— Not 3000 Years Ago[34]

This was my first published essay in which I revealed some of my childhood traumas around body and food. It received some angry pushback from commenters, as well as some sympathetic support from people who had similar experiences. I do not regret publishing it and feel like letting go of the shame is an important part of the healing process. But the reactions demonstrate just how normalized body-shaming is in our cultures.

No holiday brings out the screaming in my head as much as Passover.

There are two sets of noise that take hold of my brain at this time of year: the pre-Pesach (Passover) trauma and the Seder night trauma. Or as I have come to experience it, the trauma created by *women's* stuff, and the trauma created by *men's* stuff.

---

[34] April 13, 2016. Originally published at *Lilith Magazine*. Reprinted with permission.
https://www.lilith.org/blog/2016/04/passover-freedom-for-women-now-not-3000-years-ago/

Growing up, the pre-Pesach anxiety began as soon as Purim was over. We were only allowed to eat from a pre-determined collection in the kitchen, we were on a schedule around what rooms were already sterilized, and my mother's mood gradually devolved from the usual cold and cranky to the downright hostile. Nothing was ever right, we walked on eggshells, and life was insane and frenetic. Although I often wonder how many of my traumas are from religion and how many are from my particular family, in this case, I have come to learn that this kind of thing was going on not only my own house but also in many Jewish homes around the world. Even women of privilege engage in the panic. (I'll never forget the time, years ago, when a mother frantically came over to pick up her daughter from a play date around a week before Pesach, saying, "Hurry, I have to rush home and watch my cleaning lady do the kitchen.") Pre-Pesach insanity, it seemed, was the Women's Way, no matter how you celebrated the holiday.

I've been living in Israel for over 20 years, and it is still astounding for me to watch how this culture takes over Jewish women's lives, no matter what kind of religious observance they adhere to during the year. Conversations in shops, on the street, and online revolve around Jewish women of all backgrounds managing the minutia of obsessive cleaning, shopping, and cooking. There seems to be an uncontrolled lust for women to compare themselves to one another — who started cleaning and cooking earlier, who is having more guests, who is more efficient, who is more creative, and ironically also who has more time-saving hacks. Facebook doesn't help, by the way.

Growing up in Orthodox Brooklyn, I found that this pre-Pesach cleaning-cooking-hosting-mania was compounded by the other assault on women's bodies:

clothing shopping. Our job, as religious girls, was not only to manage the kitchen but also to look gorgeous as we did it. We prepared our shul and Seder outfits meticulously and expensively, down to the last perfectly matching accessory. But let me tell you something: there is nothing quite as dysfunctional within the female experience as surrounding yourself with copious amounts of food and then forbidding yourself from eating any of it. Women's and girls' table conversation, once we finished serving, invariably revolved around calories, points, fat content, carbs, gluten, GI, cellulite, whatever. (Each year, the measures for what we should or shouldn't eat changed, led by trends announced by *The New York Times*. This added to women's competition not only over who was thinnest but also over who was the most in-the-know about the most current dictates for how to lose weight most effectively).

Women actively and eagerly participate in this competition. It is what I think of as the Queen Complex. So many Jewish women ultimately want to be Queen. You want to show the world that you have the loveliest table, the largest number of guests, the best organization, the cleanest house, the nicest-looking family, the longest Seder—in short, that you are Mistress of the Universe. You are the best, the most special. I participated in this need-to-be-Queen for more years than I care to admit. In a world that is so gendered, where women are rewarded for the most successful act of performing femininity, you can't really blame women for wanting to be Queen. It's all we have to go by sometimes. And doing femininity well has its social rewards. Public adoration is nothing to scoff at.

Meanwhile, the actual Seder night experience created a whole other set of traumas for me. Growing up in a family of all daughters, if we were schooled in how to be Queen, my father was undoubtedly King. This was a whole other thing. Being King meant Running the Show. The King dictates what happens when, how long each part of the event should take, and who gets to talk and for how long and about what. If being Queen means women are masters over all thing's food-body-service-oriented, being King means men are masters over all things Legacy-Ideas-Throne. The Seder table is where women show off their kitchen skills, and men show off their mental prowess, their power, and their general mastery over all things Jewish or otherwise.

Memories of my father's Seder are among the most trigger-inducing for me. If I wanted to participate in a conversation, it was always exclusively on my father's controlling terms. If I said the wrong thing, anything that made someone's eyes roll, my father directed the conversation elsewhere. If I spoke too long, that was a terrible sin on society, and my father would instantly cut me off and continue his schedule. If I dared disagree on a point, I was summarily punished, reminded that girls and wives are not allowed to disrespect the men in our lives. Most family Seders I ended up crying alone in my bedroom. Sometimes my mother would come upstairs, not to comfort me but to seal my fate. "You will not ruin my *shalom bayit*," the "peace in the home," she would say.

I was never a correct girl. After all, it was always too hard for me to hold back my ideas. When I deviated from the script and asked genuine questions that were on my mind, I was being a pain. When I challenged the way things were done, asking about the supposedly educational idea that we do things "differently" at the Seder so that kids will ask questions ("The kids asked," I would say. "What is the actual answer beyond 'so you would ask'?"). I was considered a defiant annoyance. During one of the meals, I challenged my brother-in-law about the policy of his family law practice not to hire women lawyers because "women are too emotional to be good lawyers" — and as a result, I became the problem of the family, eye-rolling and all. (That was in the early 1990s, not in 1955). "Here she goes again," someone at the table would say every time I had an opinion. Then there was the body-control over the mind-control: When I wanted to eat more than a bite of potato during *maggid* because it was late and I was hungry, I was looked at as piggish and selfish. The dining room table so often felt like a trap for me, one that I tried to escape via food. I defied femininity early and often, and it never ended well.

During my early years as a parent, I made some definitive changes to our Seder. For one thing, I am not in charge of cleaning. Either we all do it together, or it just doesn't happen. I have come to terms with an imperfect measure of cleanliness in my house. It is the price of my sanity.

Over the years, my rebellion has evolved into a new vision for my own life. Our family does Seder very differently from the way I was brought up. First of all, my husband and I not only share the cooking but also sit together at the head of the table. There are no Kings and no Queens. We also don't let anyone starve. Many years ago, we adopted a practice of eating lots and lots of vegetable dips and crudités for *karpas*, so that nobody sits at the table hungry, ever. We also do not do much rote recitation and skip parts we think are boring. When my kids were small, I spent days before Passover making puppets and writing plays and songs, finding ways to make the Seder active and fun. And everyone can talk, for as long as they want. No idea is rejected, nobody is ever told that they are talking for too long.

And here's a biggie for me: nobody will ever, ever sit alone crying in their room, ever. If one person in the family is hurting, we all hurt with them. That is a year-round rule.

Dome years, we do something completely radical and have a Seder with no guests, just our kids. I realize that is very anti-Jewish, but it is also genuine. My kids don't like putting on a superficial performance, and we don't like competing. We like being true to ourselves and following practices that feel right to us.

I realize that some of my salves seem out of bounds for those still adhering to the most limiting stringencies of man-made halakhic practices, but I no longer feel loyalty to a set of rules that assume female servitude. I mean, Passover is really the height of gender irony in Judaism. The way this particular celebration of freedom has evolved over two millennia rests entirely on someone's servitude. To mark the end of slavery, certain people – and by that we usually mean women – must stand in the kitchen for weeks in advance. It's completely wacko. We mark our objection to our nation's slavery by imposing slavery on the women. Even though today many men participate in some way, the fact remains that the kitchen and house were women's exclusive job for so long, and despite many social changes, it still remains this way in many Jewish households. (No, I do not have hard data on this; just many supermarket-line conversations and Facebook feeds.)

This is my big question: How would our Jewish traditions have evolved differently without the assumption of female servitude? Would elaborate meals for 30 be such a central part of communal and religious practice if the Jewish community valued women's full participation in all parts of public ritual? Or would we have perhaps found other ways to connect and to bring the sacred into our lives? Frankly, anything that depends on stark gender inequality has lost its sacredness for me. I cannot abide by a set of rules created by men who truly see me as their instrument for their own needs, and not really a full person of my own.

I can feel all the different forms of pushback already: Men help. Religious feminism is a thing. Gender is not binary. Families evolve. Halakha is binding. It's not all religious families, just yours.

I hear that. The world has undoubtedly changed. Not all families out there are like my family of origin. Families are diverse, gender-fluid, and changing. Many women are liberated, and many people reject these traditions. But that is not the whole story. Gender roles have incredible sticking power. We are living in a world where there seems to be as much support for a woman president as there is for a Neanderthally-misogynist president. These opposing trends seem to coexist. So, despite some significant changes, I still find this season triggering. I can't really cope with the communal discourse. My instinct is to run away, perhaps skip the holiday altogether, spend a month on a remote island. My experience as a woman with my childhood memories, communal interactions, and the histories of my grandmothers and great-grandmothers on my shoulders—these do not leave me. And no matter how much men mean well, no matter how much they cook and clean, I am dealing with is a heritage that they do not have. Men—even men who share household responsibilities—do not experience the cultural baggage of generations of assumed female servitude.

As I observe my responses to my traumas around Pesach, I cannot help but wonder how other Jewish women deal with the cultural baggage. Not all women, I know. But I am reasonably confident that many other women out there also have traumas and scars from being brought up in a world that says women's servitude is an essential part of a culture of chosenness and specialness. I am confident that a lot of the noise in my head comes from women's screaming this time of year. It takes a lot of cognitive dissonances to maintain the narrative that women's servitude is a beautiful thing, part of a wonderful tradition. It also requires mechanisms for dealing with unhealed traumas, which may involve some serious dysfunction.

I hope that women out there who want something else can find a healing path, a way to let go of social expectations, follow their hearts about what is truly right for them. The feminist revolution starts that way, with women paying attention to our hurts, our scars, and our needs. It is both personal *and* political. If Passover is to be a holiday of freedom, it needs to start with freedom for women—not 3000 years ago, but today, right now.

Post-script

This essay was one of my first times sharing my real, personal pains in a published magazine. I realize that we currently live in a share-all kind of world and maybe I'm just a late arrival. Maybe I was – and am – still struggling with the shame of the self-reveal. Or maybe I always wanted to be valued for my scholarship and not my victimhood. I still wrestle with how I identify with all these different voices and the various pieces of my self – researcher, journalist, thinker, anthropologist, activist, rebel, fat woman with an eating disorder. Somehow I have to make them all co-exist. Whether the world has changed or whether my spirit has tired of hiding in the dark, the time has come for me to say what I have to say. Essays like this one

– and in fact this very book – have become milestones in my path towards wholeness. Owning all parts of myself, even the ones that feel shameful. It's a hard process, but overall a good one.

My First Girdle and Other Religious Moments[35]

I was so ashamed of writing about this that even in my computer files, this essay was saved under a pseudonym. By publishing this here, I'm letting go of my shame. And by placing these stories together in this volume, I'm starting to address the very important and potent connection between sexuality, sexual abuse, emotional abuse, and eating disorders. These issues are all intertwined in my pained and traumatized body, as I'm sure they are for many people.

My mother bought me my first girdle when I was 14 years old. The year was 1984, and I weighed 98 pounds (yes, of course, I remember how much I weighed – I can tell you exactly what I weighed at every single milestone of my life, both the significant and insignificant ones). I probably did not need the girdle; not only was I a size four at the time, I also had a flat stomach – or so my mother told my three sisters and me whenever we would try on clothes in the Loehmann's dressing room, "Elana is the lucky one. She's the only one of you girls who got a flat stomach and

---

a flat tush," she would say as my sisters and I traded outfits.

Flat stomach or not, I was excited about the girdle. Finally, I thought, I have a way to make sure that my stomach will *really* look flat, which was, of course, pretty much all I wanted in life back then. And even though my mother said I had the flattest stomach of my sisters, the constant practices of watching, measuring, and judging ourselves and others overpowered any possible benefit from that assessment.

I remember the first time I wore it. I squeezed it on underneath a purple and green long-sleeve flared dress that I wore to the synagogue on Shabbat. This was Orthodox Jewish Brooklyn, where our fashion lives pretty much revolved around Shabbat. My sisters and I would walk up and down Avenue J every Friday, buying challah and accessories, desserts and lipsticks, snacks and pantyhose. It was the 1980s, so having matching bracelets, earrings, stockings, and shoes in every loud color was of supreme importance. Getting ready for synagogue involved a jittery exchange of paraphernalia among the four girls, endless questions about which outfits make my thighs stand out, and about who has the right pair of earrings for which outfit. This transmission of religious rituals conveyed the unequivocal message that a woman's/girl's job in life and in Judaism is to look beautiful in front of the community.

So, the girdle felt like a godsend to my tiny-waisted adolescent body. I could now be assured that my stomach would indeed *look* flat, even in my purple and green dress, which probably looked great on me, anyway. I wish I could go back to that 14-year-old girl and tell her how beautiful and perfect she was, even without the girdle, even without the heels, even without clothes. It would help me receive the all-coveted comment from relatives and other women in the community: "You look GREAT!" What else could a girl want out of life?

I often wondered what people meant when they said, "You look great". Like the time I came home from summer camp having had a lot of formative experiences, some pleasant and some not. The first thing my mother said to me was, "You look great," and I remember looking at myself in the rearview mirror of the car wondering what exactly she saw when she didn't really know anything about what I was going through. And also, by the way, trying to figure out what made a person "look great."

Actually, one of the most memorable body rituals in my family took place after synagogue when we arrived home for lunch. My father would sit down at the head of the dining room table as the girls would set the table and prepare the meal. We would strut back and forth between the kitchen and dining room, serving ridiculous amounts of food while wearing our high heels and fancy dresses, like models on a runway, and ask my father, "How do I look today?" We might do a little spin, my father would look us up and down, he would assess our waists, and then he would take full aim at our *chins*. Yes, for my father, the discussion always ended up at our chins. "From the look of your chin, I can see that you probably gained four or five pounds this week," was a typical response. I can't ever remember him assessing that we might have *lost* weight that week, although I imagine he sometimes said that too. For many years (how many? Three? Ten? Thirty?), I have had a love-hate relationship with my chin. Well, mostly hate. I remember many conversations not only at home but also among girls in school about my chin – "Does Elana have a double chin? It's just a round face. Elana always had a round face. It's just a double chin. Elana has always been that way." Memories of my fourth-grade teacher pinching my cheeks assured me that, in fact, I might have been lucky to have a flat stomach, but I was unlucky to have that dreaded double chin. This chin ritual has made family photos very difficult. I prefer to wear turtlenecks or scarves, or to manipulate my hands in such a way as to cover my chin. I have had entire conversations with photographers at family portrait events where I instruct them in poses for hiding chins. Whatever happens, to avoid letting the world see my double chin. And of course, over the years, my chin has only sunk worse and worse, and taking those photos has become more tortuous. One day I may finally learn to look at my face in the mirror or look at an old photo of myself, without swimming in a pool of disgust and self-loathing—that damned chin. If I were ever going to do one plastic surgery, it would be a magical one that gave me one singular, tight, and beautiful chin.

So this was our Shabbat ritual – girls prancing around the dining room table with our fancy clothes on, serving my father food while he assessed our weight loss. Not that we ate particularly healthy food or had any real fitness awareness. In our house, the rules were that religious girls weren't allowed to take dance lessons ("Dancers perform on Friday night") or gymnastics ("The outfits are not modest") or even jog ("Jogging is bad for women's bodies," meaning breasts). On the plus side, we were encouraged to drink only water and walk everywhere. That was really the extent of helpful body messages. Mostly there was a sense that you were expected to be "naturally" lucky and thin and beautiful – but also eat as little as possible. Men, of course, could eat what they wanted, and my mother, tellingly, cooked according to what my father liked. Nobody even really knows what *she* likes – she mostly ate standing up in the kitchen. For me, I cannot remember a single meal in which there wasn't someone talking about the food we ate being fattening or having some discussion about the latest diet craze. It is so very hard to learn to eat normally when everyone is complaining about how bad the food is for you the entire time. This environment of pressuring us girls to be skinny while we were simultaneously in charge of feeding the one man at the table who was allowed to eat everything while we serving girls obsessed over dieting – it's like an Orthodox cross between The Twilight Zone and One Flew Over the Cuckoo's Nest.

Even as adults, my sisters go to my father for weight-loss approval. I was horrified when, way into my twenties, I watched my older sister ask my father how her chin looked. *Still?* I thought. *You're still asking him?* She recently had surgery to remove half her intestines to cope with a chronic stomach illness. I thought to myself, *that is the ultimate weight-loss fantasy, to just cut out half your stomach.* And then I thought, I should try it myself.

These conversations take place while preparing for the next step for the Orthodox girl – motherhood. In a world in which women are revered for a flat stomach, the greatest threat to a woman's self-image is undoubtedly pregnancy. Our Shabbat meals were punctuated with steadfast gossip about pregnancy and weight loss of women in the community. We would analyze women's appearances ad nauseum and decide who may or may not be pregnant. My father prided himself on being able to tell – by the chin of course – who was pregnant. Then there were incessant discussions about women losing weight after the pregnancy. My father was full of warnings about those women who gained too much weight and then struggled their entire lives with how they felt about themselves. "She'd better be careful," he would say about a woman. "You can see on her chin that she's gained a lot of weight." This mortal sin of gaining weight was at odds with our great mission in life, which my mother would caution as "Looking after yourself."

A woman must look after herself – which did NOT mean things that I would consider looking after myself, like going to work or getting an education or making money or getting therapy or taking up judo or marathon running, but rather ensuring that no matter what, always looking beautiful and youthful and happy. If that requires weekly trips to the hairdresser and manicurist, so be it. Looking after yourself was the primary job of a correct woman. And no matter what happens, do not let pregnancy "ruin" your figure because that would be the end of your life, pretty much.

This message came along with the other primary message to Orthodox girls: get married early and have lots of babies. How girls are supposed to manage all of these messages – be thin but have lots of babies; dress modestly but always be pretty and alluring; be young and beautiful but always serve everyone's needs; look after yourself but mostly look after your husband – is still a mystery to me. It took me more than a few years of painful trying, but I gradually realized the futility of the efforts, and I eventually gave up. Well, maybe not entirely. I mean, I'm still married and a mother. I'm just fat, and that's it. That's my freedom, I suppose.

My first pregnancy, when I was 22 years old, became a very traumatic experience in terms of my relationship with my body. I was terrified of gaining too much weight, so of course, that's exactly what I did. My doctor – an old sexist guy who was my mother's doctor would spend most of the appointment discussing my weight. He would also inject strange comments and voyeuristic questions about being Orthodox. Like, "You don't drink? You don't smoke? You've never slept with anyone except your husband? You really need to loosen up a little! *Hardy har har....*" But mainly, every appointment he would castigate me about my weight. "You need to eat less," he said to me. "Try eating Melba toast." I swear to you that every time I pass by Melba toast in the grocery store, I think about this doctor and shudder.

So, I had my doctor telling me to gain less weight during pregnancy, my father warning me not to gain too much weight during my pregnancy, and my mother reminding me to "look after yourself." It didn't help when, one Shabbat afternoon early on in my pregnancy, I walked into my mother's house where she was holding court with a bunch of friends and neighbors, and announced to everyone, "Oh, Elana, I was just talking about you. I read an article about women whose husbands make them fat. It made me think of you." I stood frozen at the door for a while.

After I gave birth to my amazing and beautiful daughter, I had gone from a size four to a size eight or ten – to my mother's horror. A few weeks after the birth, my mother took me shopping for a dress for my cousin's bat mitzvah. Her complete shame at my body size and shape was unmistakable. It is that shame which has stayed with her all these years and which pretty much defines her experience of me in every respect. She has told a few too many people how embarrassed she is of me, including my daughter and my college roommate and a board member of an organization I used to run and my former high school teacher.... She says she is embarrassed about the things that I write and say, but it's also about my body. My audacity to leave the house when I look like *this* is just unfathomable to her. And to everyone else in my family of origin. When my sister went through a particularly heavy period due to medications she was taking for her condition, my brother-in-law told me that she must lose weight because until she does, "she is embarrassed to leave the house" – as if that kind of embarrassment about *being too big* is normal and expected. Who *wouldn't* be embarrassed to walk around looking overweight? The implication was that I, too, am meant to be embarrassed to walk around in this world. I take up too much space, my shape is abnormal, and I'm abhorrent. A horror!

Two years after that dressing-room incident, after I gave birth to my beautiful and amazing son, my father sat on my couch several days after the birth and watched me. I was expecting a visit from my then 75-year-old kibbutznikit cousin, may her memory be blessed, a wonderful woman named Etka Holzberg who had toiled hard her whole life and experienced much pain and suffering, and for whom make-up and weight-loss were completely irrelevant. I loved Etka and appreciated that she was going to take three buses to get from her kibbutz to see me. But my father looked at me and said, "You look tired. You should put on make-up before Etka gets here." What I wanted to say to him – aside from challenging the incredulous idea that Etka gives a flying fuck about my lipstick – was that the reason why I look tired is *that I just gave birth* and that perhaps if he wanted me to look less tired, he could get off his behind and offer to babysit while I take a nap and maybe then I might *look* less tired because I might actually *be* less tired. Instead of saying those things, I went and put on lipstick, and later had a nice, long, private binge. Then, later on, went on another diet.

This is how it's been for the past 30 years, since that first girdle – losing weight, gaining it back, losing weight, gaining it back. I was constantly hearing my father's comments about my body, making assumptions about my life based on my weight – the "You look good" when I'm thin that assumes everything is going great, and the "Maybe things will start working out for you soon" when I show excess flesh. Waking up every day, saying to myself, "TODAY, I'm going to fix my body and lose weight." Spending tons of money on diets and trainers and gyms only to give up and fall over in exhaustion as my moods fluctuated along with the number on the scale. And then, once again, abandoning it all because I'm tired of hating myself.

My entire life has been this kind of struggle with my body. I go back and forth between desperation to lose weight and a crying need for love and acceptance. Somehow these two never seem to go together. Well, not yet anyway. I wish I could say I was over all of this, that after so many years and so much distance from my family of origin that I have successfully purged my inner being from all the voices that seek to own my body, my sexuality, my entire being. Meditation and yoga have helped a lot, as have all different forms of healing, Geneen Roth, intuitive eating, and binge-watching SVU. But so far, the scars still remain, and the journey of healing is not yet over.

Postscript
If someone else had written this, I would know how to guide her to self-love. And I have had many teachers try to do the same for me. But it never quite sticks. The texts graffitied into the crevices of my brain about my body are just stuck there. For now, anyway.

211

The Shabbat Binge[36]

This essay, another unpublished piece about eating in the darkness, is still very, very hard for me to share. But I'm doing it anyway. Some bits have appeared in other essays at this point. But this was the long, deep exploration of my own food and body torment that I kept hidden in my hard drive for many years. Putting it here in its entirety is about facing my fears and purging the poisons in my head. It is also an exercise in being kind to myself – looking at my hard truths and being okay with who I am.

It's 4:45 on a Saturday afternoon – Shabbat – and I'm staring into the refrigerator looking for something to eat. You would never know that only an hour earlier, my husband and I finished clearing up from an elaborate four-course meal for 18 people that took us a day and a half to prepare. By prepare, I mean, shop, cook, wash dishes, clean the house, and then rearrange the furniture to enlarge the table and find all the spare chairs. This is what we do, Orthodox Jewish women, week after week. You invite, you greet, you dress up, and you make yourself pretty, and you serve throngs of guests. That's

---

[36] 2014. Unpublished.

how you become Queen, by filling your house with people who you stuff with more food than they would need for a week. Orthodox Jewish women tend to have this Queen Complex, a form of reigning my making your house the center of the universe, where People Come to You. Lots of people hanging around your home and eating your food, that's what makes you Queen. Shabbat and holidays are when the Queens come out. On the days before every holiday, Orthodox streets are swathed in women's kvetches about all the work involved, with only thinly veiled brags over queendom, as in who has the most guests coming over. Your status in the community is based on how many guests you have, how much time you spend cooking, how elaborate your food is, how well-dressed and well-behaved your children are, and how clean and sparkling your house looks. One ultra-Orthodox woman I used to work with, always introduced herself as, "I am a mother of eight children, and my house sparkles like a museum." (Followed by broad smile, chest up, nod.) This is how conversations go among Orthodox women. The day after Passover seder, women – and then girls – compare how many people they had over at their houses the previous night, and how late they all stayed. It's a kvetch-brag kind of thing. The more bustling your home is, the more wholly and utterly exhausted and wiped out you are, the more social approval you get. Your status as Queen is set.

I stare into the packed void of the refrigerator, with no idea what I want, and think how sad it is that I'm still trying to be Queen. I thought I had stopped playing the game, but apparently, that desire to be Queen remains fixed in my consciousness somewhere. At least sometimes, selectively, when I'm feeling insecure or detached or guilty, or some vague and unnamed irritation pressing my buttons. This was such a day. We had over a family that has recently moved to our town of Modi'in from New Jersey. We decided that to make them feel welcome, we would invite another family as well, also originally from Teaneck, where the husband worked with my husband, and the wife and I have mutual friends. It's the right thing to do. (As right as assuming that the married, heterosexual, middle-class family is the way everyone in the world lives, but that's a whole other conversation). That is to say, it's the right *Orthodox* thing to do. In another world, I might have just invited the woman for coffee or something. Anyway, we thought it would all be lovely and charming. "Come to us for a Shabbat meal!" is the way people are meant to feel welcome. Or, maybe more likely, that was me thinking, I really wanted to be Queen, too.

I poked open one of the containers that I only recently wrapped. It's my mock-salmon appetizer that usually impresses guests but didn't garner any compliments from this group. I closed the container and decided to leave it for my husband, who enjoys it more than I do. The group was busy talking about mortgages, gas prices, schools, and the weather in Israel. One of the women barely sat the entire meal since she was looking after her toddler in my not-babyproof-enough house. Meanwhile, her husband was not inclined to help her at all, and even as I tried to enlist my own teenagers as assistants, the woman spent the entire meal chasing her child. Not only did her husband sit the whole time, but at one point, he even yelled at her – yes, yelled – "Penina! He's making a mess over there!" as if it was entirely assumed that it was *her* job and hers alone to clean it all up while he drank his scotch with the guys. *Yes, this is 2014.* Meanwhile, the other man, who had just moved to Israel, was dominating the conversation with complaints about Israeli culture – what he kept calling the Israeli "mentality", ignoring the fact that my kids are Israeli. We've lived here for over twenty years. He was angry that nobody in Israel approaches you in the supermarket to ask you if you need help, and people on the street don't smile at all. (I was thinking, Israel is the only country in the world where new immigrants expect the entire country to bow to them at every turn. Or at least American immigrants do. And anyway, you haven't been here long enough to earn the right to *really* complain.) At one point during the meal, the only people sitting were the men – including my adoring and generally very helpful spouse – while the children were all scattered and the women were in the kitchen, talking about grocery shopping and diets. I tried to get my husband's attention to save me from this and swap places, but it was a lost cause. I don't blame him, really. When everyone else around you expects the world to be divided by gender, it's very hard to be the one man to make a statement and revolt by walking into a kitchen full of gossiping women to start washing some dishes. It wasn't his fault. I knew he would make it up to me in other ways. There was definitely a message waiting for me that evening.

I pulled out another wrapped package. It was my husband's famous pumpkin pie that my oldest daughter loves. He makes it every time she comes home for the weekend. Despite all of our efforts to live a gender-equal life, Shabbat so often has a way of sending me back to Betty Draper land. I put the pumpkin pie back and pulled out the broccoli quiche that I missed because it was on the other side of the table. I contemplated the roasted potatoes – always a great comfort food, warm, soft, and heavy in my stomach. Really, I wanted some of the vegetarian meatballs that my husband is famous for. Perfect. I pulled out three containers, kicked the door shut, and started with the cold spaghetti and veggie balls. (I would get to the quiche and potatoes later).

I sat down at the table with a fork and knife and took a breath. That's what Geneen Roth, the compulsive eating guru, tells people to do. In fact, it's her book title: *When you eat at the refrigerator, pull up a chair.* The point is, always eat consciously, even when you're binging. I knew that all by heart, and so I took three deep breaths and thanked my food and my Creator. I also knew I wasn't really hungry. At least not for food. I knew in my head that it was a combination of boredom, resentment, and habit that kept my mouth eating way after my stomach had had enough. I knew all these things but continued anyway. I was consciously numbing myself with food, voices in my head of "should" and "shouldn't" drowning each other out long enough for me to bite into the coveted meatball.

This is Shabbat for me. It always has been, for as long as I can remember. The Shabbat binging – a bit of force-feeding, a bit of tedium, a bit of soothing, and a bit of recovery from being put into the box of "The Little Woman." It is that way I've been doing food for a long time.

I can imagine lots of people getting angry at me for my depiction of Shabbat. After all, Orthodox Jews tell themselves and the rest of the world that Shabbat is the most beautiful part of the week, where your house fills with kids and friends, where the prohibition against using electronics means that people connect over real conversation and maybe some board games, where we go back to our spiritual roots and feel the Creator in our midst. It's beautiful, right? Any Orthodox outreach institution that produces videos to convince Jews to keep Shabbat – like Aish and Chabad – is always full of this

216

mythology. The beautiful home, revolving around large families sitting around the Shabbat table that the woman has prepared so calmly and elegantly for a crowd of 20 – isn't that just divine! The Wissotsky Tea company recently came out with a video ad campaign that quickly went viral based on the idealization of the serving mother. Thousands of people called it "beautiful." I called it nauseating. The video, like all these descriptions of Shabbat, leaves out the part that Shabbat is also when men get heart disease and diabetes, and women get eating disorders.

Bites of potatoes swarm around my throat. I love potatoes, the warm, heavy scent caressing my tongue, traveling through my chest, filling up the holes in my heart, and my stomach. Like the bottomless pit that is my desire to be loved, my insides are never truly satisfied. That doesn't stop me from eating. Even after a whole container is finished, I'm not done. That's what hunger is, a constant wanting of *more*. I always want, I always desire, my insides and my outsides crave and all that I know what to give them is food – potatoes, bread, rice, the warm and the heavy that maybe one day will make me feel satiated and calm. I keep giving it to myself in the hope that one day I will feel better, feel happier, feel less trapped, feel freer, feel that I'm allowed to take up space. Feel *life*. That's what food, like life, is for me – it's both a salve and a punishment, a comfort and a drug, a form of self-care and a form of self-harm, a longing to notice my existence and a tool for numbing all sensation. I eat so that I can live, but sometimes I eat because I don't really want to live at all.

I've been a compulsive eater since I was 14, what someone on FB recently referred to as a "secret eater". I would go downstairs in the middle of the night, sometimes on Friday night and sometimes on Saturday night, and steal a few pieces of chicken, some potato salad, some bread kugel. I could polish off an entire tray of my mother's bread kugel in one standing. (Yes, back then, pre-Geneen Roth, I was still standing at the refrigerator). Years later, when I was pregnant, I would sometimes shuffle into the kitchen half asleep at 3:00 a.m. just to get some of the leftovers without anyone watching me or judging me. To this day, even though I don't do the middle-of-the-night binges anymore, my husband knows that my Shabbat morning breakfast is almost always leftovers from the night before. We have a vegetarian home, so there is no chicken or meat involved. But if the opportunity would present itself, I would have no qualms about eating leftover brisket for breakfast.

I started using food as a salve when I was in high school. I can say now – though I didn't have any kind of language to describe this back then – that as a teenager, I was *depressed*. I discovered this only decades later. I had this crazy experience in 2006 during an energy-healing treatment I did for my recurring shoulder pain, on a day that happened to be the day that I was presenting my doctoral dissertation to the entire education department of Hebrew University. It was a few weeks before graduation, and this was to be a very festive event. As Heidi the healer had me in a semi-conscious state, she said, "Your body is telling me that you have pains from when you were around fourteen." That's how she talks. She says the body "speaks" to her, and that all of our traumas and emotional pains are stored in our body. "Tell me," she said, "what were you like when you were fourteen?"

Had I been awake, I would have said that I was a ninth-grade student in a modern Orthodox yeshiva in Brooklyn, New York, the third of four girls in a powerful and well-known family where my father was president of everything, including the school and the shul. I might have said that I played piano and was good in math but not a very diligent student, and that I had a few scattered friends though I wasn't part of any particular social group and always struggled with a feeling of outsiderness. Maybe. But most of that description forms a kind of formal "resume" of my life. In that half-awake somewhat meditative state, where I wasn't thinking but just experiencing a connection to my inner self, I suddenly blurted out, "I was depressed." I didn't know where it came from, but I know it was true. Throughout my high school years, I was definitely depressed. I felt trapped, confused, and so often alone.

Imagine my surprise at this discovery. Calling myself depressed was only one part of the shock. The other was that my entire doctoral thesis, which looks at the identity formation of adolescent religious schools, was just a tool for me to try and uncover the truth about myself. It was no accident that I had this realization on the day I was officially completing that project. Clearly, the universe wanted me to learn that. That entire enterprise, those years of trying to understand the inner lives of religious girls who are inundated with gender messages, all of that was really a ruse, what I wanted to do was to understand *myself*.

I always struggled socially – always having some friends but never really fitting in or having a kind of group of friends where I belonged. My current therapist Inbal calls it my "group" problem, a difficulty with sustaining membership in any kind of group. There is probably no time in life when that is as problematic as it is in high school. In school, I was not studious at all, and never took a page of notes throughout high school, but I got good grades by doing what everyone at The Yeshivah of

Flatbush did at the time – photocopying one person's notes the night before the final exam. I was an expert at that, and during the final period, the local Xerox store on Avenue J had a line out the door. I was such as expert at rote memorization that during senior year after we finished our last history final, I remember asking my friend Olga, one of the ones whose meticulous notes got shared by all, what the Cold War was. I didn't know anything about history, chemistry, philosophy, or English literature. I just memorized notes very well. I got through school without ever reading a newspaper, and I'm pretty sure I had no idea who the president was. I floated through high school without anyone ever noticing that I wasn't really there. I was barely present as a person. My mind was nowhere, but nobody around me even noticed. Everyone assumed I was fine – happy even.

I played piano in the school band, which had the effect of letting me skip a lot of classes and use music as a much-needed outlet. I received good grades without working too hard at it. I joined lots of clubs, volunteered everywhere, looked like I was "involved" or whatever. I was doing what a good girl was supposed to do, and I smiled. So everyone assumed I was fine, I guess. But I wasn't really. I was exactly what all the research says about girls in school – when boys are struggling, they act out; when girls struggle, they go inward. Schools tend to notice only the acting out. So girls who struggle are usually assumed to be "fine," sometimes even "great."

As clueless as my teachers were about my inner life, my home experience was where most of my pain originated. That's where I felt increasingly trapped with no language or outlet even to express what I was going through. So much of it revolved around Shabbat.

Shabbat morning was spent with my sisters and me in elaborate dressing rituals, finding matching shoes and accessories with which to make an appearance in a synagogue. We would enter the women's section of the sanctuary, sit in the same seats every week where we would watch the services taking place in the men's section. Talking was incessant, mostly gossip about what other women were wearing, who was engaged, who was pregnant, who gained weight, which couples were walking hand in hand, and which looked like they were not "happy."

My mother taught us to be experts on invading other people's hearts by judging the slightest nuance in their face or on their waistline. We were proud of ourselves. My father always had a place on stage somewhere, either leading the services or reading from the Torah or making a speech or conducting a fundraising appeal. He was an Important Person. We had status in the community. We were a family of "leaders."

When I was in ninth grade, I developed a crush on a boy in my class. He lived on Ocean Parkway and Avenue U – I lived on 18th Street and Avenue J, so it was a long walk, but a very nice bike ride. I used to go bike riding on Sunday mornings and often passed by his house, hoping to meet up. We occasionally did, although we were both too shy for anything to ever come of it. One Friday, he said to me, "Maybe I'll bike ride to your house tomorrow."

This was a little new to me. He is a Syrian Jew, so his family had customs that allowed him to ride a bike on Shabbat, something that would be considered horrific in my house. It was all exhilarating for me. Anyway, when he mentioned that he might come by, I was over the moon. That Shabbat at lunch, I couldn't eat. I couldn't even touch the soft, warm challah that I love so much that I usually gobbled. I just sat there, my eyes at the door, waiting for him to come by. It's the only time in my life that I can recall sitting at a Shabbat table and not having the urge to eat everything in sight. I felt actually *alive*.

My sisters eventually realized that something was off with me. I didn't want to tell them. But they kept hassling me. Finally, I said, "Leo said he might come over today." Well, that was the end of everything. The needling didn't stop.

"Oooooh, look, Elana has a boyfriend!" My father joined in, too, of course. Teasing his children (and now grandchildren) about our love interests is one of his favorite pastimes. Well, Leo never came that day, and I ended up crying alone in my room from being teased. That afternoon, when I finally remembered my hunger, I had my first major binge. By then, I wasn't just hungry; I was starving.

Most weeks, I would sit at these Shabbat meals and eat and eat and eat until I couldn't budge because there was nothing else for me to do. There was nowhere to go. It was Shabbat – no electricity, no traveling, no real movement. If I left the table before it was over – which I sometimes did just because my eyelids were heavy, and I couldn't sit there anymore – I would get reprimanded. *(Who does that? Who just picks up and leaves the table before the meal is over? What is wrong with Elana? Does she hate the family that much?* My sisters would demand to know.) It was a trap. My father liked to pontificate, sharing his ideas about his communal work or about politics or occasionally about the bible portion that was read in shul. But if someone else – one of the girls – disagreed with him or tried to express an alternate opinion other than his own, all hell broke loose. Actually, it was always only *me* who did that, who tried to argue and debate, or at least just speak and share an idea. It was my mother who took it upon herself to whip me into shape and make sure that I don't "embarrass" the family by disagreeing with my father. A woman's job, she told us, is to be a quiet support for the man. The saying, "Behind every successful man is a supportive woman," was the motto of our family – only in our case, my father had five supportive women who were well trained in being dutiful and adoring. The concept of "successful woman" did not exist, nor did the idea of a woman having any original thoughts or ideas worth hearing.

When I was in college, it got even worse. Like many college students – especially political science majors like me (I read my first *New York Times* on the first day of freshman year, and that began my transformation into news junkie), I began to buy into socialist ideas. For my investment-banker father, this was extremely problematic and a personal affront. Shabbat tables became contentious. I was also exposed to feminist ideas at college, even though it would take me a few more years to start embracing feminism. When I brought home my college flatmate – who today is one of the most successful women in health care in America, the CEO of one of the biggest hospitals in Texas – my father was so impressed at how smart she is that he offered her a job as his *secretary*. That, to him, was the right place for a brilliant woman, the best she could do, to be the secretary of a man like him.

This was not 1955, by the way. This was 1990. When one of my sisters insisted that only men could be good obstetricians because women are too "emotional" about birth, I was the only one to protest, and my protest landed me running up to my room crying. When my brother-in-law described his father's law firm as hiring only men because women are too emotional to be good lawyers, once again, my protest landed me running up to my room crying. I have way too many memories of sitting alone in my room crying as the extended family sits around enjoying Shabbat lunch. To this day, one of my great traumas is the fear of being left behind by my family, where they are all laughing and playing, and they have forgotten about me.

My father's table is a cage. When I sit there, listening to one man controls all conversation and thought while women control the serving, I literally cannot breathe. The only thing I can do is eat. I eat and eat and eat, to stop myself from feeling, to stop myself from hurting, to stop my brain from moving, to stop myself from wanting to talk, to stop myself from bolting and running away for good.

So here I am, years later, still battling with three decades worth of trying to be a Good Jewish Woman. I still feel a little trapped; I still have bouts of depression, I'm still occasionally bingeing, and I'm still keeping Shabbat. Certainly, I've spent the past 25 or 30 years pulling back the layers of my entrapment, little by little, creating my liberated self. However, I'm still in process. My fourteen-year-old-self is still speaking to me. I'm not done yet.

To be sure, my husband and I have made many changes in our Shabbat lives, starting with the fact that all chores are shared – from cooking to cleaning to serving. Anyone who says, "Today I need a break", gets a break. And everyone gets to talk. All ideas are welcomed. No one person is in control of the meal or the conversation. And everyone is loved and accepted exactly as they are, without judgment. And people leave when they want to leave, although we like it when they stay. We ask our kids to invite their friends to the table, but there is no pressure. I would rather have a table full of my kids and their friends for a simple meal than entire families for an elaborate let-me-impress-you overdone feast. Some weeks we barely cook at all, and Shabbat lunch becomes tuna and egg salad sandwiches on challah – even with the kids' friends around. And our meals do not drag out for hours – not unless I do the occasional four-course meal for 20, which is getting less and less frequent. I'm much more inclined to invite a friend for coffee than for Shabbat lunch. I know that my kids are much more liberated than I will ever be. They are completely free to be who they are, exactly as they are.

Still, even with all these changes, I'm still here. I haven't let go of the Shabbat traditions entirely. I keep making Shabbat, keep making the meals. I have not adopted a secular lifestyle. I keep juggling Fridays to make sure I have time to write and do yoga even as I cook and clean. I keep buying into the idea that the whole Shabbat ritual is a special thing, that the entire family-centered, relationship-building, serene detachment from the western world has deep spiritual and religious and emotional significance. Sure, I've let go of the intensity of it. I rarely go to shul, although if I would, it would be to a Conservative shul and not an Orthodox one. I can no longer stomach sitting in a room with a curtain or partition separating men and women. I cannot walk into a "women's section" without feeling half my person crumble up and die, but mostly I just don't go. So I'm neither here nor there. The gates of the cage are open for me, but I have not yet begun to fly. I have not yet figured out what I want out of Shabbat or out of family life or out of religion or out of my life. (And it's hard to figure it out for yourself when you have the needs of four children and a husband's needs to consider. Isn't that always the excuse). So, I'm still limping along in this tradition. Still not feeling like a fully liberated human being.

And I'm still binging – less frequently, for sure, but I haven't stopped. Shabbat, for all its spiritual calm, interferes with my path of healing every week. It's a big joke in the Orthodox community that Shabbat destroys everyone's diets. There is no time during the entire week when I am more bored and going out of my mind – and thus prone to eat for the wrong reasons – than Shabbat afternoon. It's not just boredom – it's also the incessant voice of judgment. It's the chatter in my mind, the wondering if I'm okay – am I being a correct enough woman, a good enough mother, a queeny-enough balabusta? It's the drive to silence that voice and leave me alone that keeps me heading for the refrigerator and consequently hating myself. And it's one more thing – it's the desire for freedom. As much as I appreciate the idea behind Shabbat, part of me wants to be anywhere else. So I eat, to stifle all those aches, to stuff down the torment, to fill my insides with enough baggage that I won't have to feel anything.

Post-script
Some things have changed since I wrote this. I rarely make big meals anymore, and only invite people over who I know I love, and have expanded my community of friends far beyond heterosexual Orthodox couples. My Shabbat looks different, and that is (mostly) good. I also recognize my triggers and have other ways to respond besides bingeing.

Still, the scars are there. The unhealthy chatter about body still occupies my brain. And even though I am no longer Orthodox, I am not healed from all of this. Poet Yehuda Amichai wrote about his conversation with "the place on my arm where my tefillin used to go". I feel the same way. I never wore tefillin, but there are markings on my soul where I was cut out to be a certain kind of woman. And I'm still in conversation with all of those markings – no longer open wounds but still scars that affect my life and my movement. But writing about it here is part of the healing.

Choosing Not to Fast: Eating Disorders and Yom Kippur[37]

This essay, like the earlier one on body traumas around Passover, is an example of how I use my anthropologist hat to address issues that I am dealing with personally. Instead of writing about my own struggles with Yom Kippur, I spent over a year working on this article. I interviewed dozens of women and experts, and it took me a while to have the guts to complete it and submit it to Lilith. But I think this may be one of the most important articles I have ever written. It was long, so it was published in two parts. Below is Part One.

Last year on the eve of Yom Kippur, the Day of Atonement, Naomi Malka was busy. The High Holiday Coordinator and *Mikveh* Director at the Adas Israel Congregation in Washington, DC, she was preparing for a 6:00 p.m. service for five thousand people and had no time to eat. For most people who observe this holiday – which, according to the Guttman Center, is the majority of Jews – the 25 hour fast is hard enough, but to start the fast already on an empty stomach *and* running around

[37] October 11, 2016. Originally published at *Lilith Magazine*. Reprinted with permission.
https://www.lilith.org/blog/2016/10/choosing-not-to-fast-eating-disorders-and-yom-kippur/

organizing and working, that is bordering on painful. For Naomi, the challenge was even more extreme: she is also a recovering bulimic.

"My fast started without thinking about it, but by 4:30 a.m. or 5:00 a.m. the next day. I was in the room where we set up for the security guards and people not fasting, and I was in there stuffing my face," she recalled painfully. "Imagine, it was Yom Kippur, and I was so embarrassed and humiliated, and I was crying. It was a manifestation of so much stress. And then I went and threw up in the synagogue on Yom Kippur! It was just awful, and I was so ashamed about it for weeks after. That's when I realized; I can't fast. I can't be healing from an eating disorder and fast as a Jew. Those two things just don't work for me."

Jews are taught that Yom Kippur, the Day of Atonement, is the holiest day of the year. It is called in the Torah, "The Sabbath of the Sabbaths," the day when Israelites connect with their Creator rebirth their souls through fasting and praying. For some people, the day brings on swarms of difficult feelings – dread, trauma, shame, and guilt along with the severe risk of self-harm. The idea of fasting for a whole day triggers symptoms of eating disorders and disordered eating – not necessarily the same thing – and can send people into downward spirals and unraveling.

"Food's distinct role in Orthodox Judaism makes it a prime vehicle for playing out unspoken conflicts and confusion," Dr. Caryn Gorden, an expert in eating disorders in the Jewish community, writes in *Psychology Today*, "The religious regulations that demand strict observance can serve as scaffolding for the rigidity, control, and deprivation characterizing restrictive anorectic eating," as well as other disordered eating such as bulimia and compulsive eating.

Indeed, Naomi Malka is not alone. I spoke with a dozen women from different Jewish communities around the world, many of whom were not ready to go public with their stories, about their decisions not to fast on Yom Kippur. Although a 1995 study found that 1 in 19 Orthodox Jewish women suffer from eating disorders—twice the number as the American community generally—the topic is still shrouded in shame and secrecy, keeping precise statistics challenging to obtain.

"Shirley," a 27-year-old formerly Orthodox woman living in Jerusalem, told me that she had chosen to stop fasting on Yom Kippur because it "reminds me of when I was trying to diet and trying to be thin to make myself accepted, and I would starve myself. The feeling of starving on fasts can trigger me to possible suicide. That's how strong my body image shameful past is."

Shirley has been struggling with eating, food, and body acceptance for most of her adult life. "When I turned eighteen, I started to overeat and take my issues out on food," she told me. "Eventually, I gained about forty extra pounds, and that's when I began to suffer from a lot of body shaming. My relatives, my friends, and many people who were lacking boundaries would comment on how pretty I was and a shame that I was so overweight and chubby."

Shopping for clothes for Shabbat went from a time of fun with her sisters to an experience of shaming. "I started not to enjoy going shopping with my skinnier sisters and always felt like I had to wait to lose weight. Some family members told me, 'You better stop eating or you will need a large sheet to make a dress for Yom Tov.'"

230

Lisa's troubling relationship with food began when she was 12 or 13 and went on a diet to lose 20 pounds. "It was a really rigorous diet," she said. "I wound up losing the weight, but then I was at a party a year later, and because I was so disciplined and using my so-called will-power, I was at a party and ate and ate and ate like there was no tomorrow. I was so bloated; I felt so sick the next day. So I would lose weight and then gain weight, up and down, always like a thing."

Naomi Malka was also traumatized around body and food during adolescence. "When I was a teen between fourteen and seventeen, my bulimia was pretty severe," she told me. "For a long time, right before my period, I would start a binge. It would be like a four to five-day bender and eating everything off the walls. I was so dissociated that I would get into like sleeping days where I would eat without thinking, without being present at all." Yom Kippur brings all that back. "That's what fast days trigger for me. The whole starvation thing would feed into a cycle. I would just, it would catapult me into a binge that could last a few days. I didn't understand what was happening."

For Lisa, the cycle of eating and self-loathing continued for her throughout adulthood, especially around pregnancy, when she was hungry and ate a lot, but that only brought on more body shaming. "I like big meals, that's how I am. So I gained forty pounds when I was pregnant with my son. I remember going to the doctors, and they weigh you, and the doctor said that if I continued to eat the way I eat, I would become a porker. I will never forget that. So every time I would go there to be weighed, I would always cringe after that."

Oh, that sounded so familiar to me, too. During my first pregnancy, my doctor talked about my weight and nothing else. He kept putting me on diets – even though, by all measures, I was beautiful and healthy then, though I never got that message. I will always remember the way he said to me, "Eat melba toast," as if that was the key to a healthy pregnancy. Every time I see melba toast in the supermarket, I shudder.

Girls get the deleterious impact of diets and body-shaming from all directions. Naomi Malka's mother put her on a diet when she was nine. "I was on a restrictive diet when my body and metabolism were supposed to be getting set up for the rest of my life. So I have a really messed up metabolism." I can relate. My mother bought me my first girdle when I was 14 and weighed 100 pounds, to keep my stomach the desirable flat.

"When I was growing up, it felt wrong to have a body, to be short," she said. "I was supposed to be a certain weight on the scale. All of that made me overeat."

Like Naomi, the experience of being put on a diet when she was young sent Lisa on a life-long path of struggling with food and body acceptance. "When I was working at a camp, when I was sixteen or seventeen, and I was always big-chested, nothing you can do about the size of your boobs, and I remember being teased about that, and it was very, very painful and very hurtful to me. I remember covering up with a t-shirt after that for a very long time. I never really appreciated how I looked."

These women now struggle with many aspects of Jewish life, especially around Yom Kippur. "Fasting can be a horrible trigger to restart things," explains cognitive-behavioral psychologist Aliza Levitt who specializes in eating disorders, "going back to that cycle of starvation, control. Bulimics will also starve themselves, and then will get so hungry that they will binge. And it can be thousands of calories. And then if you're vomiting, that can destroy other parts of your body. It is a life and death situation."

Getting permission

Women who choose not to fast can face judgmental reactions in the community – not necessarily from rabbis, but from laypeople who are concerned about the way the decision is taken. Thus, for example, even though many Orthodox rabbis' rule to exempt people for whom fasting is life-threatening – such as recovering anorexics and bulimics – Sarah Tuttle-Singer still received some harsh pushback. The criticism was not that she didn't *fast*, but that she didn't ask a *rabbi*.

In the comments section of her essay, many posters – almost all men – criticized her for not getting rabbinic permission. One guy wrote, "One cannot simply 'decide' on their own not to fast on YK, even with medical issues. She should have gone to a Rav who, if they're in the LEAST competent, would have told her not to fast…and then, she'd have been OBLIGATED to eat."

This idea that women's great violation of Judaism is deciding for themselves runs pretty deep. I had a similar experience on my Facebook wall a few weeks ago when I announced that I was writing this article and was seeking interviewees. The first comment was a link to a halakhic document talking about women who are excused from fasting due to breastfeeding. I responded that I'm not writing a halakhic treatise, that I am a sociologist and not an expert in Jewish law, and that I wasn't looking for rabbinic opinions. The pushback was swift and sharp. "How can you write about this without a mention of the Halachot? It's Yom Kippur," wrote one commenter, which led to a thread about what the *halakha*h actually says. I'm not going into it because, as I said there, I'm not all that interested in Orthodox readings of *halakha*, which reflects a corpus of Jewish law written exclusively by men. I am interested in women's lived experiences. And anyway, eating disorders are not something that was discussed in the Talmud.

For the record, cognitive-behavioral psychologist Aliza Levitt, a specialist in eating disorders, says that all the Jewish women she has worked within Israel received permission to eat on Yom Kippur, to save their lives. Meanwhile, Shirley, who was on that thread, messaged me about how difficult that conversation was, thanking me for shutting it down.

The thread about *halakha* raised a much more interesting conversation to me, which is the way women — especially Orthodox women – are told that they are not allowed to make decisions for themselves.

Still, despite all the pressure on religious Jewish women to be blindly obedient and to repress their feelings, ideas, and experiences, some women are deciding for themselves not to fast on Yom Kippur. "Without the 'did you ask an effing *shayla*" (query to the rabbi), Shirley said. "No one asked an effing *shayla* when body shaming me."

Even when women get permission, the stigma can be sticky. An Orthodox woman named Yocheved, for example, who commented on Sarah Tuttle-Singer's blog post, described her own experience of not fasting. My doctor advised me against fasting, and I called my Rabbi in tears, telling him, "Call my doctor, tell him how important it is (to fast)! It's not life and death!"

Instead of telling my doctor how important fasting was, my Rabbi told ME how important EATING was. I told him I would feel guilty for eating on Yom Kippur. He responded that the only thing there was to feel guilty about was feeling guilty. "But what G-d wants from us first and foremost is to care for ourselves. It was a mitzvah for you to eat on Yom Kippur, as it was for me. And, like you, I have a much harder time justifying my non-fasting to my family and friends than I do to G-d."

Perhaps it is not surprising, then, that the act of not fasting arouses so much shame in people. Professor Rabbi Rachel Adler shared with me the following story. "Years ago, I was a social worker in a nursing home. People were devastated when informed that they could not fast. The medical staff told them, 'Because of your condition you don't have to fast' and then were surprised that the patients were not delighted. But those people felt that after a lifetime of fasting, they were now being told that they were no longer part of the Jewish people. Some would refuse to eat anyway and get sick. Others were ashamed to go to services. They just stayed in bed, faces turned to the wall. The *halakhah* proved valuable here. I would bring in my husband, an Orthodox rabbi, not only to explain why they were obligated to eat but to tell them exactly how to do it and give them texts of Yom Kippur blessings after meals. We also created a *kavanah* to recite before eating. Feeling obligated, connected to God, and included in the community made a huge difference. I now know several rabbis who cannot fast. You should ask them what they do."

Healing and self-care
The act of choosing not to fast on Yom Kippur is, in this setting, a brave and compassionate act of self-care, even if it comes with a price of shame and stigma. The women I interviewed are grappling with different elements of healing and recovery.

One woman, "Hannah," is healing through parenting, by breaking the cycle of abuse through food that she experienced as a child. "I changed how I parented my children and cooked different meals for each child according to their preferences," she said. "I learned to accept mine (and their needs) and not berate myself for my sensitivities. I also grew to despise fasting as a way of augmenting my pain and suffering. Hunger began to be the symbol of what I endured as a child. I haven't fasted in many years and have found other ways to induce a spiritual state."

She also issued a challenge to educators. "I wonder how educators can help students better understand their individual connection to the tradition and what it is truly intended to accomplish for the body/soul."

Naomi Malka has made spiritual healing around the body part of her life's mission. Through her work at the Adas Israel Community *Mikveh*, the only progressive *mikveh* in DC, she has created educational programs that teach body love and body acceptance to groups of all ages.

Ultimately, my conclusion from all this is that the reason why so many women are choosing not to fast on Yom Kippur is not really about eating disorders. In fact, I would say that eating disorders and not-fasting are two expressions of a deeper problem in the community. This problem is that the way many Jewish practices are kept communally is unhealthy. The women I talked to are struggling within varying forms, and not-fasting is just one of many acts of self-care along the way to healing.

Does Judaism Generate Eating Disorders?[38]

This is part two of my series on women not fasting on Yom Kippur.

Many women who struggle with traumas around food and body shaming have stopped fasting on Yom Kippur. Cognitive-behavioral psychologist Aliza Levitt says that for many women, food is like a drug. "Like with any other drug, you can't just take food away. It is a matter of life and death. Eating disorders have a high mortality rate, and you have to take that into account."

It's more than that. The trauma of food triggered by Yom Kippur reflects a deeper problem in Jewish culture when it comes to food. The overemphasis on food in excess in Jewish life — so often served by women — combined with family surroundings in which body commentary is the norm, can launch different painful relationships with food and body.

---

[38] October 11, 2016. Originally published in *Lilith Magazine*. Reprinted with permission.
https://www.lilith.org/blog/2016/10/does-judaism-generate-eating-disorders/

One key aspect of Jewish culture that disorders women's relationships with their/our bodies is the expectation of feeding, serving, and managing everyone's appetites. "As a mother and a wife. There is an expectation that I will put food on the table. And that is really hard for me. To be so engaged with food," says Naomi Malka. Malka is High Holiday Coordinator and *Mikveh* Director at the Adas Israel Congregation in Washington, DC. She is also a recovering bulimic.

Shabbat meals are often a place where many eating disorders take shape. "Lisa," a woman interviewed for this article who wishes to remain anonymous, remembers, "All these meals, the abundance of food, you make tons of dishes, and then you sit around and eat all this food, and you just sit and grab, and the longer you sit, the more you grab."

The emphasis on sitting around for hours on Shabbat and holidays, surrounded by copious amounts of food, is a risk factor for Jewish women, according to eating disorder specialist Tanya Berg. In an article for *National Eating Disorders*, she writes, "Preoccupations with food can exacerbate eating disorder issues for those who struggle. Eating disorder thoughts and pressures tend to be stronger during holiday times. The individual might 'save' her calories during the week to indulge at the Shabbat or holiday meal; however, this usually leads to either bingeing or further restricting due to the intense fear of overeating. Those who struggle may begin to omit traditional Shabbat foods, or participate but purge later."

"We don't expect men who struggle with alcohol addiction to serve drinks for two hours every evening, but we give no thought to assigning at least two hours a night of food preparation (plus 17 holidays, 52 Shabbats and numerous life cycle events each year) to women who struggle with disordered eating behaviors and/or obesity," eating-disorders consultant Dr. Marjorie Feinson said at a conference of the Renfrew Center on eating disorders in the Jewish community. The Renfrew Center has a program specifically designed for Orthodox Jewish girls.

The language of discipline, control, and willpower can forge unhealthy relationships with one's body. In that sense, kosher rules can exacerbate the issue. As Kate Bigam writes in *Jewish Women's Archive*, although many women are fine with kosher restrictions, "for others, Orthodoxy offers the perfect guise under which to develop anorexia, bulimia, binge eating, and other serious disorders." She explains, "because Orthodox Judaism enforces a litany of rigid food rules and restrictions – no mixing meat and dairy, a bevy of off-limits foods and brands – Orthodox women who keep strict kosher learn from an early age to resist temptation and adhere to stringent meal guidelines. For the sake of religiosity, they become experts at saying no to foods that might otherwise appeal to them – and in some cases, such as on Yom Kippur and Tisha B'av, to saying no to food, period."

What distinguishes eating disorders among religious women are factors such as, "the mixed and contradictory obligations embedded in the religion, the importance of food, the significance of family and the shidduch (matchmaking) phenomenon," writes Dr. Caryn Gorden, an expert in eating disorders in the Jewish community, in *Psychology Today*, "as well as incompatible demands to observe a traditional, spiritual way of life, while functioning in a modern, secular world."

Religious women have multiple expectations around them—to be thin yet covered, to have large families, with pregnancies in quick succession, to serve tons of food but not overeat. Dr. Gorden writes, "There are laws dictating the modest clothing women are permitted to wear, married women must cover their hair when in public, and women are allowed only limited contact with men, including their husbands. The observant female's attempt to reconcile these contradictory imperatives can catalyze the body shame and sexual discomfort that often underlie eating disorders."

The Shabbat table was also a place of trauma for "Hannah," a 42-year-old autistic mother of three who has severe food allergies. She told me that she is triggered by "memories of years of fasting." She spent her childhood "being beaten at the family meal table for refusing to swallow and gagging basic foods."

"Shirley" described how the body-shaming engulfed her on Shabbat-especially around the issue of getting married. "'It's not healthy,' they would say. Or 'You'll never find someone who will want to sleep with you. Boys don't want just personality. They want looks. Try eating only one slice of challah.' I can go on, but if I told you all of it, we would be here forever."

So much of this was familiar to me. Staying thin so that boys would like you, incessant observations of how looked, magnifying-glass inspections of how our chins looked, our waists, our hair—all this was standard fare in my house growing up. And the challah thing that brought up some recordings in my head. Discussions about how many pieces of challah I should eat were the mainstay of my Shabbat table growing up, too. Challah was a comfort for me around the table, in which the girls in the family served copious amounts of food to the men sitting around the table before we sat down and started counting each other's calories. We would sit at the table for hours, and for me, the soft, warm, white bread provided some kind of internal salve that I was desperately craving.

"Orthodoxy privileges traditional gender expectations: a good *shidduch* (marital match), marrying young, having many children, skillful domesticity and physical appeal while in modest dress. How can a woman balance the requirements of secular success with those of significant domestic responsibility?" Dr. Gorden adds.

Shirley's response to the shaming was to starve herself. "I started to go on these 500-calorie diets where I would starve my body to lose weight," she told me. "I eventually lost forty pounds. I remember going to a wedding and being surrounded by around twenty girls who were yelling and screaming about how gorgeous and skinny I was." However, that only emphasized how stuck she was in the cycle of gaze and shame. "The next day began the binge. Eventually, I gained fifty pounds back."

Food, religion, and abuse

There's more. For many women, these experiences with food are part of larger patterns of abuse. Some women shared with me how the abuse contributed to their tricky relationships with food. For Hannah, for example, who experienced food with forced feeding, the experiences of body control at the family table made her see fasting as "a major relief from the mealtime trauma."

Similarly, "Chaya," a 43-year-old social worker who converted to Judaism 20 years ago, shared with me how Yom Kippur was used as a particular excuse for inflicting harm by her physically and emotionally abusive ex-husband. "One of the worst experiences of abuse happened half an hour before Kol Nidre one year, after which I crawled into bed and refused to get out," she shared with me. "He then sickeningly was super nice to me and convinced me to get out of bed because it is the holiest night of the year – which is ironic that he would do that to me right before the holiest night of the year." As a result, she no longer wants to have anything to do with fasting or Yom Kippur. "It makes me feel negative about being Jewish."

Indeed, there is a strong correlation between eating disorders and abuse. According to the National Eating Disorders Association, 30% of people who have an eating disorder have been sexually abused, because body shame often sparks eating disorders. Body-shame can trigger habits of self-harm, like resulting in starvation, purging, or binging. And anorexia, or extreme fasting, can be a means of trying to gain control where a girl feels that she has no control over what is happening to her body.

Chaya also struggles with body issues because of the abuse she experienced in her marriage. "He would stand me naked in front of a mirror and point out all my so-called 'disgusting parts of my body,'" she shared. "He called me a disgusting fat pig every day," she recalled, echoing Donald Trump's toxic language about women. "He would stare at my naked body in the mirror and physically touch the parts, and saying to me, 'Look how disgusting you are,' 'Look at this,' pointing to my belly, 'Look at this,' pointing to my breasts." Chaya is now remarried and free from abuse, but the scars of physical and emotional abuse remain. In this case, it is also a case of spiritual abuse, in which religion is used as an excuse to inflict harm.

There are other stories of Yom Kippur being used as a form of emotional-spiritual abuse. Abusers can use the emphasis on penance as a form of emotional manipulation and blame, where an abuser reminds his or her victim about all their "flaws" or "sins" about all the apologies that she needs to be making. It is hard to know how common this form of spiritual abuse in the Jewish community is because there is no research on it that I know of, but is out there in Jewish life, and still unnamed and unacknowledged. My history includes some very painful spiritual abuse around Yom Kippur.

In fact, the lead-up to Yom Kippur this year, coming at a time when the world is watching Trump move and speak like a sexual predator, is especially triggering for women like Chaya. "It is all crazy-making," she told me. "It is the accumulation of my lived abuse, assaults, dismissiveness, egotistical, mansplaining, sexist, misogynist, 'women don't know anything' experiences as a woman all wrapped into one person."

Post-script

In this two-part series in Lilith, I left out one significant bit of information. I, too, do not fast on Yom Kippur. What I was really trying to do was tell my own story without having to face the world. But maybe it's time for me to let go of that shame.

I stopped fasting in 2009 after a particularly traumatic experience of emotional abuse that took place around Yom Kippur eve that left me shaking. Two days before Yom Kippur, my mother called me up because she felt it was her duty to remind me what a terrible person I am, how every single person she knows and every member of our extended family had been waiting for an apology from me, some since I last saw them when I was a teenager, and how "everyone" wanted to know when was I going to grow up, change my ways, and apologize for everything I have done for the past 25 years. I was 39 years old at the time. On Yom Kippur, my job was to apologize to the entire world for, you know, existing.

I had already learned to tune out my mother's abuse, through therapy, meditation, and support networks. But this particular attack, coming as it did on Yom Kippur eve, invoking the very serious work of forgiveness as a tool to hurt me at the core, this was hard. It tore at my relationship with religion and spirituality, as well as to the whole process of fasting and repentance, because my mother used Yom Kippur as a weapon. And it was also, despite its seriousness, completely meaningless. The idea that "the whole world" was offended by me and has been for my whole life left me with no actual constructive commentary that I could potentially use for self-reflection. Truthfully, I didn't even know what she was talking about. I still don't.

As a result of this attack, I cut my mother out of my life. I told her never to call me or speak to me again. It was a freeing and correct response, even as it left me trembling. That kind of response carries its own impacts. Although my father tried in his own meek, sexist, and patronizing way to repair this – by calling my husband and having a conversation among men about the women problem, a tactic doomed to fail with me – my decision has remained. And it eventually extended to the rest of my family of origin. In fact, not a single one of them has ever asked me why I did this. Not one. They talk to each other about all the things they perceive as being wrong with me – that I'm "angry" that I "have an agenda", that I'm "sick" or just "not nice". I have heard all these ideas coming through the grapevine. Not one member of my family of origin ever asked me why I may be angry. I cut them out not so much because of the abuse but more emphatically because none of them ever do the real work. By work, I mean, engaging, listening and self-reflection. It is much easier to point to me as the problem in the family, leave me on the side of the road, and move on.

FOOD AND FAT

That fateful Yom Kippur when I finally spoke back to the abuse and told my mother to get out of my life, I was relieved but also deeply traumatized. I went to shul and tried to stick to some kind of normal, but that was the end of Yom Kippur for me. I was sitting in shul next to my friend Ariella, wearing the purple tallit that I love, trying to be present with the congregation. But I started to shake. My whole body was just shaking. Despite everything I knew, despite my deep desire to participate in my heritage, I couldn't do it. I ran home in the middle of the Torah reading.

And what did I do when I got home? Someone unconscionable. I headed straight to the refrigerator, Yom Kippur be damned. It was just too hard. Too hard to care for my own emotional and spiritual needs while I was also battling with my food demons. Food has always been my drug of choice, and I desperately needed something to soothe the pain. I could not do it all – the self-deprivation, self-flagellation, and actually living.

Or maybe I just didn't care. It felt like the entire religion was a bit of a scam. If this was how religious Jews kept the supposedly holiest day of the year, what was it all worth? The whole religion lost its meaning and its purpose.

I have occasionally tried to return to Yom Kippur, though mostly through spiritual practices and not through fasting, which is just too big of a trigger for me. I don't actually see any spiritual point in fasting, especially as it turns every conversation into a kvetch about food instead of about the personal process. I spend Yom Kippur eve doing the Hawaiian Ho'oponopono exercise with my children in our garden, which is often more powerful than reciting hundreds of pages from the Machzor. I do this, with some joy and some sadness, always reminding myself to tend to my own needs. I don't know how I feel about the religion right now. But I do know that I will never fast again. Ever. I'm learning to feel my own hungers and feed them.

ELANA SZTOKMAN

Yom Kippur is still a hard day for me. Cutting off one's family of origin was like removing a gangrenous limb. It needed to go because its poison was killing you. But you're still missing a limb. And it's your own fault it's gone. I don't regret the decision, but it makes me sad.

Why I Hate Hearing 'You Look Great'[39]

This essay should have come with an "unpopular opinion" warning. When I wrote it nearly ten years ago, I was still at the beginning of processing my body issues, so that the essay may have come out a bit rough around the edges. I certainly got some angry pushback from friends who said, "But I LOVE when people tell me I look great." Today I realize that those are women for whom the system works, and not necessarily who I'm writing for. Still, even as raw as this essay is, I still mean every word.

The words "You look great" are one of the conversation starters that I most despise. When someone says that to me, it always feels like what they are saying is that the last time they saw me, I looked terrible. Or is it that they are surprised to see me not bed-ridden or comatose? Or, maybe, they simply have nothing interesting to talk about other than our

---

[39] April 4, 2011. Originally published at the *Forward*. Reprinted with permission.
https://forward.com/sisterhood/136713/why-i-hate-hearing-you-look-great/

superficial appearances. Regardless, I hate it because it reminds me how much people are constantly looking at each other and judging others' entire lives based on thinness, youthful appearance, and shallow versions of beauty.

I thought of this last week as someone remarked to me that she had seen my daughter and that my daughter "looks great." My first thought was, *duh, of course, she looks great; she's an active thirteen-year-old and has a beautiful spirit, and she looks exactly how she should look.*

My second thought was this: Why are you observing and judging my daughter's appearance? What are you looking for? What are you expecting to see? And what does "great" even mean? Does it have any meaningful interpretation at all?

My next thought was you don't even *know* my daughter at all. If you encounter another human being and come to all kinds of conclusions based on the person's appearance, you have not actually connected deeply with the other person at all, other than to judge her. The more I thought about this tiny little comment, the more I felt violated, on behalf of my daughter but also vicariously for myself.

It reminded me of the time when I was around my daughter's age and came home from summer camp, only to hear certain relatives say, "You look great!" I remember looking at myself in the mirror after those exchanges thinking, "What do they see?" I didn't know what "great" meant. All I knew was that I had a lot of really fun, new, and exciting experiences over the summer – as well as some hard ones – none of which I had not even shared with those adults, that they had no idea who I was or what I was doing, but they decided

248

that I "looked" great. Today I think that what they really meant is that my face was thin, my chin and cheeks were hallow, and maybe my skin was clear and tanned. Mostly, I feel like they were just looking at the size of my chin. Anyway, it was a formative moment, and I remember the confusing feelings associated with it as if it happened yesterday.

I know this little rant may sound a little extreme because after all, the "You look great!" opener is so common, but it just really makes me bristle. I don't want anyone looking at my body, watching, measuring, or evaluating it. I certainly don't want anyone to make entire determinations about who are what I am, whether I am "successful" or "doing well" in life or otherwise, based on how my hair is coiffed, how well my make-up is done, or how thin my waist happens to be at that moment. But this is what's happening all the time, at almost every social event, and it shapes our entire culture.

Lately, I've been writing about the male gaze on the female body. But the fact is, there is a female gaze on the female body as well. It's about this: women seeing other women and determining how they measure up. It's about women seeing how other women "take care of themselves."

That's another expression that I abhor. When we hear about a woman who "takes care of herself," we are basically talking about spending a disproportionate amount of time, money and energy on plucking, waxing, Botox, mani-pedis, hair dye, tips, straighteners, extensions, lenses, creams, tucks, fixes, facials, make-up and Spanx — not to mention clothing, shoes and endless accessories. To take care of oneself means to make a massive life investment into the beauty industry to be guaranteed a spot on the receiving end of the "You look great!" exchange. It's more about investing in how we *look* than in how we *are*. What a waste of women's lives.

As I read about how this beauty industry, the one so destructive to women's spirits, is frighteningly on the increase rather than on the decline — as illustrated by last week's *New York Times* piece on the increase in breast augmentation surgery — I cannot help but feel a profound sadness and loss. Wasted human energies, how all that time and money could be used to bring more humanity into the world.

Compounded by the events around us, the war, terror, and human catastrophe that have cut short so many lives, these thoughts leave me to wonder what will be said about women — about me — after we die. I wonder how many women will be left with nothing to write on their tombstones other than, "She always looked great. She really took care of herself." It breaks my heart.

I do not want to be on the receiving ends of superficial judgments at all. I do not want to be gazed upon and measured, especially if what's being measured is how my body looks. However, I will say this: If you're going to judge me, don't look at my body but just at my hands. Look at what my hands produce in this world, my creations, and creativity. Judge me not by how I look but what I do. My arms and hands that work and write and hug. In the end, that's all I really am.

Post-script

Wow, this was one of my most hotly contested essays ever. I'm pretty sure that I lost friends over it, in particular friends who relish the benefits of their own successes at navigating societal beauty demands. Put differently, friends who like being told that they look hot. That status comes with a lot of benefits, and it was very risky for me to question it. As I said, women for whom the system works are not the people who I can easily have these conversations with.

Now that I've shared more personal essays in this volume, this essay makes more sense. Although I wasn't sharing my real truths yet, after I published essays like this, other women would share their truths with me.

I have since read blogs and essays that make the same assertions that I made here. And each time – as was the case when I originally published this as well – the women who struggle most with this issue are grateful for the sharing. It seems we belong to a secret club of women who are living with something so hard to define and even harder to justify. Like, "What?! You don't like receiving compliments? What's wrong with you?"

Today I know that the reactions to this kind of "compliment" among the women in my secret club reflect a triggered response characteristic of complex-PTSD. It all comes from years of experiencing a form of emotional-sexual abuse in which your body is the fodder for communal and family commentary and judgment. It's not just your body – it's also your sexuality, your behavior, your personality, your life choices, your worth. All of this belongs not to you but to the people around you – your parents, your teachers, your rabbis, and others – often the people who were supposed to be protecting you. You may live for this for years, sometimes decades. At some point, your whole being rebels and all you want is for the entire world to stop looking at you and stop talking about your body – all of it. That's what this is about.

I have also come to understand that excessive body commentary, even when well-meant, is a form of verbal-emotional abuse. When it is also connected to sexuality – be thin but cover up; be attractive but not sexually alluring; men are always watching you, so watch that chin or waist or butt – then it is also a form of emotional-sexual abuse. It has the same kind of impact as long-term sexual abuse, of devastating one's own relationship with one's body and one's sexuality. It can destroy one's ability to be fully present, to trust, and to be sexually free and whole. These issues are all connected. But because body commentary is so ubiquitous – and sometimes can sound like a compliment – it's hard for us to admit how damaging it is.

There is a lot more to say about this, and I'm currently using my anthropologist's hat and conducting research about this issue – that is, emotional-sexual abuse, or non-contact sexual abuse. We need to talk about this more seriously.

Barbie's 'Real' New Body Still Ain't Too Real[40]

As I work through these issues, something is shifting when it comes to body acceptance. More women are speaking out. Awareness is growing. But we're not quite there. Yet.

The announcement this week that Mattel is launching a new line of Barbie dolls with "realistic" bodies was greeted with cheers in the feminist community. It was a welcome response to a decades-long struggle against the ubiquitous commercial messages that an ideal woman should have a ridiculous body size and shape – unattainably thin limbs, a waist narrower than her neck, and leg-torso proportions that would make it impossible to stand up straight in real life. The fact that Mattel finally listened felt like a victory for the body-acceptance movement. Score one for Real Women.

That feeling lasted for about a split second until I looked at the new line-up of dolls. The new so-called "diversity"

[40] Originally published at the *Forward* on January 29, 2016. Reprinted with permission
https://forward.com/sisterhood/332390/barbies-real-new-body-still-aint-too-real/

is better than the original Barbie, but only by a small margin. Yes, there are dolls with wider hips, dolls with different color skin and hair, and dolls that are shorter and taller (although I cannot imagine anyone complaining that Barbie was too short, but perhaps that is my own 5'0" bias). Despite these variations, there is still something uncannily Barbie-like in the new line-up: they are all still *perfect*.

The new colors and proportions have not tampered the overall Barbie's image of perfect beauty and perfect body-ness. There is not a single bulging waist or tummy, not a single unattractive bit of flab anywhere on any of the bodies, no massive thighs, no double chins, non-cellulite, no thick ankles or calves, no muffin tops, no women who "look" a little pregnant but are actually just a few months or years postpartum. The idea that wide hips constitute body-size "diversity" is a frightening concept; for many women, those wide hips are not a function of fitness or obesity but merely a fact of nature. When I look at this line-up, I still see only thin, beauty-obedient women.

The new Barbies are all still remarkably pretty, according to standard Western and Hollywood embedded concepts of prettiness. The faces have golden proportions, perfect skin, big long-lashed eyes, perfectly groomed and unfrizzy hair, and a general impression of perkiness. None of the Barbies has a wrinkle anywhere to designate real-life expressions – like thinking or talking or fighting for social justice. There is not a lash or pore out of place, no blemishes, no zits, no frown lines, and no indication that these dolls are meant to do anything other than to be someone's eye candy. The dolls are also all still designed to be at their best in dresses and high heels – the way they presented almost exclusively in the publicity photos. The idea that women may prefer non-stiletto shoes in real life, or that some women cannot walk in heels at all, still has not occurred to the doll-makers. We are still presented as ideally legs and lashes. The message from this new line is less about presenting a realistic diversity of women's bodies and lives and more about showing that women with slightly fewer conforming bodies can still achieve a Barbie-like allure of beauty perfection.

Imperfect women – who are probably the majority of women in the world – are still not seen by the Barbie-makers. This includes women with disabilities, as well. There are still no Barbies in wheelchairs or with walkers, no Barbies with hearing aids or walking sticks, none with missing limbs, or any kind of disfigurement. I suppose I should not be surprised. In a world where a pimple or a freckle or a frizzy look are threatening, I can only imagine how completely invisible disabled women would be.

Having said all this, I can hear some of the pushback already. They are just dolls, it's just play, girls can do what they want with the dolls, girls can add freckles or cut hair or make the dolls become famous soccer players, etc. I can also hear the idea that under these criteria, it is *impossible* to include everyone.

So first of all, play is not just play. Mountains of research demonstrate the importance of play in helping children formulate identity, manage their environments, and absorb cultural codes and cues. When children do not see themselves represented in books and toys, they receive very clear messages about their place in the world. Similarly, children who are not exposed to the "other" in society learn to believe that that other does not exist or is not significant in their world. Peggy Orenstein, in her phenomenal book *Cinderella Ate my Daughter*, scans some of the most important studies about how children are affected by body images that they see in books, magazines and toy stores. The impacts of the too-perfect body pressure coming from the commercial world on girls' self-concept are real and can be devastating.

Second of all, it is not so hard to try and achieve real diversity. This is just a smokescreen. Toy companies could do it if it were an actual value to them. The obstacle is not that it is too "hard" but rather that toymakers just not that interested in selling to the "imperfect" market. Not only are "imperfect" women unseen by the doll makers, but we are also unseen by salespeople and marketing directors. We are simply not viewed as potential or valued customers. Just like the clothing makers who refuse to create large sizes because they do not want to have large-size women as customers, so, too, I believe that toy-makers do not want to see imperfect women as customers. That is the only real explanation for their unwillingness to deviate in any meaningful way from beauty standards. The dolls are all eye candy because companies want customers who are eye candy.

The good news is that somebody somewhere in Mattel is listening to these conversations. This is a good first step and leaves me with some hope. But we have a long way to go before women deemed imperfect – whether due to body shape, disability, or an unwillingness to do the perky thing – are truly seen as complete and equal members of society.

Post-script
I realize that it may seem like a silly thing to focus on Barbie dolls. It sounds so trivial. But these issues are all connected – how we consume our culture and how we feel about ourselves.

Also, I think that when I write articles like this, I am using the Barbie doll to talk about myself. Meaning, I am describing my own experiences, whether that was my 5-year-old self playing with dolls or my teenage self sitting in a women's section in a Flatbush shul, or my 50-year-old self watching bad Netflix movies. It is about how those cultures impact our selves. I am describing what it is like to participate in a culture that has a particular view of who you are and who you are supposed to be. Even the most rebellious among us will likely absorb at least parts of those cultures. We can't help it. We are drowning in it.

Here is my truth. I have spent my entire life hating my body. My. Entire. Life. I don't think that there has been a single day in my life when I woke up and did not wish my body to be different. Thinner for sure. No chin, oh my God. Flatter stomach. Thinner thighs. Stronger arms. Bigger eyes. Every single day. I pass by the mirror and, no matter what, I think awful thoughts. I think thoughts that I would never think about another woman because it would be too cruel. I do all that all the time, every day. I also dress in a way that reflects all that. I cover my body with layers of loose clothes. For many years, I wore black all the time. Even today, I don't wear belts or tight jeans, even though in theory I would love that. Because I'm too busy hating my body. This is the reality.

And I'm writing these words for public consumption for the first time in my life. It's not about the Barbie. It's about me. I'm writing about me. It's a vital step in releasing the shame and fully embracing a path of compassion and healing.

A Large and Lovely Beauty Pageant[41]

Here is an example of what healing and empowerment may look like. Or at least a start.

"My name is Heli Buzaglo; I'm 24 years old from Afula, a fat girl, FAAAAAAAAT but beautiful (or at least that's what everyone says, including the mirror on the wall)." Thus opens the blog of one of the contestants in the 16th annual "Fat and Beautiful" beauty pageant in Israel.

The pageant, held mid-December in Beersheba, was open for women weighing more than 176 pounds. In advance of the voting, the Internet was swamped with homemade videos of self-described beautiful fat girls in heavy makeup, sexy lingerie, and suggestive poses. In yet another, *American Idol* transposition, young women begged their viewers to "SMS Yarin, (contestant's name) number 995! I love you all!"

---

[41] December 30, 2009. Originally published at the *Forward*. Reprinted with permission.
https://forward.com/news/israel/122188/a-large-and-lovely-beauty-pageant/

Women (weighing up to 264 pounds) from all over Israel participated in the pageant. Although casual wear and evening wear were two of the categories in which the women competed, the swimsuit competition was absent from the pageant.

The winner was a 22-year-old security guard, Moran Baranes, from Beersheba, weighing in at 205 pounds. She was awarded beauty products, jewelry, a trip abroad, and an annual membership to a gym.

Post-script

Here, too, I was not really writing about Heli Buzaglo but about myself. I was wondering out loud whether I could love myself as a 'fat' person. Whether I could even admit out loud that I am fat, and that I have been fat for a long time. Whether I could say that out loud without cowering in shame for being a failure. Like, if I have been fat for so long, despite trying so hard to be otherwise, doesn't that make me unworthy? Embarrassing?

Even as I write these words, I still have mixed feelings about whether embracing the word 'fat' is empowering or self-otherizing – whether it is subversive and shame-releasing, or using a label that others have constructed for me. I'm not sure. I'm experimenting here even as I write these reflections. Can I say that I'm not fat but just okay? Can's I say about myself that I am just beautiful, exactly as I am, right now? That is what I want. I don't want to call myself fat or anything. I just want to be okay and loving with myself exactly as I am.

On another issue, there is at least one line in here that has definitely changed in ten years: my assumption that girls who pose suggestively are preparing for life as a porn star. Although I have never chosen to engage in that myself, I would not condemn it today quite the same way I did back in 2009. I think that maybe it is actually empowering, and a step towards healing ourselves bodily and sexually.

Overall, I love connecting with women promoting their sexuality, especially those whose bodies are deemed subversive and incorrect. I remember the time my then-teacher of yoga announced to the class that it was very important for us to flatten our stomachs because thinner women are more sexual. I literally fell out of my pose when he said that. I left the class and never went back to him. Because how we look to men has nothing to do with how we feel inside. And that is the whole point. It's about reclaiming our own sexuality as an internal, personal experience.

I feel like my sexuality and body ownership were stolen from me by my religion, my family of origin, my teachers, my rabbis, western culture, a zillion dietitians, and even my yoga teacher. I have spent the past 10-15 years trying to get it back, to own my own sexual feelings and sensuality.

The process is not over, but at least I understand now what I want. I permit myself to desire. I allow myself to love myself, exactly as I am. That is a vital powerful step.

Rebellions

*"I am not free while any woman is
unfree, even when her shackles are
very different from my own."*
— Audre Lorde

*O*ne of the sights that breaks my heart is when I see an Orthodox woman sitting on the beach in layers of clothing while her husband and children wear bathing suits and play in the water and the sand. Sometimes when I see a young Orthodox couple walking down the street, he in shorts and a tank top and she in a long skirt, long sleeves, and heavy wig, the unfairness burns inside of me. I remember being that woman, a 22-year-old young married sitting at the side of the pool during my honeymoon, wearing a long robe over my bathing suit that would never see the light of day while my husband splashed around in the water. What a honeymoon.

The language and practices of "modesty" are not only about the length of the skirts or sleeves. They are an entire vision of women and girls who do not move through the world the same way that boys and men do. Girls who wear skirts are unlikely to do somersaults on the grass, climb trees, or speed down the hill on their bikes with abandon. Women who adhere to these body practices, for the most part, do not audition for Broadway musicals, do not run for public office, and do not try out skydiving. In many communities, they are even unlikely to give a speech in shul.

Yet, a lot has changed since my honeymoon in 1992. Orthodox women have started noticing the effects of these confines, and some have been stretching boundaries. Orthodox girls who become leading athletes. An Orthodox woman who sings on The Voice. An Orthodox woman who takes boudoir photos. And Orthodox women speaking in shul, and more.

I have been writing about these trends for a long time, and at certain points, I was even part of them. In fact, on a certain level, when I write these stories, I am always in some way *writing about myself. I may not be an athlete or a singer, but I have spent most of my adult life breaking open many the artificial restrictions that I was socialized into from early on in my own way, and sometimes, living vicariously through others.*

But I am not alone in any of this – even if sometimes I felt like I was. Many women are breaking open the boxes that they were socialized into – not only Orthodox women, not only Jewish women, in fact not only women. People of all genders and all backgrounds are doing this vital work of talking back to their cultures and recrafting their own identities based on their own dreams and desires. I deeply identify with those processes, and find inspiration from the many creative ways in which people everywhere are engaged in that reinvention. In fact, I might even say that the process of breaking free from socialization and recreating one's own identity is in many ways the essence of life.

This section looks at several examples of people doing this work. Listening to people's stories about the ways in which women and girls emerge from those boxes to rebuild visions of themselves and their cultures leaves me with hope and optimism. And strengthens my own sense of freedom and connection with myself.

Why Orthodox Girls Don't Figure Skate[42]

I had a lot of interests over the course of my youth that I was never allowed to pursue because it wasn't "done" by religious girls – dancing, gymnastics, even jogging. (I know, go figure.) As an adult, I gradually reclaimed some of my passions, but in others I remain an observer – an avid observer for certain, but still an observer. Thankfully, my daughters have all the freedom to pursue their hearts' delights, and they do! There is karma after all, if we're lucky enough to see it through to the next generation. I am blessed.

This is one of my favorite seasons – Olympic figure-skating season. For me, every other sport, in or out of the Olympics, holds a very distant second place, if at all, on my scale of interest. When I read in Gia Kourlas' *New York Times* piece that she is always met with laughter when she tells people that she is a former figure skater, I was incredulous. After all, if I were to

[42] February 28, 2010. Originally published in the *Forward*. Reprinted with permission.
https://forward.com/sisterhood/126376/why-Orthodox-girls-dont-figure-skate/

meet a professional figure skater, my response would undoubtedly be, "That's so cool!" while inside, I would be thinking, *I'm so jealous....* I cannot imagine anyone laughing.

Figure skating is among the many professions that seem like they will never be open to an Orthodox Jewish girl. It's not just the outfits that reveal far more thigh and shoulder action than the average day school dress code. Although, interestingly, the lovely Israeli pairs' team, Alexandra and Roman Zaretsky, tried hard to transform Orthodox attire into an ethnically intriguing skating costume; they did not quite pull it off, in part because all the above-the-knee skin made it a bit inauthentic and in part, because it's hard for me to idealize so-called "modest" women's attire as something quaint, like an Indian sari or Sioux headdress. Mostly, though, it's simply hard to imagine an Orthodox Jewish couple dancing with such ardor. It's of like trying to imagine President Obama knitting, or Rabbi Ovadia Yosef doing yoga.

There are certain aspirations that are pretty much unacceptable for Orthodox girls – Broadway actress, astronaut, cellist with the philharmonic, President of the United States, university president, Surgeon general, bus driver, sanitation worker, policewoman, pilot, *mohel*, *shochet*, and a Rabbi (though that may be changing). Sure, there are lots of seemingly reasonable excuses given – some professions demand working on Friday night, some demand "indecent" clothing, some are too "physical", and some are just, well, *pas nisht*, or not done.

There are moments in my life, though, when I get that pang. That sort of "what if" melody rising through my chest. What if I had grown up in a world when these ambitions were acceptable for religious girls. I was not allowed to take dance or gymnastics because it's not for religious girls (although today that has changed). I was also told that girls are not supposed to jog or run, due to some vaguely expressed issues around bouncing boobs. (This, too, has thankfully changed, although the sight of women jogging in long skirts is still jarring). I remember being completely enchanted by Broadway musicals when I was in my early teens, and my experience seeing Kevin Kline, Linda Ronstadt, and Treat Williams in *Pirates of Penzance* has stayed with me all these years. I still sing the score to my (mostly embarrassed) children. I can also recall the times when I, in my naïve youth, would dream about trying to pursue drama and being told, "It's not for religious people – there are performances on Friday nights." Sure, I was probably being saved from the fate of discovering the hard way how terribly I sing (a minor obstacle in the mind of a 14-year-old). Nevertheless, there are pangs. The same pangs I have when I watch the figure skating and fantasize about spinning, leaping, and floating on the ice to glorious music as the cold air rushes around me. When I watched Kim Yu-Na in her gold-winning performance, I found it so beautiful that I actually cried.

When these stultifying conversations take place in religious homes, I think there is a profound impact on the lives of girls. It's about passion. The subtext of all these conversations is that passion, creativity, and drive to absolutely pursue a personal dream – a dream, that is, other than that of being a nice, sweet wife and mother – is simply not for a religious woman. Our dreams, we are told, are selfish and self-serving. Dedicate your life to serving others, and your life will be meaningful. Religious girls internalize this to the extreme, squashing passion and desire, and redirecting our need to excel into excelling at the home. Create the best Shabbat meal, have the most children, have the cleanest house, be the thinnest and most beautiful, be the best mother, *daven* with the most *kavannah*, most successfully balance everything, like super-woman. Our passions go anywhere but towards ourselves.

I think about my friends, so many women spending vast portions of our lives on cooking, mothering, chauffeuring, dishes, and laundry. I think of all the dreams that are set aside during all those hours of labor. Sure, we all love our children and would not trade them for anything in the world, but a life that requires, say, 8-10 hours a day of ice skating — or sculpting, or writing an operetta — sometimes feels so out of reach. Many religious men manage to love their children and still pursue their dreams, but religious women – not so much.

So I watch these amazing figure skaters with swelling awe and envy and think about all the passions of women I know and wonder what will be with them.

Post-script
Since this was published, Orthodox Jewish girls have entered some athletic and artistic fields for the first time. Here are a few examples:

In 2014, Anya Davidovich, a sixteen-year-old Israeli American figure skater, represented Israel in the Winter Olympics. She was part of the first-ever pairs team to compete for Israel in the Olympics and the only female member of Team Israel. She and her partner finished 15th in Sochi.

Naomi Kutin, an Orthodox high school student in New Jersey and a professional powerlifter, broke the world record for lifting three times her body weight when she was just nine years old. She is an outspoken advocate for women in sports and Orthodox Jewish girls achieving their dreams, and is considered to be one of the strongest women in the world of her weight class.

Amalya Knapp, a tenth-level gymnast from New Jersey and high school student, is outspoken about keeping Shabbat while winning many medals.

Sarah Avraham, an Orthodox, Indian-born, Muay Thai kickboxer living in Israel, was the 2012 Israeli women's champion in Thai boxing.

It's all very exciting and encouraging. Maybe things are changing after all. I can only hope that these girls are free from tormenting socializations, and that their experiences become not the exception but the rule.

An Orthodox Jew Leads Toledo to a Women's National Basketball Title[43]

Stories of girls breaking down the restrictions imposed on them continue to enthrall and inspire me. Here is a story about an Orthodox Jewish girl who became a basketball star.

Naama Shafir, a junior guard, poured in a career-high 40 points to lead the University of Toledo to victory in the Women's National Invitation Tournament championship. She was crowned the basketball tournament's MVP, and then she walked about two miles home.

Shafir, an Orthodox Jew from Israel, did not want to break the Sabbath.

The University of Toledo's 76–68 triumph over the University of Southern California on April 2 marked a historic moment for Toledo — its first postseason championship in school history. The win also marked the

---

[43] April 6, 2011. Originally published at the *Forward*. Reprinted with permission. https://forward.com/news/136770/an-Orthodox-jew-leads-toledo-to-a-womens-national/

climax of a historic season for Shafir, the first female Orthodox Jew to earn an NCAA scholarship and to play American women's Division I basketball.

Indeed, Shafir is arguably the only Orthodox woman athlete prominent in the public eye right now, but to get to this point, she had to overcome unique barriers of language, religion, and gender.

"The game was one of the most incredible moments of my life," Shafir told the Forward. "There were over seven thousand people there, and during those seconds when the game was over and the whole crowd ran to the court, I experienced an unbelievable high."

The 21-year-old star is the fourth of nine children born to a family in the town of Hoshaya in Emek Israel in the Galilee. Like Shafir, almost all of Hoshaya's residents are traditionally observant. Shafir began playing basketball in the Emek Israel girls' basketball league when she was in fourth grade, and her talent became readily apparent. Outside the league, she often played with the boys her father recalled, she also excelled.

"Naama was always a very special girl, and she has grown into a wonderful young woman," gushed her coach from Emek Israel, Liran Barel. "She is a natural leader, and she is very creative in her game, very courageous and very humble."

The Emek Israel league, a mixed club of religious Jews, secular Jews, and Arabs from around the Galilee, is considered one of the best in Israel. The league's makeup has imbued it with a commitment to pluralism and accommodation that respectfully nurtured Shafir's talents. Out of consideration for its observant members, the league refrains from practice on the Sabbath.

"To coach someone with this kind of talent and ambition is a gift that most coaches don't get in their lives," Barel said. "It's a privilege."

It was late on a Saturday night in Israel when the Toledo Rockets faced off against USC in the championship game. In Hoshaya, the Shafir house was packed with people, and after the game, celebrations continued long into the night. The family had to wait until 4:30 a.m., when the Sabbath was over in Toledo, to call Shafir and congratulate her personally.

In Toledo, the entire basketball program adapted its practices to accommodate Shafir's religious needs. There are no practices on the Sabbath, and whenever there is an away game, the team traveled together on a Friday before sundown. To mitigate religious concern regarding modesty, Shafir also wears a T-shirt under her sleeveless jersey. The team stocks a storage freezer in a nearby eatery with kosher meals. The Rockets are also planning a trip to Israel this year.

"The college has been incredibly supportive," said Itzik Shafir, Naama's father, who visited different colleges with his daughter before she settled on Toledo. She had been offered several scholarships, but he wanted to ensure that the one she chose would respect her lifestyle.

Shafir, who is 5-foot-7 and led the Rockets with an average 15.3 points and five assists per game this season, is not the first Orthodox Jew to play American basketball. Tamir Goodman, an Orthodox Jew from Baltimore, once ranked among the top 25 U.S. high school players, and he received public attention for refusing to play on the Sabbath. But he has since moved to Israel and retired from basketball.

More than Orthodox men, women face additional challenges, such as religious demands to wear loose clothing that covers knees and elbows. In some circles, an expectation not to play in front of men, as Rabbi Shlomo Aviner, a prominent Orthodox Zionist religious leader, has ruled.

Shafir received rabbinic approval to pursue her dream from Chaim Burgansky, rabbi of Hoshaya. "The halachic rationale is based on the fact that although the *Halakha* says that it's forbidden to jump and run on Shabbat, someone who derives pleasure from it can do it. But exercise is forbidden," he told the Forward in an e-mail. "Practice is in the category of 'exercise' and therefore forbidden, but the game itself is fun for the player. Who wants to sit on the bench?"

This would not be possible in Israel, Burgansky hastened to explain, since holding a mass-spectator sport there on the Sabbath would involve Jews in desecrating the holy day. "But outside of Israel, it's non-Jews, so it's not a problem," he said.

Burgansky stressed that his ruling was a personal one for Shafir, addressing the specific situation confronting her. "I would under no circumstance give permission to hold a basketball tournament on Shabbat from the outset," he said.

Few Orthodox women have made such strides in sports. According to the Jewish Women's Archive, although Jewish women and girls have participated in sports throughout American history, in fact, Senda Berenson was known as the "Mother of Women's Basketball" in the 1890s — there is little if any history of Orthodox women with advanced athletic careers.

"Religious girls are not exactly encouraged in sports," said Shira Amsel, founder of a basketball league in Israel for observant Orthodox women and girls. "Sports are not considered 'feminine' or 'religious.' We're taught to be quiet and modest and to get married, which is nice, but it's also important for girls to have a positive body image." Shafir is a "great role model for girls in general, and especially religious girls," Amsel said.

Shafir's athletic achievements in America stem from a decision she made at 18 that required considerable courage: to leave her small community, where everyone knows her and follows her career closely, for Toledo, where she knew no one. At a time when many of her classmates were entering the Israeli army or going to Sherut Leumi, the voluntary national service, Shafir headed for a town in the American heartland with only a small Jewish community and few who are traditionally observant.

"Coming here was the most important decision of my life," Shafir said.

"She barely knew English," her father recalled. "The first few weeks there were very difficult. It took her months before she was able to sit in class and understand a lecture."

Three years later, her English is excellent, her studies are going well, and she is majoring in business. And in the process, she has taught people a bit about Israel.

"She is Israel's best ambassador," her father said.

Like the University of Toledo, Israel has adapted its practices for Shafir. After she left for America, Science and Technology Minister Daniel Hershkowitz expanded the regulation that said women could serve in Sherut

Leumi only until the age of 20, allowing them to serve until age 24. This was done explicitly to accommodate Shafir, who felt that she could not pass up the opportunity Toledo offered her but wanted to return after college to serve.

After Sherut Leumi, though, Shafir doesn't know what she will do. "Anything is possible," she said.

Meanwhile, her advice for athletic Orthodox girls is this: "If you have a dream, it's not a question of 'either-or.' You can do both. You can be religious and fulfill your dreams."

Post-script

At the height of 5'0", I am admittedly not someone for whom basketball was ever a great aspiration. But I deeply admire those who fall in love with something amazing that their bodies can do, and who work hard to push forward in strength and grace.

More than that, though, what I love here is the process of talking back to rabbinic language and authority. So much of what is taken as Judaism is just someone's opinion. Judaism has always been a salad of diverse traditions – except, of course, when it comes to gender. Part of the process happening here, then, in which women and girls push back against being excluded, is that ideas of authority, truth, and tradition are shifting as well. Whose lives get to inform the law, whose needs get to be considered, whose ideas get to be included in the spectrum of legitimate thought – these issues are also changing as women and girls demand the rights and the space to live fully. That is what truly excites me.

Former Gur Hasid: 'A Hole in the Sheet' Saved My Life[44]

The notion that ultra-religious Jews have sex through a hole in the sheet is mostly a myth – a persistent one. Here is a story of a woman who escaped the ultra-Orthodox life, and who decided to share her secrets with the world.

Sara Einfeld says, "A hole in the sheet" saved her life.

The 25-year-old former Gur Hasid and mother of two from Ashdod said in an interview in last weekend's *Yediot Aharonot* that she was choking in her life, "a carbon copy of masses of other ultra-Orthodox women, all about kids, cooking, husbands, and meeting friends to talk about kids, cooking and husbands."

Then she discovered the *Internet* and began blogging anonymously at "Hor Basadin," literally, "A Hole in the Sheet." She says, "That was when redemption came."

---

[44] October 16, 2009. Originally published at the *Forward*. Reprinted with permission.
https://forward.com/sisterhood/116979/fomer-gur-hasid-a-hole-in-the-sheet-saved-my-life/

In the past two years, much has changed for Einfeld, the article reveals.

She ran away from home, got divorced, earned driving licenses for auto and motorcycle, started a job as a messenger, got a few tattoos, was disowned by her parents, and became something of a virtual guru for other ultra-Orthodox women.

Her blog grapples with issues around Orthodox women's restricted lives, including depression, frustration, confusion, and forms of rebellion. "Ultra-Orthodox women always want to please," Einfeld writes. "First their parents, then their husbands, but mostly God. But really, they don't really know what they want from their miserable lives."

Einfeld's rebellion began while a Bais Yakov high school student when she dared to wear thinner socks than usual and read non-Jewish books. At 18, she came home one day, and her mother told her she found a match for her. Einfeld spoke to the boy for two hours, "and the next time we met was under the huppah."

Over the next four years, Einhorn did what she was expected – had two babies, and lived the hasidic life, but battled depression. To cope, she began to blog in early 2007 and discovered many women felt the same way. A year later, faced with the harrowing prospect of a third pregnancy at the age of 23, she decided that she could no longer live a double life and, taking her two children, ran away.

Einfeld is now not at all religious — "I drive on Shabbat, and eat on Yom Kippur, but I cook a Friday night meal and light candles," she reports — and her blog attracts throngs of readers. While some attack and others to "return" her, many express a sad yearning, commiseration, and immense gratitude for the forum.

Last weekend's public "coming out" in Yediot, which included a provocative photo of her upper back with nothing between her skin and the camera other than a shoulder tiger tattoo, a nose ring, and her snood, caused a considerable stir in Israel.

Hasidic writer Eliezer Hayoun calls it "The Sara Einfeld Carnival" and claims that she is really on her way "back" to being a Hasid. Tali Farkash, a religious writer at Ynet, decried, "the nasty habit of confronting the past by turning all haredim into miserable people in a closet," which "has become a bit pathetic." Farkash concedes, however, that, "Contrary to what the many haredim who read the article will say about Sarah, every word there is true."

I'm sure there are many happy haredi women out there, whatever happiness means, but the debate over whether Orthodox women are "happy" always reminds me of the "Happy Slave" from Plato's "Lysis"– the idea that even in oppression some people seem to be okay does not take away from the fact of their oppression.

Einfeld concludes her blog with a heart-wrenching poem written by one of her readers:[45]

> I still cry when I remember
> Me
> A young women who tried to explain to a
> yeshiva scholar
> Who sat across from her
> Next to the dark wooden table in the living
> room. Who made charts and asked, So
> what's bothering you?

---

[45] Translation from Hebrew throughout this post is mine

And wrote down: That we don't pass objects
from hand to hand
That you don't call me by name
That we have intercourse according to
predetermined times because that ruins
everything. And then I was embarrassed
To tell him that I want
Him to hug me tight, to give me a little kiss
on the lips and say,
I love you. And when I tried to tell him, I felt
dirty. And how I cried one day so hard until
I banged my head against the wall over and
over again
Harder and harder. And he
Closed the steel door quietly
And in fast steps with his hands folded
behind him and his face locked to the
ground He went to the Shteibel
Learned Gemara, or an hour of halakha.
And I wanted to die, I wanted to die, I
wanted to die. Because our sages (or rather,
his sages) also said, "O hevruta o mituta,"
Either in a pair, or death

Einfeld responds to this poem, "There are women in this country who have never flown on the wings of love ... Everybody thirsts for love."

Post-script

Today, an entire community of formerly Hasidic women and men come together in organizations and online in order to share experiences and support one another, such as Footsteps *in North America,* Hillel: The Right to Choose *in Israel, and many Facebook groups. Several poignant memoirs have been published about Hasidic "escapees" as well, such as Leah Lax's* Uncovered, *Leah (Jericho) Vincent's* Cut Me Loose, *Chava Abby Stein's* Becoming Eve, *and others. The genre of the Hasidic escapee has also been immortalized in popular culture – including several Netflix shows and a character on* The Good Doctor.

But that emergence of a social or cultural trend is only part of the story. Another part of the story is that many people still remain stuck in religious or social-cultural expectations and do not see a way out. In addition, there is often still intense and angry pushback when people choose to leave, and it is hard to know how much that has changed.

Moreover, I would argue that while the story arc of escaping from ultra-Orthodox society has many dramatic elements with a certain voyeuristic appeal – such as issues of sexuality, dress codes, social seclusion, asceticism, and language differences – some people in more modern communities also struggle, perhaps less dramatically, in less externally visible ways, and with less attention. Over the years, I have met many women who, like me, emerged from modern Orthodoxy in mid-adulthood and forged a different path. My friend, Rabbi Dr. Reverend Haviva Ner David has also written about this journey. But as opposed to our haredi or Hasidic counterparts, our journeys often look less stark from the outside and have fewer of those clear demarcation lines. And we have no organizations, no symbols or signs, no meeting places, and no name to help us clarify our story arcs. There is no organization where women who left modern Orthodoxy because of trauma or sexism gather to discuss and share. We don't even have a Facebook group. It is not yet recognized as a thing, as a trend.

But I think it should be. Because even though I was brought up studying secular subjects, watching television, speaking to boys, and wearing jeans, those factoids mask deeper gendered socializations that ended up leaving me with many traumas, as I have been exploring in this book. Sometimes it feels almost hard to explain. Even as I write these words and compile these essays, I have voices in my head dismissing me, telling me that I grew up with all the freedoms in the world and I have nothing to complain about. But I know that my reality is far more complicated than that.

ELANA SZTOKMAN

So even though my story is hardly "dramatic" compared to those of haredi escapees, I do think that there are probably a lot of other women out there like me who can use a social circle for sharing and healing. I hope that my writing helps that happen.

When Religious Girls Become Beauty Queens[46]

*Girls are torn between multiple pulls on their bodies –
cover up, but not too much. Be attractive, sexy, and thin,
but don't be a slut. For religious girls living in a modern
society, those competing pulls can be even stronger. Here
is a story of one young woman making her way in the
quagmire.*

Maayan Madar won the title "Miss Gedera" in
her local beauty pageant. And then she was
kicked out of school. The 18-year-old, who is
finishing 12th grade in a state religious high school in
Israel, was told by her principal that her participation in
the pageant went against school rules. Most importantly,
the principal reportedly said, "Madar wore a strapless
dress."

"I don't think the school has the right to interfere in my
personal life," Madar, who is now a local celebrity, told

[46] April 15, 2011, originally published at the *Forward*.
Reprinted with permission.
https://forward.com/sisterhood/137100/when-religious-girls-become-beauty-queens/

reporters this week. "And anyway, before I entered the pageant, I made sure that there was no swimwear competition, and that the dresses were not low-cut." In fact, Guy Harari, the pageant producer, said he arranged in advance with the head of the municipal council of Gedera Yoel Gamliel —himself a religious Zionist man — that the pageant would not have "immodest" components out of respect to the large religious community in the town.

Her parents are incensed about the principal's actions, and Madar was worried about her future. She was meant to matriculate in a few months, and she is not sure what will happen to her next. The Ministry of Education has come out in support of the principal but said in an official statement that it is still "investigating the matter."

Meanwhile, the religious Zionist community in the mixed town of Gedera had mixed reactions to these events. "I'm a religious woman," a Gedera resident named Esther told Ynet, "but with all due respect, this is not Iran…The girls were lovely. Too bad, the Ministry of Education ruined the occasion and destroyed the girls' experience."

Leah Barak, a former school principal in this sector, disagreed. She said that participation in a pageant "does not suit the world view of religious education" even if the girl claims to be maintaining modesty, because "there will always be a question to what extent she defines modesty, and whether her definition meets with the standards." It is not entirely clear what kind of standards Barak is referring to, although I suspect it has to do with assumptions about the girl's sexual behavior. The implication seems to be; if a girl dresses like this, we must wonder what else she's doing.

This is not the first-time religious girls have challenged their boundaries of modesty by entering the beauty industry. Last year, Modern Orthodox young woman Esther Petrack famously removed her sweater on national television while competing to become "America's Next Top Model," revealing a bra/bikini top. Hardly the stuff of the ulpana upbringing. In Israel, Hava Mond is a successful religious model who has described her life as a panoply of cleavage, miniskirts, and morning prayers. Although Petrack was heavily criticized in the religious community for not being more steadfast in her public commitment to observance (though her mother says that her comments were badly edited), I'm not sure that the navigation of *halakha* is the most troubling aspect of these girls' choices.

Dr. Beverly Gribetz, a veteran educator of religious girls and founder of the Tehilla religious girls' high school in Jerusalem, once shared with me an astute insight into what this all may mean for religious education. She said that she often hears religious educators lamenting the fact that girls walk around in slacks in the mall during their free time. "The problem is not that they're wearing slacks; the problem is that they're spending their free time in the mall."

Maayan Madar's principal should not see Madar's clothing as a rejection of religion but should see Madar's beauty queen aspiration as a failure of her own educational system. Rather than expel a student for succeeding in what she set out to do, the school should be asking itself why this was her goal, why this is the best value system she came out with in terms of girls' roles in society, why her teachers were unable to transmit an image of religious womanhood that was more attractive than becoming a beauty queen. This is a failure of the religious education system — and actually the entire

Israeli education system — and a victory for superficiality, for the reality television-high fashion culture from which the religious community is hardly immune or exempt.

All I can say is, at least Madar won the competition. She should emerge with at least some social capital that may enable her to do other things. Maybe she'll get a university scholarship or a car. Or at least a chance to earn her way as a weather girl. And at least she has some ambition for herself. I'm glad she is insisting that she has to finish school and matriculate. Maybe her story will offer a surprise ending.

Post-script

Since this essay is from 2011, I was curious to find out what happened with Maayan Madar since then. I used all the tools at my disposal and found nothing – no news items about her, no social media presence, and no contact information. She won the beauty contest, was kicked out of school for it, was allowed to finish following public pressure, and then disappeared from the public eye.

The truth is, I'm not entirely mourning the exclusion of religious women, or anyone else, from beauty pageants. I'm not hanging placards for women's rights to be sexualized, commodified beauty objects. Eurovision winner Neta Barzilai expressed a similar sentiment when she refused to perform at a major beauty pageant in Israel. That said, I do think that women, girls, and everyone else, should be free to pursue their passions and dreams. While women can do better than dream about being Miss Universe, it is still a platform and some beauty queens have gone on to do great things with the power that the tiara gave them. Mostly, though, I'm an advocate for freedom. And while the world is changing in many ways, in other ways change remains slow, and people should be free to pursue their own power in whatever ways speak to them.

Where Women of All Shapes and Sizes Do the Hula[47]

My work in Hawaii in 2010 was one of the most spiritually and emotionally uplifting experiences of my life, one in which I discovered the word "healing." I wrote a series of articles about it in the Forward. Here is one essay in which I confront issues of body size and dance.

One of the most life-altering events I experienced in Maui was going to an Uluwehi Guerrero concert. Uluwehi, or Ulu as he is known to his friends, is a beloved Hawaiian folk artist who is dedicated to preserving not only Hawaiian language and music but also the entire Hawaiian culture and heritage. Leslie Granat, a fabulous Jewish philanthropist, and businesswoman — a Brooklyn-bred Maui resident and one of the major sponsor s of Ulu's concert — told me that if I could go to only one Hawaiian concert in my life, this should be it.

---

[47] September 16, 2010. Originally published at the *Forward*. Reprinted with permission.
https://forward.com/sisterhood/131384/where-women-of-all-shapes-and-sizes-do-the-hula/

ELANA SZTOKMAN

Indeed. Ulu, a massive man with a captivating voice and gentle presence, sits at the back of the stage surrounded by a row of ukulele players on his left, other string instruments on his right, a 40-person choir to the side, and dozens of hula dancers in front of him. He tells stories – ancient and contemporary – about every song, while dancers dressed in hula skirts, leis, and peony hairpieces fill the stage with their dances. Every bodily movement matches not only the music but also the words — with hand motions for birds, for trees, for relationships, and even for a hilarious fly-swatting song.

I had the distinct honor of sitting at Leslie Granat's table during last week's communal Rosh Hashanah dinner at the Jewish Congregation of Maui. (Read my previous dispatches from Maui here, here and here.

Dressed in Hawaiian regalia and emoting with warmth and hospitality, Leslie introduced me to Pono Fried, Ulu's partner, producer, and songwriter. Pono is a Jewish man with ties to the East Coast and Israel whose mother, Joyce, was also in town visiting from Riverdale, N.Y., for the concert and was bedecked in jasmine leis that were handmade by her son. Pono (born "Barry"), whose taken name means "righteous" in Hawaiian, is the musical genius responsible for much of Ulu's success. He puts his heart and soul into the music, although he seems a bit tired. "Tell Pono what you loved about the concert," Leslie encouraged me, intimating that Pono and Ulu can use some *hizuk* or encouragement.

So I told him. I said that I love the way dancers come in all shapes, sizes, and ages. I love that older women are given respect as owners of knowledge and tradition. I love Ulu's humor and warmth — he has a knack for making you feel like you're an old friend of his sitting in his living room — and the way his stories express

Hawaiian traditions of care and connection to the earth. I absolutely loved the choir as well as the musical accompaniment. And I loved the entire spirit of Hawaiian culture that I just couldn't get enough of.

Leslie, who has studied hula, explained that this is all much more than dance. The *halau*, or troupe, do meditations beforehand to connect with the spirits and earth and messages of the songs, they spend weeks collecting blossoms for their own leis and hairpieces, they make their own hula skirts from grass, and every single movement has meaning that connects to the music. Ulu, who teaches many groups of all levels, does not make any public appearances without the *halau*, as a way of acknowledging their centrality in his mission. Perhaps most poignantly, Leslie explained that the reason why body shape is not important in Hawaiian culture is that "when Hawaiians see you, they see your heart and your spirit, not your body." Wow. So obvious yet so elusive elsewhere in the U.S. and Israel.

These descriptions have me smitten.

At Leslie's house, I encountered the most color-infused art I've ever seen, including many pieces that she painted herself. Right next to her door hangs a painting of a woman laughing, a painting that I totally fell in love with. I thought to myself, "That's the spirit that I'm seeking in life." If I were to stare at that painting every day as I left my house, it's possible that life would always be okay.

Hawaiian culture, in its purest form, is love. "That's exactly what aloha means," Pono explained as we chatted after Rosh Hashanah services, "and that's the ideal." Although contemporary Hawaiian culture is distanced from the ideal, the origin is ever-present. Perhaps Ulu's and Pono's work in maintaining a heritage that's slipping away is making them tired — a feeling that some American Jewish leaders may identify with, struggling to protect our own ancient heritage that is at risk of getting lost. I told Pono that I'm taken in by the whole concept of aloha, with its layers of meaning and expression. "You really need to move here," he smiled.

It's tempting, I said, adding that Maui is now permanently etched in my heart. But my real work is in Israel. That's where my home is, and that is where the Hawaiian spirit of aloha is so desperately needed.

I believe that Judaism, in its purest form, resembles Hawaiian culture. Our first paragraph of the *Shema* starts with *v'ahavta*, urging us to love God with all our heart and spirit. Hillel encapsulated the Torah as "Love thy neighbor as thyself — all the rest is commentary."

We are told 36 times to be kind to the stranger. This is the essence of Torah. As I prepare to return home, I am bringing with me the spirit of aloha and a strong desire to bring Judaism back to its core of love.

Post-script

Leslie Granat died a few years ago, but her memory lives on in me. Her invitations and parties. The water-color sunset she painted that hangs in my living room. The hand-made hula earrings she gave me for my birthday. The memories of large-ladies-only skinny dipping in her pool. And of course, her many lessons about Hawaii, about living in the moment and enjoying all the world's bounty.

I am still connected with friends on Maui and hope to return one day. My dear friend Shayna Nechama Naveh, who has since become an ordained rabbi, is a spiritual teacher and healer on Maui. My friend and soul-sister Zita worked on healing with me and has incredible spiritual power. Judith Elam looked after my daughter when she traveled there last year. Janine

Holstein is building a new Jewish school. There is beautiful activity that connects the Jewish and Hawaiian cultures. I still follow Pono Fried on Facebook, as well as his partner Uluweihi and am looking forward to one day bringing my family to enjoy Ulu's music and Pono's wonderful tours. I also remember Pono's mother, who recently passed away, who also loved Maui. Pono's tributes to his mother are moving, and remind me of what motherhood can be.

I grew so much from my experiences there, and I am deeply indebted to all those who made it all possible. Maui is with me every day.

Watching My Daughter Fly[48]

I rarely write about what my children are doing. But here I made an exception – with my daughter's permission – because the experience of watching what she does with her body was and still is enthralling for me. Healing, vicariously, through my kids. The story is less about her and more about me.

I have a knack for embarrassing my children.

Like when I sing along while they listen to "Funkytown" with their friends (is it my fault 80s music is the new retro fad?) Or when I start doing the hip-hop line-dance to Mary J. Blige's *Just Fine* in the middle of the living room. "*Ima*, please stop," is what I usually get in response. (Just for the record, my oldest daughter secretly loved the dance and had me show it to her, but she'll never admit that to her friends).

So I speak, sing, and dance to my heart's delight, but invariably endure that unmistakable look of desperately

---

[48] November 9, 2009. Originally published at the *Forward*. Reprinted with permission.
https://forward.com/sisterhood/118614/watching-my-daughter-fly/

seeking out the nearest rock to crawl under. Ah, motherhood.

One day they will hopefully all grow up and find me charming and endearing. I just hope I'm still lucid when that day comes.

Recently, though, the embarrassment reached new heights when I did something so mortifying that my beautiful 12-year-old daughter actually went running to the other side of the park. No, I did not regale her friends with stories of her toddlerhood or even break into my favorite rendition of the Major General Song from *The Pirates of Penzance* (which would have likely sent many mothers running as well).

What did I do that was so degrading? I shrieked.

I couldn't help myself; it just happened. Like a primordial expression of wonderment upon seeing fire for the first time, I uttered this shout of enormous glee, a loud, powerful pronouncement emerging from somewhere in my gut, a language-less expression that there is something utterly phenomenal and extraordinary in this world. I imagine many other parents would have done the same in my situation. After all, I had just watched my daughter do a *flik-flak*.

A *flik-flak* is Hebrew for a "back handspring." It doesn't quite have the same ring to it in English. *Flik-flak* is much more expressive, almost a visceral description. It's the sound of a body flipping over itself backward and forward over and over in a line, like a slinky: *flik- flak-flik-flak-flik-flak*.

Oh, sure, the girls in the Olympics make it look easy, but let me tell you, to be two feet away from this lovely little creature — the same creature, mind you, who once lived inside my body, who I once held because she could not yet walk or talk never mind flip in the air — this little body practically flying in the air, well, it was just beyond anything I have ever experienced. The shriek just came.

I think it emerged from that place in my soul that wishes that I, too, could fly through the air. Of course, I can't. I'm terribly unathletic and always have been. In my mind, however, I easily imagine myself flipping and twirling, flick-flacking my way through the heavens. And then I invariably open my eyes.

But my daughter, my God, she actually did it! The vision just swept me away in its majesty.

So my shriek may have startled her – I suppose it startled me too. But I think it reflected something deep in my sense of what it means to be a woman. It's about the passion and desire to fly, to feel the wind rushing around my body, to be free.

Some of us may have grown up with restrictions as girls, emergent women confined by strictures and conventions.

We were educated to be women – which means, for some of us, we were educated to serve, but our daughters… our daughters… they may yet fly.

Post-script

Ah, watching my daughter fly. I wrote this a long time ago, but the story has swelled. Yonina, who is now 23, has done many things that I wished I could do at that age. She traveled the world on her own, she surfs and dances and does all kinds of physically challenging activities like acro-yoga and wall climbing, she wears exactly what she wants, she lives on her own, she decides exactly what she eats and where she wants to go, and is completely free. I didn't know how much I craved all that until I saw her live it.

There's more. Most recently, she has mastered pole-dancing. Not the strip-club kind but the artistic-athletic kind. (We have talked about what a shame it is that the sex industry co-opted such a beautiful, powerful form of dance.) Watching my daughter on the pole has been an unexpectedly uplifting and inspiring part of my life. Watching her spin upside down, her back arched and her arms ready to embrace the sky, I can feel all of my insides opening up. It's like suddenly I can breathe again.

I asked Yonina what pole-dancing feels like, and she replied, "Like I'm free." Exactly.

Yonina has been a wonderful teacher and mentor for me on my journey. She is teaching me to be free in myself, that I am allowed to own my body, to love my body, and to be exactly who I want to in this world. And along the way, she is teaching me pole-dancing.

Reflections

"No woman should be told she can't make decisions about her own body. When women's rights are under attack, we fight back."
— Kamala Harris

Orthodox Feminism: Where to from Here[49]

The following is a synopsis of the talk I gave at Limmud Modi'in in 2014 titled, "Orthodox Feminist Narratives". By then, I was not really Orthodox anymore, but not yet out of the closet about it. This talk marked a moment of transition, between looking backwards and looking forward.

O rthodox women have complicated lives – beautiful and enriching, certainly, but also very complicated.

To be sure, there is a lot of beauty in being an Orthodox woman. You are encouraged to have a rich family, a busy community life, and relationships that are active and sincere. You are often part of a larger synagogue or communal system that provides meaningful routine and structure. Indeed, your life is a constant search for meaning and genuine religious expression. Your week is punctuated by Shabbat, which ideally involves festive ritual gatherings, singing, prayer, joyful relaxation, and

---

[49] June 13, 2014. Originally posted on my blog *A Jewish Feminist*.

http://jewfem.com/index.php?option=com_easyblog&view=entry&id=429&Itemid=499

elaborate meals with friends and strangers. Your lifecycle events are swathed in ceremony that links you to ancient heritage and hopefully to God. When you give birth, you get lots of food. When you sit *shiva*, you get lots of food. When someone is sick or having a *simcha*, you get lots of food. You never have to be alone if you try hard enough, and at key moments, you are unlikely ever to be hungry. You are busy and loved and adored, as people sing your praises every Friday night and at every bar mitzvah. You are thanked excessively for keeping the home. You are adored for your inner beauty – *sheker ha-chen v'hevel hayofi* (loveliness is a lie, and beauty is hollow) – revered for your kindness and supported in your efforts to be good to all.

This beauty, however, has a flipside. In exchange for all that "internal" beauty, women are indeed expected to keep that beauty to themselves. Covering up is key – covering your body, covering your hair, covering your voice, covering your passions, covering your difficult feelings, covering your aspirations. The covering is compounded by a certain silencing and invisibility, so that you're only a partial participant.

You may desire to *create* – to express yourself in singing, dancing, or writing a commentary on the Talmud – but you have to be careful and search hard to find outlets for those desires if they exist at all. Cupcakes yes; nude paintings, no. Elaborate Shabbat tables, yes; publicly traded shoe company, unlikely.

You may have *passion* and *desire*, but those scary feelings need to be kept in line. You want to be an exuberant davener, or overachieving wife and hostess, great; want to be a professional swimmer, gymnast, or figure-skater, probably not. You want to study Talmud, sure; you want to be the rabbi of your shul, unlikely. Although, in some places, that may finally be changing.

You may have the desire to *lead* – to lead services, to lead synagogue, to lead the seder – but you have few if any approved outlets for that desire. Leading groups of women, yes; leading men, no. Leading children's classroom, of COURSE; leading a cultural institution, not likely. Sharing recipes, amazing; sharing new and innovative ideas, forget it.

For Orthodox women, there are many added layers to this. Who owns knowledge, who runs the ritual, who is in charge of public connections versus who is in charge of home and family planning – these all remain highly gendered. Moreover, if by chance, you don't really fit into the social expectations of Orthodox women – maybe you're not married, maybe you don't have children, maybe you're gay, maybe you just really aren't into Shabbat that much, maybe you don't like shul, maybe you've just never been the feminine or dainty type, maybe you're too introverted to do all that expected socializing, maybe you're a terrible cook or not a 'maternal' type, maybe you hate skirts or just really crave walking down the street in shorts and a tank-top – if you don't fit in with expectations along any of these lines, your life as an Orthodox woman may be fraught with quiet or at times overwhelming pains and internal struggle.

And... all that body cover. Sure, you may have a gorgeous *sheitel* that's nicer than your hair. Sure, you may really love the idea that your hair "belongs" to your husband. You may like the idea that you are not expected to look like Britney Spears – you can hide the crinkles in your thighs and your chubby arms and not worry about it. Maybe all your friends also wear skirts and scarves, so you don't think about it too much, and you like belonging to a great community of women. Or… maybe you hate it and wish you didn't have to do it. Perhaps you really do want to wear jeans and a t-shirt, just once. Or maybe you really do get headaches from the *sheitel* and wish some rabbi would let you all off the hook from this thing already. Maybe you're tired of sitting on the beach watching your sons and husband frolic while you sit still on your chair in your skirt and hat. Maybe you wish that you could stop hating your body and constantly thinking about how to cover it, and just learn to be as you are, to love and accept your body as it is, whatever that happens to be. Maybe you're just tired of all that communal obsession about your body….

Like I said, being an Orthodox woman can be very complicated.

What's more, even among educated, active, firy, smart women, the home front is often a place of regression. This is not just among Orthodox women, but also women around the world.[50] In heterosexual marriages, gender roles at home are more entrenched than any of us would care to fully admit.

The Orthodox feminist movement has done some important and impressive work on changing the lives of Orthodox women over the past 20 years. Women have made significant inroads to change both publicly and privately. Women now have opportunities to learn, to teach, and to write Torah. Women have created all kinds of wonderful and beautiful rituals around bat mitzvah, birth, and more. Women's tefilla groups and partnership

---

[50] The Corona lockdowns have unfortunately clearly demonstrated women's regression at home, and the negative impacts on women have been widely documented.

minyanim have given women outlets to take part in prayer worship in meaningful ways. And of course, Yeshivat Maharat has created a whole new landscape for women's religious leadership, which is nothing short of thrilling.

Yet, with all this great movement for social change, I believe that the Orthodox feminist movement has been missing a key component of the work that Orthodox women need. What has been missing throughout the history of Orthodox feminism is attention to the inner lives of Orthodox women. That is, *I think that the next vital step in the movement for Orthodox feminism must focus on the healing that Orthodox women desperately need.*

Because let's face it. Orthodoxy abuses women.

I realize that perhaps my family experiences are not the norm. Many people over the years have tried to tell me that it's not all that bad. There may be a certain truth to that. But it does not change the underlying truth that the culture of Orthodox Judaism systematically and routinely abuses women and girls in a myriad of painful ways. Women who grow up and live for years or decades in a system that continually justifies their silencing and exclusion as the word of God are forced to make all kinds of internal adjustments to function normally. They may not describe themselves as abused. They may even take offense at this characterization. But the fact is that these are practices of abuse. The culture pounds away messages about what women are or should be. If any individual man would force his wife to live according to the assumptions of Orthodoxy – that she is not allowed to speak or sing in public, that she doesn't count when we count people, that men pray every day for not being a woman – we would be able to say clearly that this woman is abused. But because we are so used to hearing that this is "Torah" or this is "*halakha*," because the entire culture does it, we brush off the impact of these practices on the inner lives of women. We don't call it abuse. We accept it all as normal and expect women just to adjust. Many do. Perhaps even most do.

But the question that looms is a big one: How do all these practices impact a woman's sense of self, her sense of who she is, what she is capable of, and where her passions can be expressed? The culture collectively stifles women's spirits, and we have not yet really asked the question about what that process of stifling does to women's beings.

Sure, there are many Orthodox women who are doing great. Probably most women are doing okay – working, pursuing careers, building great communities, living happily on a day-to-day basis. We all accommodate and work within all kinds of limitations, we all negotiate with our surroundings, and many women even manage to thrive. And many women will disagree completely with my entire characterization and say that this doesn't apply to them, and they have never felt a negative thought about Orthodoxy in their lives. More power to them. If you've never felt stifled or contained or hurting from Orthodoxy, I am glad for your good fortune and wish that all women merit being able to feel that same joy every day. Nonetheless, many other people struggle with different aspects of a culture that is abusive toward women and perhaps don't even know how to name their pain.

In fact, I think that even many of the most enlightened and activist Orthodox feminists can use a journey of healing. In my experience with Orthodox feminists, I have found that even while women are fighting for things like, say, getting women into leadership positions, they themselves may still be sunk in unexamined patriarchal practices and abuse. I cannot begin to describe how agonizing it is for me to watch Orthodox feminists treat each other with the kind of abusive assumptions that men have been using against women for millennia. All this internalized sexism....Women hurting women simply because that's what they are used to. It is excruciating.

Until we start to work on our own pains, our own healing, our own histories of feeling abused, Orthodox feminism will be stuck in an unhealthy place, and Orthodox women will not get the help that they really need. We have to start unpacking how the community educates women and men into relationships and identity. And we have to move from thinking about change "out there" in the world to change "in here" – in our spirits and in our souls.

I think that the next stop for feminism, not just Orthodox feminism but for feminism all around: *healing from the deep painful, personal impacts of patriarchy*. It's about looking at the deep damage to the self. Fighting the patriarchy is not just about career (though that, too), not just about money (though that, too), not just about women in leadership roles (though that, too). It's about what happens when people are systematically prevented from living fully, according to their own consciousness and needs. It's about transforming the world in order to allow space for all human beings to fully thrive, as they want, need, and deserve to.

Post-script

When it comes to public roles, things have improved for Orthodox women. Women are becoming rabbis and getting jobs that were once out of reach. Still, I wish I could say that the public changes for women are also reflected in private changes. I'm not sure. I belong to many social media groups for religious women, and they are often not encouraging. Abuse and trauma still seem rampant, and expectations of over-giving and under-receiving still dominate. Covid lockdowns made all of this worse, not just for Orthodox women but for women everywhere. Two steps forward, one step back.

Moreover, I think that many of these issues extend beyond Orthodoxy. Women everywhere are still getting stuck in childcaring and other aspects of the mental load and emotional labor. So many women are not where they should be in their lives, a fact documented by mountains of research about persistent gender gaps in wages, career advancement, and the double-shift. Overall, I think many women are still struggling, Orthodox or otherwise. And while ceilings are being broken and roadblocks are being removed, many of us have not yet achieved the freedom that we need and deserve in order to pursue the urgencies of our souls.

For me, I'm definitely on the journey. I have changed in many ways. But there is still quite a bit of work left to do.

What is My Story?

Having re-read my writing on body – modesty, hair, fat, sexuality – my strongest take-away is that it's time for me to be kind to myself. Perhaps, in a way, I am rebirthing myself. Or parenting myself – giving myself something that I have needed for a long time that I never had: permission and freedom to just *be*, exactly as I am. It sounds so simple, and should not feel so radical, but apparently it is.

Today, I can see that I was fully socialized into a system that sought to own me, use me, and manipulate me – all under the guise of living out a destiny or "chosenness" or divine servitude. I bought into much of that rhetoric for a long time, which is why it was so hard to pull away from it. After all, there were a lot of beautiful things along the way, and certain benefits that derived from a willingness to be obedient and conforming. Many aspects of life that human beings cherish – family, togetherness, security, meaning, and purpose – come along with playing these roles well. Some of it worked for me along the way, until they didn't. The system still works for many people who are committed to it. I am not one of them.

It took me several decades to pull back the layers of hurtful socialization. It was a gradual process, one of trying and testing, of retreating and returning, of questioning and accepting and questioning again. Ultimately, I need to conjure up the courage not only to ask myself hard and truthful questions, but also to listen to the answers. The process is one of listening to those whispered voices in our heads telling us what we know to be true but are too afraid to follow because we don't know where they will lead us. It took mountains of honesty and courage – and a willingness to live with the loneliness of the path – in order to actually step out of everything I was taught, let go, and begin to think for myself. A willingness to face the pain – not an easy path.

No wonder so many people choose not to take those steps. I understand well why many people choose to stay rooted in the patriarchy, and even dedicate their lives to defending it. It can be a very comfortable life – as long as you are willing to look away, to not question too much, and to adopt the party-line, the collective patriarchal responses.

I spent a long time working on external changes before making the *real* changes in myself. All those years as an activist, educator, and researcher were not only about social change but also about using the cover of public action to avoid facing the hardest truths. I fought for the rights of agunot before asking myself what I'm chained to. I wrote about emotional abuse that others experienced way before embarking on the excruciating process of examining my own personal history with abuse. I fought for women's right to teach, to learn, to lead prayers, and to speak way before I examined the places in my life where I was still silenced and invisible. I supported many women in their struggle for body love and body acceptance before I learned how to do that for myself. I celebrated so many other women who desperately needed to be celebrated way before I was able to say, "I need that, too."

That is not to say that public advocacy is not crucial; of course it is. The real solution to these problems undoubtedly lays in systemic change. For me, it was easier to do that work than to ask myself how I was faring. While I was building organizations, reforming synagogues, conducting research, and at times lobbying at the Knesset, I was very possibly neglecting myself. I was fighting for cultural and political change while struggling to undo the real damage of living in the patriarchy.

What did this look like? In may case, it meant continuing to spend time judging myself, criticizing my body, internalizing other people's views about my life choices, and even hurting my body in many ways. It meant continuing to live according to halakhic rules even though I knew that the halakhic system does not even recognize my person as an equal human being. The Torah doesn't even talk to women – we are merely objects in the landscape – and yet, I continued to be an agent of that system. I revolved my week around hosting and serving far longer than I enjoyed it. And I often put everyone else's needs before my own.

This is what internalized patriarchy looks like. It's about feeling like we owe the world something – to look "good", to act "right", to serve the collective. It is where my own right to live according to my dreams and desires does not even exist.

One of the most telling experiences I had about how trapped I was in this deeply internalized patriarchy was in the Facebook exchange about women's head covering that I described in one of my essays. When a woman wrote that she covered her hair for 17 years and hates every minute of it, and I responded that she might want to consider stopping doing something she hated, I wasn't expecting quite the pushback that I received. It wasn't just that what I was suggesting was against *halakha*. I was told that clearly I wasn't Orthodox, and then I was expelled from the group because clearly I did not understand the purpose of an Orthodox-only sharing. One of the commenters even wrote, "We can't just do what we *want*. If we did that, would anyone keep Shabbat? Would anyone fast on Yom Kippur?" My first thought was that our tradition seems to be hanging by a thread. After all, if people felt that they could say no, apparently they all would. But my second thought was that somehow my comment hit on the core of what it means to be part of the group. It is all about conformity. The second that a person – a woman – thinks for herself, or expresses loyalty to her own needs, she is no longer Orthodox.

That exchange encapsulates my story. After a lifetime of hearing about how many things I *must* do or *should* do for the sake of the nation or the family or the collective, I realized that the one person missing from all that was *me*. I chose this radical path of prioritizing my own needs, desires, and comfort, over those of anyone else. I stopped listening to people who think that it is their job to tell me what is wrong with me or my body or my mind or my personality. I started listening to the only person in the world who is fully capable of knowing what is right for me in this life: me.

And that is the very definition of being not Orthodox. Possibly not anything else. The prioritizing of my self over the collective possibly expels me from many groups.

I think the best way to describe myself right now is that I am in recovery from religious-spiritual-emotional-sexual abuse. I think that the entire Orthodox Jewish culture is abusive to girls and women and that this is a form of spiritual abuse because it uses religion as a tool of violence. It is not an accident that a good portion of my writing over the past ten years has been about sexual abuse. I often wondered about this myself, because I thought to myself, "I was never raped," so why should I care so much? But what these essays have shown me is that there are many forms of sexual-emotional abuse and that some of them are systematic and even communal.

My story is in some ways an escape from Orthodoxy, but not only. Many people grew up in cultures that torture and abuse women and girls' bodies at every turn. Many have been making choices, like me, to reclaim my body despite all that. It has less to do with Orthodox culture per se and more to do with the conscious decision to live awake, with honesty and compassion for oneself.

My next volume will be dedicated to the issue of sexual and emotional violence and abuse. It is absolutely imperative, and I have a lot to say about it.

Meanwhile, the writing process is cathartic. Getting out of the closet about my experiences and sharing in the light of day is certainly terrifying, but also liberating. Like taking off a heavy backpack that I have been carrying around for way too long. I do not need to carry it all anymore.

Some 20-something years ago, my friend Dr. Karen Abrams asked me why I identified with chained women. Back then I did not know how to even think about the question. But today, I know. I understand. I've unchained myself. Well, mostly.

307

Perhaps that is my story. It is a story of a girl who wanted to fly and did not know why it hurt so much every time she tried. Until finally someone asked her if she had ever really considered the chains. The chains. All the chains. All kinds. Well, she noticed that a lot of women around her had chains on. She started talking about other women's chains, writing about them, getting degrees in how to understand women's chains. But she kept hurting. Until finally, someone said to her, "Hey, what about the chains around yourself?" And at first she was like, *whaddayamean*?! But eventually she started noticing that she, too, had chains around her. And once she started paying more attention to herself, she not only had a better understand about the chains around so many other women – she also started to fly. It's what she wanted all along anyway.

Today, I refuse to be small. I refuse to cover myself. I refuse to disappear. I refuse to self-silence. I refuse to let anyone tell me what it means to be me, what I should or should not be, especially if it's premised on ideas about my gender or someone else's idea about God. I'm having no more of that. I am finally ready to be fully me, on my own terms. Ready.

Epilogue

*"What would happen if one woman
told the truth about her life?
The world would split open."*

— *Muriel Rukeyser*

I am standing on the edge of the sand at the Palmachim beach, a pastoral spot some 30 kilometers south of Tel Aviv. It is the morning of Yom Kippur eve in the early autumn, and the water is still warm enough to soothe my ankles as the tide came in. This has been my own pre-Yom Kippur ritual for a few years now. I need a way to escape the communal pressures to do what everyone else is doing, and to stay away from the superficial and meaningless Facebook posts, "If I inadvertently hurt anyone of you, well, sorry." The people who are really supposed to ask for forgiveness never do, and the whole episode feels like a sham. I seek meaning, yet my own history continues to get in the way. I find solace and refuge in nature, in the water, in my family. But some days still have their challenges.

Forgiveness. It's so important, but also so hard. The things that are supposed to happen don't happen, but I work on forgiveness anyway. Not in synagogue. Not in the presence of anyone else. And not out loud. Just me and my heart. I forgive in my heart – I forgive those who hurt me, and I forgive myself. Sometimes it's harder to forgive than to ask for forgiveness, I think. It's particularly hard to forgive those who don't ask for forgiveness. Or maybe that's just me. Maybe, like a lot of women, I've already apologized way too much in my life for things that I shouldn't have had to apologize for. I feel like I've spent years apologizing for just being. I'm over all that. I'm not apologizing. But I am still trying to forgive.

I feel the sun on my face, the wind in my hair, the water on my legs, the sand on my soles – all four elements enveloping me at once. I close my eyes, take a deep breath, and connect to myself. *Who am I?* I don't really know. I am of this earth, and the earth fills me, yet I don't really know who I am. I'm reworking my entire relationship with the person I was taught to be. I am not sure how much of it I still want. Shabbat, Judaism, community, family, God, being "good" – all of these concepts which were once core to my identity have combusted. They have mostly caused me pain. I trusted, I invested, I submitted and obeyed, and was hurt over and over again. The truth is, even in this book of essays, I have not yet written about some of the deepest pains. I haven't even drilled all the way down yet. But this has definitely scratched the surface. I'm getting there.

I enter the water and let myself surrender. I do a water meditation that my friend Zita taught me on Maui in 2010, about embracing what we want to keep and releasing what we want to let go of. Later on in the afternoon, I will gather with my children and we will do a Ho'oponopono exercise on healing relationships and forgiveness while we have the pre-fast meal. Then I will bless them, send them off to synagogue, and retreat to my room with a good book. I've kept the parts of Yom Kippur that I want – connecting with myself, connecting with my kids and my spouse – and left the rest behind.

On the beach, I can think clearly. I can feel who I am. Being in the water, I can feel something that I did not allow for many, many years: *pleasure*. I've discovered that, in the world of healing from trauma, the opposite of pain may be pleasure. Joy. Allowing myself to live in the moment and fully feel what I feel, unmediated. Nobody else interpreting my experience. Nobody else telling me what I should or should not be doing or feeling. Nobody inserting their own needs into my life. Just me, my body, and the earth. Serving myself.

I've been actively seeking out things that give me pleasure, and it's a whole different way of living.

Swimming in natural water... Sleeping in.... Binge-watching SVU.... Singing karaoke.... Eating creamy chocolate ice cream..... Reading books about society and culture.... Yoga.....

One of my first experiences of allowing myself to feel happened in yoga. I found a teacher who would say, "What does your body want right now?" It was a crazy question. He would come over to me and ask me to adjust my position so that it would be more comfortable. I was shocked that such a thing was allowed, as if to say my job was to suffer through, to deal with my own inadequacy. He was insistent. At every pose, he would ask, "What is your body feeling *right now*? What does it *want*?" Want? What do you mean *want*? For a year, I cried my way through the class. It was so radical to listen to what I want, to serve my own needs, to attend to my own comfort. "It's okay for you to be comfortable," he would insist. I cried through that – until I realized that I really *am* allowed to be comfortable. I *am* allowed to live for myself. I *am* allowed to listen to myself.

Once I started listening, I heard myself whisper things. One day I decided to paint the walls in my house. I had been drawing during boring meetings, I often doodled women's bodies in awkward positions to the horror of the people around me, and hid my drawings away. Anyway, drawing is purposeless, I would tell myself dismissively. I needed to be responsible and do what's expected, to work and make money and act like an adult in meetings. One day, after my yoga teacher taught us about the different mandalas, or symbolic representations, of the chakras, or energy centers, I found out something interesting. The heart chakra

312

mandala is the same shape as the Star of David. One of my meditation teachers, the magnificent Inbal Gal, had been using a golden Star of David as a meditative tool and it resonated with me. So one day, I decided to paint a Star of David slash heart-chakra mandala on the wall of the room where I often worked. It was painting as meditation, painting as spirituality, painting as taking ownership of my space. I just did it. I stopped overthinking and overanalyzing, and just did it.

The experience of randomly painting the wall was liberating from a personal-growth perspective but rather mediocre from an actual artistic perspective. I thought to myself, *I would love to take an art class* – but I did not understand back then the significance of hearing the words "what I would love" erupting inside one's own brain. Today, I know that those are sacred words. *Sacred*…. It took me a few good years between the time I decided I wanted to paint and the time I enrolled in an actual class. Enrolling in a leisurely painting class felt, well, *indulgent*. The idea of spending so much time and money on something not important – or rather, on something just for *fun* – was overwhelming. Plus, you know, the class featured nude models, which was far beyond my comfort zone. Eventually I did it anyway. The first day I drove myself to old Jaffa to the Avni Art School, I felt like I was flying into outer space. Like I was sneaking away into a new world. *Heaven.* I drove straight into heaven. And it introduced me to the healing power of art for art's sake. Or of anything for its own sake. Of me for my own sake.

Once I really started listening to that sacred inner voice of desire, I discovered so many things that give me pleasure.

Painting.... Planting sweet potatoes in the garden... Eating fresh pomegranates... Having a foot massage... Organizing my books.... Talking gender about pop culture.... Playing music with my kids...

Once I allowed art for pleasure's sake, I found myself returning to music. Playing piano was one of my few pleasures of youth. I started bringing music back into my family life. Singing, playing piano, making music with my kids. One of our favorite pastimes is playing the musical game Encore, especially on Shabbat afternoon when I am so often bored and agitated. We sing, we laugh, we chat, we let go. I'm teaching them by example how to live in joy, that it is okay to be happy in the moment. It's not sinful or irresponsible. It's actually *living*.

This year, I took up singing lessons with the awesome Rabbi Dr. Minna Bromberg. Like my first year in yoga, this experience also makes me cry often. Releasing my voice is not just a metaphor. It is a real, visceral experience of allowing what was not allowed for so long. I release the self-consciousness, the actual muscles that have gotten used to holding myself back. I'm so done with that.

I also reclaimed playing the drums. I wanted to play the drums since I was 7 or 8 years old, but was not allowed. (*Too noisy. Takes up too much space. Too expensive. Plus, you'll never stick to it. You don't stick to anything.*) It took me 40 years, but I finally started learning the drums – different kinds of drums, the darbuka, the tabla, the dholak. Drumming gives me immense body-centric joy, and wakes up my pumping blood.

Playing Encore with my kids... Taking a nap on the swing.... Playing piano and singing at the same time... Writing music…. Listening to great women singers like Beyoncé or Sia or P!nk….. Gender-analyzing pop-culture…Pizza and ice cream…. Laughing with my entire stomach…

The more I dive into new practices, the more I want to learn. I'm the kind of person who doesn't trust easily – I need to look under the hood, so to speak. If I'm enjoying something, I'm going to dive in deeper before I take it all on.

In yoga, for example I decided to dig deeper – and also find a new teacher. Even though some of my classes were amazing, I also experienced sexism, body-commentary, and fat-shaming in class. The same teacher who taught me that I'm allowed to feel comfortable also made inappropriate sexual comments, and after four years of practice, I left him. But I missed the yoga, the breathing, the listening to self, the allowing, the accepting my body as it is. So I decided to go to India, to Rishikesh, and spent a month in an ashram doing yoga and meditation all day. I also studied yoga teach-training for a year, which took me to Europe, to Hungary, to an ashram in a little village called Szolad two hours outside of Budapest off the Balaton Lake. (I eventually left the teacher-training because here, too, I encountered unbearable sexism, and also discovered that the school of yoga I had been practicing all these years was founded by a guru who is a pedophile and a rapist. Yeah, that happened….I will yet write about my spiritual quest while averting the pitfalls… so many pitfalls.)

Learning to listen to myself came in fits and starts, with the hard things interspersed with the uplifting. I still do yoga regularly, but I am no longer searching for a teacher and do not ascribe to a school. I am not interested in gurus any more than I am interested in rabbis. Still, I take what I enjoy and leave the rest. I love the traveling.

ELANA SZTOKMAN

Visiting new places.... Ireland... Rwanda... Paris...Thailand... Budapest.... Standing in a waterfall... Learning languages.... Fresh snow.... Great views from the tops of mountains that took a lot of effort to reach.... Picnics in the forest...Hawaii...Maui...

O, Maui, How do I love thee? Let me count the ways. Ten years ago, in the liberating but confusing period right after I cut ties with my mother, I received a miraculous opportunity to go to Hawaii for work. It was magical, wondrous, and completely freeing. Even though there were many voices in my head telling me not to. So many voices of "shouldn't". Even though my father heard about it and called me up to tell me that only a terrible mother would leave her children over the High Holidays. (They have a *father*, I thought, while I cried.) Never mind, I hung up the phone, released all those voices – I ignored them and listened to the other voices, the ones that celebrate life and celebrate me, including, by the way, my kids, who still think it was awesome – and continued on my journey, fully present. On Maui, I learned to feel the air, to smell the sky, to hear the spirits, and of course to enjoy the sunset.

Sunsets... Walking barefoot on the sand..... Chatting with a friend about our processes.... Bike riding... Cooking with lots of spices, especially when someone else is cleaning up.... Surprise parties.... Dancing at my kids' weddings....

Once you've let go of the need to be what other people expect you to be, when you let go of every "you should" in your brain, the world is a completely different place. I realize that I have been trained from day one into a life of servitude. I have been acting out the fantasies of men (and their gatekeepers) for so long that for years I did not even know that I was allowed to even ask myself what I want. *What do YOU want?* I meet women all the time who

316

continue to struggle with this very thing. As if to say, it never occurred to them that they were allowed to do what is right for them. It makes me sad but also invigorated because I can see a clear path forward.

The realization that women are people – that even mothers are people – has also helped me re-embrace motherhood, from a new perspective. I've released many western patriarchal ideas about what it means to be a mother and have come to a place where I just want to have relationships with the people in my circle. They are all incredible people, and I just want to be a person in their orbit.

Watching my daughter move... Singing Disney songs with my kids.... Swimming.... A great hug..... Buying new clothes... Eggrolls.... Hot chocolate with whipped cream.... Getting a massage....Giving a massage.....

One of the things that often stopped me from doing what I want was getting dressed. That is, doing things like putting on a bathing suit or bike shorts and appearing in public. For so many years I wore only black, and very loose clothes. The body shame did not only affect my sense of how I looked, but also limited my actual activities. It's such a shame that I didn't get on the bike more often, or go to the beach more. What a waste.

Well, I'm done with that. I go to the beach whenever I can, and do not let the outfit issue hold me back. Around the time I returned from Maui, I started buying brightly colored clothes. In India, I bought the most beautiful colorful clothes that have no fashion equivalent where I live. And not only that, I love to wear tight jeans and low-cut shirts, even if I'm a size 14. Forget that. I have hips. Thank God.

*Making new friends …. Writing…. Dancing around the
kitchen like I'm Beyoncé… and more…. The things I still don't
talk about in public…*

Oh, I love dancing. When I was young, I wanted to take
dance lessons, but I was taught that religious girls don't
"dance" because it's not modest. What my mother meant
was that dancers have *sex*, although she would never say
it quite in those explicit words. She would say, "Look at
their outfits!" But her big fear was that I would have sex.
I mean, regardless of whether it's true that girls who
wear leotards also have lots of casual sex with strangers,
and whether or not that's the kind of thing to say to an 8-
year-old, it was an unarticulated subtext for this and so
many other discussions.

I also wanted to do gymnastics, but that was also *pas
nisht* – not done. When I was in kindergarten, my favorite
pastime was swinging upside down on the monkey bars.
Throughout elementary school, I could not sit still. The
principal, Rabbi Kahana, used to send me on errands
around the school to keep me from irritating my
teachers. Today they would probably put me on Ritalin.
But back then, nobody knew what to do with this strange
girl who just needed to move. I mean, I gave them lots of
clues. I said, *Let me dance! Let me move! Let me fly!* But
nobody did. I mean, sure, we had Israeli dancing. I
participated in that whenever I could. But I only
understood much later in life – after I had tried things
like belly dancing and the hula – why Israeli dancing was
so unsatisfying.

It's about the hips. When I was in my late thirties, I took
up belly-dancing, taught by a fat woman. The class
allowed me to explore my body without too much self-
consciousness. In this small space where everyone was
imperfect but joyful, it was all good. I discovered that my

hips know how to move, and it's fun. I love that. I also discovered that you can dance without counting steps. The Israeli dancing that was allowed for girls in my house was all about feet. It was a regimented exercise of stepping in the right way. It didn't actually involve much of the body at all. Whereas belly-dancing involves often no steps at all. You stand in one place and move yourself like a slinky. Each body part becomes alive, especially the ones that I'm used to reprimanding for being too big. In belly-dancing, big is good. The bigger the hips, the more emphatic the movement. The more you *feel*.

I moved on from belly-dancing to Biodanza, a kind of sensual free-movement that also teaches me freedom, passion, and expression. I was going to an all-woman's class before Covid hit, and I'm hoping to start again soon. In the meantime, I always have my kitchen, where I shimmy, dougie, and twerk to my heart's delight. And sometimes I get out of my kitchen entirely. My husband, in fact, has pretty much taken over Shabbat cooking entirely, and realizes that one of the most helpful things he can do for me is to get me out of the kitchen. That's love.

The dancing has not only taught me to love my hips; it has also given me permission to do what pleases me. This sounds like an obvious thing, but it's not. One of the biggest lessons I have given myself in my path of healing is that I'm allowed to do what feels good to me. I am allowed to want and I am allowed to desire. And giving in to my desire is not sinful. It is, in fact, divine.

Giving myself permission to answer my own needs is one of the greatest acts of both freedom and self-love. If I want to sleep, I sleep. If I want to eat, I eat. If I want to do nothing, I do nothing. My body is entitled to need things, and it is okay for me to give it what it wants.

In fact, I am also allowed to *ask* for what I love. That is also radical in the patriarchal culture that surrounds us. A woman is allowed to not only want but to ask her surroundings to accommodate *her*.

So here I am, fifty years old, only now fully understanding that my needs count, that wanting is a beautiful thing, and that giving in to my desires makes me feel alive. That makes me swing my hips, *yeah*!

Acknowledgments

As a book that collects my essays from the past 25 years, this project would not have come to fruition without the many editors and publishers who decided to take a chance and publish my writing. I'd especially like to thank the very special Susan Weidman Schneider at *Lilith* who is a mentor, cheerleader, and feminist leader par excellence, and Gabrielle Birkner founding editor of The Sisterhood blog at *The Forward*, who gave me a huge boost for a few good years.

Special thanks to feminist activists, friends, mentors, and counselors over the years who shared different key parts of this journey with me: Dr. Chaya Gorsetman, Erin Griver, Rabbi Professor Rachel Adler, Beth Cohen, Shirley Glance, Di Hirsch, Dr. Roberta Levy-Schwartz, Sally Berkovic, Dr, Karen Gerber Abrams, Nechama Munk, Ilona Fischer, Loolwa Khazoom, Dr. Elisheva Zerem, Aviva Janus, Judith Djemal, Jessica Kaz Hoffman, Dr. Susan Weiss, Dr. Melanie Landau, Hanan Ablassi, Josie Glausiusz Kluger, Gladys Teitel, Segal Hirsch, Dr. Sharon Weiss-Greenberg, Miriam Isserow, Naomi Eisenberger, Professor Alice Shalvi, Dr. Ariella Zeller, Elise Rynhold, Ruthie Lang, Annie Eisen, Susan Goodman Jackson, Devora Blachor, Heather Stone, Hannah Katsman, Pamela Becker, Rivka Hellendal,

Rabbi Dr. Minna Bromberg, Jackie Bitensky, Inbal Gal, and Re'eli Kimchi.

Special thanks to Barbara Dobkin for supporting my research.

Thanks to all my readers over the years who have given me valuable feedback and opportunities for improvement.

Huge shout-out to my amazing children and extensions – Avigayil and Matan, Effi and Sophie, Yonina, and Meital as well as Tari and Amos– for always being willing to engage with me, even when we disagree, and even when it's hard. And none of this would have happened without the ongoing love and encouragement from my super-supportive husband, Jacob, who always puts my well-being first.

Finally, I would like to acknowledge the good grace of my Creator, with gratitude and awe that I have come to this point in this life.

Dr. Elana Hope Maryles Sztokman
December 2020

About the Author

Dr. Elana Maryles Sztokman is a Jewish feminist author, anthropologist, educator, consultant, and activist. A two-time winner of the National Jewish Book Council award, and winner of the Gourmand Award in the category of fundraising for her work on behalf of women in India, Elana is Founding Chair of the founders of the Kol Hanashim Women's Party that ran for the 2020 Knesset, and was number four on the list. She also serves as the Vice Chair for Media and Policy of Democrats Abroad-Israel, and was the 2016 Scholar-in-Residence for National Council of Jewish Women. Elana speaks, teaches, and works with people and organizations around the world on gender, culture, and building compassionate communities.

This is her fifth book.

www.ingramcontent.com/pod-product-compliance
Lightning Source LLC
Chambersburg PA
CBHW022043020426
42335CB00012B/521